THERAPEUTIC APPROACHES TO THE CARE OF THE MENTALLY ILL

Edition 3

David S. Bailey, Ed.D., A.B.P.P.

Diplomate in Clinical Psychology, American Board of Professional Psychology; Clinical Director, Department of Clinical and Neuropsychology, Northeast Georgia Medical Center and Laurelwood Psychiatric and Substance Abuse Hospital, Gainesville, Georgia; and Consultant, Department of Human Resources, State of Georgia

Deborah R. Bailey, R.N., B.S., M.S.N.

Vice-President, Nursing Division, Northeast Georgia Medical Center, Gainesville, Georgia

F. A. DAVIS COMPANY • Philadelphia

F. A. Davis Company
1915 Arch Street
Philadelphia, PA 19103

Printed in the United States of America

Last digit indicates print number: 10 9 8 7 6 5 4 3 2 1

Publisher, Nursing: Robert G. Martone
Production Editor: Jody E. Gould
Cover Design: Donald B. Freggens, Jr.

As new scientific information becomes available through basic and clinical research, recommended treatments and drug therapies undergo changes. The author(s) and publisher have done everything possible to make this book accurate, up to date, and in accord with accepted standards at the time of publication. The authors, editors, and publisher are not responsible for errors or omissions or for consequences from application of the book, and make no warranty, expressed or implied, in regard to the contents of the book. Any practice described in this book should be applied by the reader in accordance with professional standards of care used in regard to the unique circumstances that may apply in each situation. The reader is advised always to check product information (package inserts) for changes and new information regarding dose and contraindications before administering any drug. Caution is especially urged when using new or infrequently ordered drugs.

Library of Congress Cataloging-in-Publication Data

Bailey, David S.
   Therapeutic approaches to the care of the mentally ill / David S. Bailey, Deborah R. Bailey.—Ed. 3.
     p. cm.
   Includes bibliographical references and index.
   ISBN 0-8036-0552-8 (alk. paper : pbk)
   1. Psychiatric nursing. I. Bailey, Deborah R. II. Title.
   [DNLM: 1. Mental Disorders—prevention & control. 2. Mental Disorders—therapy. WM 400 B154t 1993]
   RC440.B245 1993
   616.89′1—dc20
   DNLM/DLC
   for Library of Congress
                                                93-16296
                                                CIP

This book is dedicated to Donny Bailey. The Vietnam war left him physically scarred and mentally tormented. That torment caused him first to try to make the real world fit his unrealistic perception of it and, failing that, he sought to escape through agents which numbed his senses and dulled his pain. His life ended tragically on the eve of his twenty-fifth birthday. His pain is gone, but those of us who remember him also remember his pain and hope that we can help diminish such pain in others.

Listen

When I ask you to listen to me
and you start giving advice
you have not done what I asked.

When I ask you to listen to me
and you begin to tell me why I shouldn't feel that way,
you are trampling on my *feelings*.

When I ask you to listen to me
and you feel you have to *do* something to solve my problem,
you have failed me, strange as that may seem.

Listen! All I asked, was that you listen.
not talk or do—just hear me.
Advice is cheap: 10 cents will get you both Dear Abby and
Billy Graham in the same newspaper.
And I can do for myself; I'm not helpless.
Maybe discouraged and faltering, but not helpless.

When you do something for me *that I can and need to do
for myself,* you contribute to my fear and weakness.

But, when you accept as a simple fact that I do feel what I feel,
no matter how irrational, then I can quit trying to convince
you and can get about the business of understanding what's
behind this irrational feeling.
And when that's clear, the answers are obvious and I
don't need advice.
Irrational feelings make sense when we understand what's
behind them.

Perhaps that's why prayer works, sometimes, for some people
because God is mute, and he doesn't give advice or
try to fix things. "They" just listen and let you
work it out for yourself.

So, please listen and just hear me. And, if you want to
talk, wait a minute for your turn; and I'll listen to you.

Anonymous

Preface to the
Third Edition

This edition marks the 17th year of publication of this book. We would like to thank the tens of thousands of you who have chosen to use our previous editions. We continue to be grateful for your loyalty and your support of our efforts.

Certainly, we live in a different world than that at the birth of even our second edition, much less the first. Thanks to the demise of the Soviet Union, we are undoubtedly safer in terms of the potential for mass destruction. However, that reduction in anxiety is offset, and perhaps even exceeded, by the increase in the sense of personal danger imposed by such events as the Los Angeles riots, the shooting of an abortion clinic physician, the phenomenon of drive-by shootings, freeway shootings, the bombing of the World Trade Center, and acts of almost unbelievable violence commited by various religious extremists as a means of venting assorted frustrations. Surely, as we become a world culture, there must be a means of accommodating our differences without the necessity for violence, particularly against innocent bystanders. Clearly, we must all do what we can to manage frustration in ourselves and others without resorting to tactics that are destructive to our people and to our society.

We, the authors, feel as limited as almost everyone else in terms of what we can do. However, beyond the exercise of personal responsibility, which is incumbent on all of us, we do have professional mental health skills with which we endeavor to help others more effectively manage their individual angers, frustrations, impulses, cognitive distortions, perceptual inaccuracies, and various other manifestations of mental illness. In some cases, what we see—and what you as you enter your training will see—is not mental illness but simply intolerance, difficulty profiting from experience, unwillingness to delay gratification, aggressive use of denial, or the use of rationalization to the point of justifying one's extreme or inappropriate behaviors.

How does one know the difference between mental illness and simple instances of misjudgment, behavioral excesses, disregard for the rights of others, and deliberate acts of violence? We hope that for the past 17 years we have helped the tens of thousands of students who have used our book to recognize those differences and to manage more effectively the behaviors associated with various mental disorders.

In this edition, we have updated all chapters, added extensively to the diagnostic section, and have added a new chapter on eating disorders, written by a nurse with many years of experience in that specialty. We have (cleverly) retained those apsects of the book for which we have received the most positive feedback. Those features include the straight-forward, down-to-earth, in-the-trenches, practical style and the specific recommendations for dealing with certain behaviors and situations. We hope you will benefit from our changes and additions. As always, we would appreciate hearing from you if you have suggestions or comments.

Let us wish you good luck in your studies and in your life. Whether or not you choose mental health as a vocation, the things you will learn in your mental health rotation will benefit you and those around you if you exercise that knowledge. Some may see the acquisition of this knowl-edge as a mixed blessing, because along with that knowledge comes the personal and professional responsibility to use it as effectively as possible. We encourage you to do what you can and to advocate that others do the same. The axiom of the gestalt is that the whole is greater than the sum of its parts. Let us not forget, however, that the integrity of the whole depends on the stability of its parts.

David S. Bailey
Deborah R. Bailey

Contents

**PART I   INTRODUCTION TO MENTAL HEALTH CARE
SETTINGS**   1

Chapter 1   Introduction to Working with the
Mentally Ill   3
Chapter 2   Personality Development   13
Chapter 3   Basic Concepts of the Mind   27
Chapter 4   Legal and Ethical
Considerations   49

**PART II   UNDERSTANDING THE PATIENT'S
DIAGNOSIS**   63

Chapter 5   Introduction to Diagnostic
Considerations   65
Chapter 6   The Psychotic Diagnostic
Categories   85
Chapter 7   The Personality Disorders and
the Sexual Disorders   95

PART III   THERAPEUTIC TREATMENT ACTIVITIES . . .   119

Chapter 8   Communication Skills   121
Chapter 9   Drug Therapy   143
Chapter 10   Electroconvulsive Therapy   165
Chapter 11   Other Therapies   175

PART IV THERAPEUTIC APPROACHES TO SPECIFIC
         POPULATIONS. 185

            Chapter 12 Care for Aggressive Patients . . . 187
            Chapter 13 Care for Anxious Patients 203
            Chapter 14 Care for Suspicious Patients . . . 213
            Chapter 15 Care for Depressed Patients . . . 221
            Chapter 16 Care for Suicidal Patients. 229
            Chapter 17 Care for Patients Who Have Lost
                        Contact with Reality 247
            Chapter 18 Care for Patients with Neurologic
                        Deficits. 255
            Chapter 19 Care for Patients with Eating
                        Disorders 265
            Chapter 20 Care for Chemically Dependent
                        Patients 283
            Chapter 21 Geriatric Psychiatric Care 307
            Chapter 22 Crisis Intervention 321

APPENDIX A Answer Keys 331

APPENDIX B Patient's Bill of Rights 345

INDEX. 349

Introduction to Mental Health Care Settings

1

Introduction to Working with the Mentally Ill

LEARNING OBJECTIVES

Student will be able to:
1. Evaluate own feelings and attitudes about mental illness.
2. Compare own personal views with those commonly held by practitioners in the mental health field.
3. Understand the importance of the relationship between the mental health worker and patient.
4. Increase the awareness of own anxieties related to caring for the mentally ill.

---

*ATTITUDE INVENTORY EXERCISE**

Before you begin to use this book, take a few minutes to examine your own feelings and attitudes about mental illness. React to the following statements and decide whether you believe them to be true or false. Let your feelings be your guide.

True or False. Circle your choice.

T F 1. People who enjoy working with mentally ill patients are somewhat mentally unstable themselves.

T F 2. Most people who are emotionally disturbed are overly active.

T F 3. Mental illness may develop suddenly.

T F 4. Mentally ill people are also mentally deficient.

---

*Slightly modified from Dreyer, S., Bailey, D., and Doucet, W.: *A Guide to Nursing Management of Psychiatric Patients.* C.V. Mosby, St. Louis, 1975.

T   F   5. People who have been mentally ill may recover from their illness and live a normal life again.

T   F   6. People who have mental illness should not marry or have children.

T   F   7. Heavy consumption of alcohol may be a symptom of mental illness.

T   F   8. People who work with mentally ill patients soon realize that their own emotional problems are insignificant.

T   F   9. Most mentally ill patients are dangerous and may kill others.

T   F   10. People who are wealthy rarely become mentally ill.

T   F   11. Most people doubt their own sanity at one time or another.

T   F   12. Most people who are mentally ill have a certain look that identifies them as being disturbed.

T   F   13. The largest number of mentally ill people come from underprivileged families.

T   F   14. The actions and speech of most mental patients are revolting and disgusting to others.

T   F   15. The main reason that people are committed for psychiatric treatment is to protect the community.

T   F   16. It is usually necessary to put emotionally ill patients in seclusion rooms.

T   F   17. Hereditary factors determine whether or not a person becomes mentally ill.

T   F   18. Physical disease may influence emotional balance.

T   F   19. People who are mentally ill are often very sensitive to the happenings in their environment.

T   F   20. Working with mentally ill patients may often cause one to become mentally ill.

T   F   21. Learning about mental disease, psychiatry, and the functions of one's mind is harmful to well-adjusted, normal people.

T   F   22. Unfortunately, not much can be done for mental patients aside from administering to their physical needs and hoping that they will get well.

T   F   23. Mentally ill patients have no sense of humor.

T   F   24. To convince patients that they should behave in a socially acceptable manner, it is necessary to use punishment.

T   F   25. Mentally ill patients often have feelings and emotions similar to those of normal people.

T   F   26. People who are mentally ill can be dangerous to themselves.

T   F   27. Working long hours causes mental illness.

T   F   28. Withdrawal from normal activities may be a sign of mental illness.

T F 29. A person may handle anxiety by becoming mentally ill.
T F 30. Mentally ill persons develop strong sexual urges and are unable to control their behavior.
T F 31. Mentally ill patients who are doing well and seem capable of assuming responsibility for their behavior should not be allowed to do so because they may suddenly become ill again.
T F 32. It is easy to identify the needs of the mentally ill.
T F 33. Symptoms of mental illness may be deeply hidden within a person.
T F 34. Children should be protected from all frustrating situations.
T F 35. Experiencing feelings of inferiority is a sign of mental illness.
T F 36. Early recognition and treatment do not affect the course of mental illness.
T F 37. Today mentally ill people have no problem being accepted by other members of society.
T F 38. People readily admit that they need help for emotional disturbances.
T F 39. Members of the medical and nursing professions accept and have an understanding attitude about mental illness, just as they do about other types of illness.
T F 40. People whose behavior is deeply disturbed are best treated in the back wards of state hospitals.
T F 41. Attitudes and feelings about mental illness learned previously may affect one's ability to deal effectively with mentally disturbed patients.

GENERAL DISCUSSION

Using the Mental Health Attitude Inventory that you have just completed, compare your views with those commonly held by practitioners in the mental health field (answers are given in Appendix A). If your responses differ significantly from the views held by mental health practitioners, you should not feel too uncomfortable. Even in this day of extensive organ transplants, intergalactic exploration, rescuing of wayward satellites, and extensive use of laser beams for surgery, a large part of our population still attaches a great deal of fear and shame to mental illness.

Although it is true that some unhealthy attitudes toward mental illness still exist, considerable gains have been made during the last hundred years or so in treating persons afflicted with mental disorders. We no longer consider them to be under spells or curses, or to be possessed by demons. For the most part, mental illness is now viewed as a sickness that can be caused by a wide variety of factors.

Although it is difficult to pinpoint a specific reason for a person's becoming mentally ill at a particular time, we do know that factors such as physical illness, one's work, family crises, broken love relationships, repeated disappointments, and prolonged frustration are frequently associated with a person's loss of ability to cope with the demands of day-to-day living. Many authorities believe that although one cannot inherit a specific mental illness, one may inherit a predisposition to certain types of mental problems. Whether or not one develops the illness to which one is predisposed depends largely on personal life experiences and the environment in which one lives. The question of why a particular person becomes mentally ill under certain conditions while another person exposed to the same conditions manages to continue to function is a puzzling one.

Probably the most reasonable explanation lies in the fact that different personal experiences cause a difference in what a person perceives as stressful and how much stress a person can tolerate. Some people are afraid of all snakes, some are afraid only of poisonous snakes, and some do not fear snakes at all. Some people fear heights; some do not. It is the way an individual views a situation that determines his or her response. The mentally ill patient often has learned many inappropriate behaviors that must be unlearned or replaced with more acceptable ones. Such relearning frequently takes a great deal of time, and hospitalization or prolonged outpatient treatment may be required.

Thanks to recent medical advancements leading to the development of more effective drugs and improved treatment methods, many psychiatric patients are able to return home to their families in a matter of days or weeks following hospitalization. Others do not require hospitalization at all but are treated as outpatients or in day care programs. Some continue to perform their jobs and receive therapy in evening programs. It is no longer necessary for mentally ill patients to go to large institutions many miles from their homes and families in order to receive treatment.

With treatment, many patients are able to make a complete recovery and some are even better adjusted than before their symptoms appeared. Others are helped to function more effectively but may need to remain on medication for prolonged periods and avoid certain stressful situations that might cause their symptoms to reappear.

Most people, however, are still extremely concerned about what their friends, relatives, boss, and neighbors would think if they were hospitalized for mental illness. Because of these fears, many people who need help will not seek it and those who are hospitalized are extremely concerned about the confidentiality of information. Until they develop a trusting relationship with staff members, they may be very reluctant to disclose any information about themselves. Trusting relationships are not built quickly. Mentally ill patients are very sensitive to how other people feel and react toward them. Perhaps this acute sensitivity is one of the reasons they have become ill, for in our society it is extremely important to be accepted, well liked, and a member of the group.

Because mental illness affects all races, ages, and socioeconomic groups, any of us, if subjected to enough stress, may suffer an emotional crisis. In fact, new workers in the mental health field often worry about their own "wellness" because they see many similarities between their patients and themselves. At one time or another, everyone has minor mood swings, gets depressed, or feels anger, anxiety, or fear. We all occasionally mistrust others. How many of us, at one time or another, have said of ourselves, "I'm going to go crazy," or have said to a friend, "Are you off your rocker?" The difference between being mentally healthy and being mentally ill lies in the frequency and intensity of inappropriate behavior and often in the public's tolerance of such behavior.

New mental health workers often experience considerable anxiety because they feel they do not know what to do for their patients. Physical health team members work in a more structured environment: they have tests to run, medicines to give, patients to be bathed, and diagnostic and treatment procedures to perform, and their patients are generally cooperative. However, mental health workers must realize that often their primary contribution to a patient may be simply that they are there and available to listen if the patient wishes to talk. In their book, *Psychiatric Nursing in the Hospital and the Community*, Burgess and Lazare (1973) state, "It takes some time to realize that listening to that which aches in the heart of the patient may touch him more profoundly than a back rub."

This brief overview of selected general factors related to the mental health field is intended to provide the mental health worker with a framework within which to view mental illness as it is seen by people currently active in this field. It may be helpful to keep these points in mind as you study the other chapters in this book.

REFERENCE

Burgess, A., and Lazare, A.: *Psychiatric Nursing in the Hospital and the Community*. Prentice-Hall, Englewood Cliffs, NJ, 1973.

ANNOTATED BIBLIOGRAPHY

Andrews, M.M.: *Cultural perspectives on nursing in the 21st century.* Journal of Professional Nursing, 1992, 8(1):7–15.

Explores past, present, and future issues and trends in transcultural nursing.

Barker, P.J.: *The conceptual basis of mental health nursing.* Nurse Education Today, 1990, 10:339–348.

Explores the historical roots of mental health nursing and its effect on current nursing styles.

Fabrega, H., Jr.: *Psychiatric stigma in the classical and medieval period: A review of the literature.* Comprehensive Psychiatry, 1990, 31(4):289–306.

Explores how mental illness was viewed in the classical and medieval periods and how this has affected the view, and therefore the treatment, of mental illness today.

Kadner, K., and Brandt, K.: *Homeward bound: Broadening student experience with home visits.* Journal of Psychosocial Nursing and Mental Health Services, 1991, 29(9):24–28.

Discusses the importance of exposing students to mental health care in home settings where patients can be followed for longer periods of time.

Lowery, B.J.: *Psychiatric nursing in the 1990s and beyond.* Journal of Psychosocial Nursing, 1992, 30(1):7–13.

Discusses the major advances in the mental health field and the rapid changes in psychiatric nursing due to these advances.

Mound, B., Gyulay, R., Khan, P., and Goering, P.: *The expanded role of nurse case managers.* Journal of Psychosocial Nursing and Mental Health Services, 1991, 29(6):18–22.

Discusses the dramatic changes in nursing practices as care for the mentally ill has shifted from the hospital setting to the community.

True or False. Circle your choice.

T   F   1. One may inherit a predisposition to certain types of mental illness.

T   F   2. Mentally ill patients are usually very sensitive to how other people feel toward them.

T   F   3. The treatment of mental illness is usually a very clear-cut process.

T   F   4. Any person, if subjected to enough stress, may have a "mental breakdown."

T   F   5. Minor mood swings are signs of mental illness.

T   F   6. People do not inherit mental disorders but may inherit a predisposition to certain types of mental problems.

T   F   7. Trusting relationships are easily established with the mentally ill.

T   F   8. If you feel you have said the wrong thing to a patient and thus caused the patient harm, you should continue to apologize until the apology is accepted.

T   F   9. It is not normal for a mental health worker to be disappointed or angry with a patient.

T   F   10. It is usually quite simple to pinpoint specific reasons for a person's becoming mentally ill at a particular time.

Fill in the Blanks. From the group of terms listed in Column B, select the letter of the most appropriate term(s) to complete the following sentences in Column A.

Column A	*Column B*
1. The difference between being mentally healthy and mentally ill lies in the _____ and _____ of inappropriate behavior.	a. decrease b. increased c. response d. intensity e. sensitive
2. Mentally ill patients are very _____ to how people feel and react toward them.	f. frequency g. available to listen
3. It is the way a person views a situation that determines his or her _____ .	h. insensitive i. confused j. aware of the problem

4. New drugs have helped to

   _____ the length of
   hospitalization of the mentally ill.
5. Mental health workers must realize
   that often their primary contribution to
   a patient may be simply that they are

   _____.

Multiple Choice. Circle the number that you think represents the best answer.

1. As a member of the community, the mental health worker can help reduce the loss to society that often occurs when someone becomes mentally ill by:
   a. Increasing the public's knowledge of the mental health services available in the community.
   b. Remembering that the mentally ill are permanently disabled.
   c. Having a personal attitude of acceptance in regard to mentally ill persons.
   d. Alerting the public to the early signs of mental illness through education.
   (1) a and c.
   (2) b and d.
   (3) a, c, and d.
   (4) All of the above.
2. To be an effective mental health worker, it is important that an individual:
   a. Understand the basic dynamics of human behavior.
   b. Be willing to explore his or her own feelings and reactions.
   c. Be able to give patients sound advice.
   d. Be able to work effectively with other members of the psychiatric team.
   (1) a and c.
   (2) a, b, and d.
   (3) a, c, and d.
   (4) All of the above.
3. Which of the following statements are true about community mental health centers, day care programs, and halfway houses?
   a. They offer care to patients without removing them from their communities or families for long periods of time.
   b. They prevent the regression and dependency of patients that often occur due to long-term hospitalization.
   c. They are rapidly growing approaches to care of the mentally ill.

    d. They will probably help patients learn to cope with the environments in which they became ill.
      (1) a and b.
      (2) b and d.
      (3) a, b, and c.
      (4) All of the above.

4. In working with an emotionally or mentally compromised patient, effective measures include:
    a. Acceptance of the patient as a unique and worthwhile individual.
    b. Support and understanding of the patient's feelings.
    c. Recognition and reinforcement of the patient's strengths.
    d. Prevention of regression on the part of the patient.
      (1) a and d.
      (2) b and c.
      (3) a, b, and c.
      (4) All of the above.

5. The aim of psychiatric treatment is to:
    a. Relieve the patient of symptoms.
    b. Return the patient to home and family.
    c. Help the patient become a better adjusted individual.
    d. Prevent the patient from becoming psychotic.
      (1) a.
      (2) b.
      (3) c.
      (4) d.

2

Personality Development

LEARNING OBJECTIVES

Student will be able to:
1. Recognize the stages of personality development.
2. Identify the developmental tasks related to the stages of development.
3. Define *id, ego,* and *superego.*

Before discussing various reasons for abnormal behavior, one must have a basic understanding of how a human being learns to behave in a normal (socially acceptable) manner. Because an individual's personality and perception of self are key factors in determining the type of behavior the individual exhibits, this chapter presents a basic overview of personality development.

Although events occurring throughout life may affect emotional adjustment, most experts in the field of mental health believe that the experiences that occur during the first 20 years have the most significant impact on the development of the personality. Some even say that the first 6 years of life are the most crucial. Regardless of which opinion is correct, all agree that the early life experiences of an individual directly influence mental health.

For the sake of discussion, the stages of personality development are usually divided in the following manner: infancy (birth to age 1½), toddler period (ages 1½ to 3), preschool period (ages 3 to 6), school age (ages 6 to puberty, which usually occurs between ages 11 and 13), adolescence (end of puberty to age 18 or 20), and adulthood (from age 18 or 20 on). Each developmental stage serves as a building block in the foundation of personality. If a stage is completed successfully, the foundation remains firm; but if there are serious problems during any of the stages, the personality structure is weakened.

One should remember that individuals develop at their own rates and that no two human beings are exactly alike; however, each of the stages listed above has certain tasks that most people will accomplish during that stage. For example, one of the developmental tasks of the toddler is to learn to walk, and most children will learn the basics of walking between the ages of 1 and 3. On the other hand, most of those same children will still be refining their ability to walk after they have entered the preschool stage and are busy conquering the tasks of that period.

INFANCY

Most authorities believe that normal newborns possess all the basic ingredients (genetic inheritance) to become biologically functioning human beings; however, the ability to use inherited potential will depend on life experiences. For example, if a child has the genetic potential to become a great pianist but is born into a poor family, never hears a piano, and never has a chance to take piano lessons, this great genetic potential will likely go unrecognized and unused. On the other hand, a child may have the finest music lessons and the best piano that money can buy but have no genetic potential or musical talent. That child will develop, at best, into an average piano player.

Although a new computer is mechanically ready to function and solve all sorts of complicated problems, it cannot begin to function until it is fed, by a human being, a massive dose of raw information, facts, and formulas (programming). A human infant functions in much the same manner. A 5- or 6-year old child will have great difficulty learning to read unless someone, usually the child's parents, spends 5 or so years programming the child's "computer" (the brain). They do this by saying over and over that a chair is a chair, that a cow is a cow (not a "moo"), and that a stove burner is hot, as well as by providing the child with a large variety of learning experiences, such as trips to the zoo, the store, the fire department, and so forth.

Newborns also have no concept of morality. They are gradually taught right from wrong over the first few years of life according to what their parents consider right and wrong. Sigmund Freud considered the newborn to be a "bundle of id." Simply stated, *id* is Freud's term for that part of one's personality that is unconscious and contains all of the "wants" of an individual (e.g., to eat, to sleep, to be comfortable, to have fun, and to do pleasurable things). In other words, infants want their basic needs (food, diapers changed, sleep, attention) met at the exact moment they want them, regardless of whom it inconveniences (usually Mom and Dad at 2:00 A.M.). Gradually, throughout the first year of life, infants learn that there are others in the world and that despite their mother's best efforts, it takes a few minutes to warm a bottle or change a diaper.

If one observes 3- or 4-month-old infants demanding a feeding, one can see that most cry, indicating their hunger need, but become quiet when their mother takes the bottle out of the refrigerator and begins to warm it. These children have begun to trust the mother to follow through in meeting their needs, and thus they begin to develop feelings that the world is a good place in which to live and grow. On the other hand, if the infants are allowed to cry for hours before being fed or are constantly abused and neglected, they begin to mistrust people and to feel that the world is not a very likable place. If deprivation and neglect are severe enough, infants or young children withdraw from the world of reality into a world of fantasy, which feels less threatening. Therefore, in the first year of life, infants need as little frustration as possible in order to learn to trust their environment and to feel good about themselves and the world in which they live.

An unfortunate characteristic of children is that they tend to blame themselves for failures of their parents and thus develop feelings of inadequacy that may affect them all their lives. For example, when parents divorce, young children often feel that they are to blame, and so they plead with the parents to stay together, promising never to be bad again. This sense of being able to make all sorts of things happen is apparently a carryover from early infancy, when young babies, being unable to see well enough to distinguish themselves from others, feel that they themselves meet their own needs. Of course, by the time they are 4 to 6 months old, infants can recognize their mother and see her as the source of relief for all their tension; therefore, they transfer their feeling of omnipotence to their mother and expect her to cure all ills. For example, you have probably heard a young child ask his or her mother to make the rain go away or to make an injured finger stop hurting.

Although not omnipotent, the mother (or mother substitute) plays an extremely important role in the life of an infant. Infants need the psychologic satisfaction that comes from being held close to another human being while being caressed and talked to in a gentle, caring way. The mother figure is the first love object for all humankind. An infant is completely dependent on her, and thus the mother-child relationship is perhaps more intense than any other relationship in one's life. In the more serious psychologic illnesses, one frequently finds a flaw in the mother-child relationship along with other causative factors. Often to their dismay, young children soon realize that neither they nor their mothers are omnipotent. Ideally, this realization occurs gradually as children begin to master more of the skills of daily living that allow them to feel more in control of their environment and thus less insecure and dependent.

TODDLER PERIOD

Between the ages of 1 and 2½, children begin to develop a sense of autonomy. In other words, they begin to view themselves as individuals in their own right, apart from their parents, although still dependent on them. Children now have minds of their own and want to try to handle reality in their own ways. Parents tend to remember this stage of development well, for it seems that all of a sudden the quiet, cuddly, agreeable, helpless, dependent, clinging little infant has become a tyrant who states over and over, "no, no, no," while refusing all offers of help and scurrying around as if in training for the Olympics.

Unfortunately, many parents fail to recognize and accept this stage for what it is—the child's first attempts at establishing independence and self-reliance. The parents may feel threatened. The ensuing battle is made especially ridiculous by the fact that one of the warring parties is 2 years old and the other is an adult. An insecure parent may be heard yelling, "No 2-year-old is going to say 'no' to me!" What parents may fail to realize is that the world is a frustrating place for toddlers. They are quite interested in their world and want to do a great many things; however, they are too short to see much of what is going on, cannot walk or climb well enough to get where they want to go, cannot dress themselves, and, most of all, are constantly being told what to do by someone four or five times their size.

The world is also frustrating for adults who have children. This is especially true when parents are faced with the delicate task of toilet training. It is hard for most adults to believe that they once thought freedom constituted being able to mess in their pants whenever they wanted to do so, or that they once felt that fecal material was something special they had created. This, however, is apparently the way many toddlers view it. Toddlers are unable to look ahead and realize that when they are toilet trained Mom and Dad will take them more places. They must also be taught by their parents that their feces are not artistic creations, that they smell bad, and that they belong in only one place—the toilet.

In other areas of muscle and motor development, this conflict of interest does not exist, because the child and the parents are in agreement concerning their goals. Parents are delighted when their children learn to walk, and they encourage and reward them for doing so. In regard to being toilet trained, children want to please their mothers and fathers and at the same time want to retain their freedom. Having both positive and negative feelings about the situation, the child experiences conflict. However, in the end, the child's desire to please the parents usually wins out, and the parents' attitude about fecal material is adopted.

This stage of development would progress much more smoothly if parents would not attempt to begin toilet training until the child is physically capable of being trained and psychologically receptive to the idea. Voluntary control of the anal sphincter muscle does not develop until a child is 18 to 24 months of age, and by that time the child is usually beginning to show signs of disgust at having "accidents." Serious psychologic problems may occur if a mother tries to toilet train a child too early, if a mother is excessively preoccupied with neatness or cleanliness, or if a mother is overly permissive and enjoys rearing a child with no shame, guilt, or need to conform to the norms of the surrounding society. Humans do not live in isolation; therefore they must conform to some extent to societal norms. This socialization process takes place in infancy and childhood, and when parents fail to assume their responsibility for making sure that socialization does indeed occur, the child usually has a great deal of difficulty adjusting as an adult. For example, people who are considered antisocial or sociopathic because they function as a "bundle of id," wanting what they want when they want it, regardless of whom it inconveniences or hurts, frequently had overly permissive parents. Society does not tolerate such behavior well, and sociopaths often spend their lives on the fringes of society or in and out of jail or mental institutions.

PRESCHOOL PERIOD

By the end of the toddler or muscle-training period, the child's motor and intellectual skills have greatly increased. Three-year-olds have fairly good vocabularies that enable them to tell about their experiences; they can ride tricycles, run with only a few falls, dress themselves if the buttons are big and in the front; and they can generally stay dry through the night. These accomplishments boost self-esteem and help children feel good about themselves. They are then ready to learn more about the world outside their families. It is during this period (ages 3 to 6) that the ego and superego begin to function. The *superego* is that part of the personality that is called the conscience. It is composed of all the "controls,"—the "shoulds" and "should nots"—that we learn from our parents, churches, schools, teachers, and so forth. Its structure depends largely on the type, quality, and severity of discipline.

Parents frequently do not realize how critically they behave toward their children and how little room they allow for mistakes. If a child mispronounces a word, they may ridicule and try to force the child to say the word correctly. Later they wonder why the child is so quiet and seldom talks. Parents tend to forget the words they mispronounce or the times they stutter. If Johnny spills a glass of milk, he may be called "clumsy" and be punished. His parents react to the inconvenience of cleaning up without realizing that they caused the problem by not understanding that a 2-year-old child's hand cannot reach around a large milk glass. Events such as these chip away at feelings of self-worth, especially when parents add injury to insult by saying over and over that the child is bad or that the child should be ashamed of himself or herself. It would probably be much better if parents would identify only a child's *behavior* as inappropriate or unacceptable, rather than calling the child either a "bad boy" or "bad girl" (or in opposite circumstances, a "good boy" or "good girl"). It is the behavior that is acceptable or unacceptable, not the child.

By the time children are 5 to 6 years of age, parents no longer have to be physically present to enforce discipline. The children have incorporated their parents' scoldings into their own minds, and before starting to do something, they hear that still, small voice (the superego or conscience) saying, "You'd better watch out; you know how clumsy you are, and if you break that toy you're going to be a bad boy."

Of course children need to be disciplined, but discipline needs to be given consistently, in small doses, and only when absolutely needed. Proper environmental structure tends to reduce the need for excessive discipline because children know what is expected of them. Children need to learn to respond to reasonable limits. If there is no discipline, children fail to develop a sense of right or wrong and will lack respect for other people and their belongings. On the other hand, if discipline is too severe, children become afraid to try anything new or different, experience extreme guilt and shame, and, in effect, become maladapted persons who are afraid of the world. Individuals need a well-balanced personality. They need a conscience (superego) that allows them to make changes and mistakes and to be successful in give-and-take situations with other people. Yet they must be able to accept blame when they are wrong and change their behavior when it needs changing without becoming so guilt-ridden that continued functioning is impossible. This is where the ego plays its major role.

The *ego* is conscious and functions as the "manager" of the personality. It deals with reality and must manage the impulses or demands of the unconscious id and superego and help find acceptable ways to meet those demands in the conscious world of reality. Of course, the ego must have help in its managerial role. It gets that help from the psychologic defense mechanisms that are discussed in the next chapter.

The preschool period, which has been called the "family triangle period" by some authorities, is the first time that boys and girls encounter different conflicts and achievements. By age 3, the baby no longer exists, and the child looks like either a little boy or little girl. Members of each sex are acutely aware of their own bodies and the physical changes that are occurring. The genital area is now the body region of emotional significance, and both boys and girls seek a sexual type of pleasure through manipulation of their external genitals. This occurs in nearly all normal children and is even seen in infants, although more randomly and less purposefully.

Unfortunately, many parents react negatively when they find their child masturbating and may resort to various threats and punishments in order to stop the behavior. Some parents verbally instruct the child to stop, stating that masturbation is not nice or may be harmful. Other parents may resort to threats of cutting off the child's penis or retaliation from supernatural beings, because they feel masturbation is a sin. Most children usually stop masturbating or continue with it less frequently and more discriminatingly due either to fear or to a desire to please their parents. In either case, a great deal of guilt is produced and must be handled by the child. The guilt is often handled by *repression*—an unconscious forgetting of threatening events. Unfortunately, the individual does not really forget the event; rather it becomes part of the individual's unconscious, where, although not remembered, it may motivate future behavior.

SCHOOL AGE

Psychologically, the early school years are quiet and peaceful ones for the child. Some authorities have even gone so far as to describe the span of time between ages 6 and 10 as the "golden era of childhood." At this point in a child's development, sexual frustrations and problems of the previous stages have usually been at least partially resolved. Most children have given up masturbation in return for parental approval and are actively attempting to become more like the parent of the same sex, instead of trying to possess the parent of the opposite sex (sometimes called an "oedipal conflict"). The child, therefore, has greater energy to devote to other areas of interest; thus great social and intellectual strides are made in this period. During this stage, the child is extremely interested in learning, and sexual curiosity has been replaced by intellectual curiosity. Instead of daydreaming about sexual achievement, the child seeks success in real-life social interactions.

The school-age child identifies with the parent of the same sex and also begins to identify with other children of the same sex. Boys greatly prefer the company of other boys and girls enjoy being with other girls. Individual friendships are extremely important, but the school-age child begins to become interested in group activities and membership as well.

ADOLESCENCE

The onset of puberty (10 to 14 years of age) is actually the beginning of adolescence. Sexual development once again becomes of prime importance. Masturbation is usually resumed, if it was ever discontinued, or increased. Girls begin their menstrual periods and boys experience nocturnal emissions (wet dreams). Both sexes begin to have romantic fantasies involving sexual contacts with members of the opposite sex. Instead of the parent of the opposite sex, who captured their interest during the family triangle period, their partners in these sexual fantasies are often classmates, older friends, movie stars, or other idolized individuals.

During puberty, it is of prime importance that the parent-child relationship be a good one. Ideally, all children should be given adequate sex education, especially in this day of AIDS and other sexually transmitted diseases, before the onset of puberty. As new and drastic body changes begin to occur, children need to be able to discuss their feelings with their parents. They have questions that need to be answered and fears that need to be expressed and understood.

Because actions often speak louder than words, the way parents relate to each other and their acceptance of their own gender greatly influence adolescents' acceptance of their own developing sexuality. For example, the way a young girl accepts the onset of her menstrual period is largely influenced by the way that her mother has accepted her own sexual and reproductive functions. Fears, inhibitions, and tension related to menstruation are often passed on to daughters and surface in physical complaints such as severe cramps and headaches, moodiness, and incapacitation during a portion of the menstrual period.

Adolescence is a stormy period for both teenagers and their parents because both have ambivalent feelings about the changes that are taking place. Parents are not sure they want to give up control of the adolescent and allow development of greater independence. On the other hand, the adolescent is not always sure he or she wants to assume the responsibility that goes with more independence. There is a great deal of security in having parents make decisions and be responsible for one's care. One of the major problems between parents and adolescents occurs when the adolescent wants the independence without the responsibility. Such dependence-independence conflicts probably account for much of the adolescent's often irritable and erratic behavior. One moment he or she is the most responsible, mature creature one could ask for; the next moment, he or she is childish and irresponsible.

Although most adolescents are not emotionally capable of engaging in a mature and responsible sexual relationship, they are capable of developing emotionally satisfying relationships that provide companionship and the opportunity for experiences and affection with members of the opposite sex.

Because adolescents are still deeply involved in trying to establish their own feelings of self-worth and are working through feelings of inadequacy and dependence at a time when they also long to be independent and self-sufficient, "love" relationships are likely to be based on what the "loved" person does to strengthen the adolescent's own self-esteem. You have probably heard a young man brag to his fraternity brothers about his date with one of the college cheerleaders, or a 16-year-old high school sophomore bragging to her friend about the guy she is dating who just happens to drive a shiny sports car.

Peer approval is extremely important to the adolescent. A girl often wants to be asked out on lots of dates in order to appear popular because this increases her status in the eyes of her girlfriends. A boy may accomplish the same thing by bragging about his sexual accomplishments to his male friends.

"Falling in love" usually begins to occur around age 16 and is likely to happen a number of times before young adults experience the type of relationship in which their wish to receive is overcome by their wish to give. These fleeting relationships, however, are important because they help adolescents develop their ability to form close relationships based on give-and-take situations, an ability that ultimately leads to the establishment of a lasting relationship.

When the individual at long last has conquered the possessive feelings of early childhood and has changed the love object from a parent to a person of his or her own peer group, the point of establishing mature relationships is reached. With this initial act, the individual prepares for the transition from adolescence to adulthood and goes out to face the world carrying all that he or she has learned to be, a small fear of being alone, and a hope for the future.

ANNOTATED BIBLIOGRAPHY

Baker, H.S., and Baker, M.N.: *Heinz Kohut's self psychology: An overview.* The American Journal of Psychiatry, 1987, 144(1):1–9.

> *Attributes the development of mental illness to inadequate parenting, parental abuse, and unmet needs in childhood.*

Carrey, N.J., and Adams, L.: *How to deal with sexual acting-out on the child psychiatric inpatient ward.* Journal of Psychosocial Nursing and Mental Health Services, 1992, 30(5):19–23.

Discusses the causes and patterns of sexual acting out and provides interventions for modifying these behaviors.

Florenzano, R.: *Chronic mental illness in adolescence: A global overview.* Pediatrician, 1991, 18:142–149.

Provides information on prevalence and types of chronic mental illness seen in adolescence and discusses current trends in child psychiatry.

Hayes, F.S.: *The McCarthy Scales of Children's Abilities: Their usefulness in developmental assessment.* Pediatric Nursing, 1981, 7(4):35–37.

Describes the use of the MSCA as a tool in the developmental assessment of children aged $2\frac{1}{2}$ to $8\frac{1}{2}$.

Kaufmann, P.M., Sparrow, S.S., and Leckman, J.F.: *Children with tics and nonverbal learning disability: Preliminary MRI findings.* The Clinical Neuropsychologist, 5(3):248.

Discusses the neuropsychological profile similarities observed in children with tic disorders and children with nonverbal learning disability.

Lefley, H.P.: *Culture and chronic mental illness.* Hospital and Community Psychiatry, 1990, 41(3): 277–286.

Discusses the effect of cultural beliefs and practices on the development and long-term prognosis of mental illness.

Pontious, S.L.: *Practical Piaget: Helping children understand.* American Journal of Nursing, 1982, 82(1):114–117.

Describes the differences in the perceptions of a child who is in Piaget's preoperational stage (ages 2 to 7), and the child who is in the concrete operational stage (ages 7 to 12). Offers insights for dealing with the child in each stage.

Rubio-Stipec, M., Bird, H., Canino, G., Bravo, M., and Alegria, M.: *Children of alcoholic parents in the community.* Journal of Studies on Alcohol, 1991, 52(1):78–87.

Provides information on how alcoholism and adverse family conditions increase the risk of maladjustment in children.

Thomas, A., and Chess, S.: *Genesis and evolution of behavioral disorders: From infancy to early adult life.* The American Journal of Psychiatry, 1984, 141(1):1–9.

A study evaluating the effect of temperamental characteristics and environment on psychological development from birth through adulthood.

Ullmann, R.K., Sleator, E.K.: *Attention deficit disorder children with or without hyperactivity.* Clinical Pediatrics, 1985, 24(10):547–551.

Discusses the importance of knowing a child's specific problems when treating them for attention deficit disorder.

Fill in the Blanks. From the group of terms listed in Column B, select the letter of the most appropriate term(s) to complete the following sentences in Column A.

Column A	Column B
1. Some experts say that the first _____ years of life are the most crucial.	a. life experiences b. 6 c. mother-child d. less threatening e. 3 to 6 f. 6 to 10 g. sibling h. husband-wife
2. One's ability to use all of one's inherited potential depends on _____.	
3. If neglect is severe enough, the infant or young child withdraws from reality into a world of fantasy that feels _____ .	
4. The _____ relationship is perhaps more intense than any other relationship in one's life.	
5. From the ages of _____, a child's superego develops rapidly.	

True or False. Circle your choice.

T F 1. All human beings develop in the exact same pattern and almost at the same rate.

T F 2. The mother figure is the first love object for all humankind.

T F 3. If there is no discipline, children fail to develop a sense of right and wrong.

T F 4. Adolescence appears to be an easy developmental stage for teenagers and their parents.

T F 5. Peer approval is of little importance to the adolescent.

Multiple Choice. Circle the letter or number that you think represents the best answer.

1. What is the outstanding characteristic of growth and development?
   a. It occurs at a uniform rate.
   b. Each individual follows a unique pattern.
   c. It is a simple process.
   d. It rarely influences behavior.

23

2. What is the most important factor in the home environment of a child?
   a. Assurance of proper nutrition.
   b. Provision of play space.
   c. Atmosphere that lets the child feel secure.
   d. Protection from overstimulation.
3. A basic factor contributing to the security of a child is:
   a. The knowledge that he or she is an individual.
   b. The setting of realistic boundaries and limits.
   c. Allowing dependence on the mother for the child's needs.
   d. Allowing the child to have what he or she wants.
4. Growth and development of children are influenced by:
   a. Heredity.
   b. Cultural heritage.
   c. Environment.
   d. The way their parents treat them.
      (1) a.
      (2) a and c.
      (3) b, c, and d.
      (4) All of the above.
5. The fact that boys fight and generally display greater aggressiveness than girls is probably best explained on the basis of differences in:
   a. Social expectation.
   b. Endocrine balance.
   c. Inherited predisposition.
   d. Hereditary factors.
6. The freudian theory of personality development divides the mind into three basic parts. Of the terms listed below, which one is *not* a basic part?
   a. Ego.
   b. Libido.
   c. Id.
   d. Superego.
7. The ego is that part of the mind that:
   a. Helps the individual deal with reality.
   b. Constantly attempts to satisfy its own demands.
   c. Is concerned with morals, values, precepts, and standards.
   d. Represses painful thoughts from consciousness.
8. A 2-year-old child is frequently negativistic and resistant to adult demands. This behavior is usually regarded as an indication of:
   a. Inconsistent techniques on the part of the parents.
   b. Overindulgence on the part of the parents.

    c. Too much strictness on the part of the parents.

    d. A growing awareness of self on the part of the child.

  9. Independent behavior is learned from a mother who:

    a. Is permissive and allows the child to do as he or she desires.

    b. Is fearful of injury or of the child's getting dirty.

    c. Permits exploration and experimentation but sets limits.

    d. Rewards accomplishments and avoids restrictions.

10. The best advice to give parents on the subject of toilet training is:

    a. To wait until the child indicates that he or she is ready via behavioral cues.

    b. To begin bladder training around 15 months of age.

    c. To use their discretion.

    d. To place the child on the potty for 15 minutes at the same time each day.

11. The best way to manage the aggressive behavior of a 2-year-old boy is:

    a. To tell him he is a bad boy and that you will not love him if the behavior continues.

    b. To rechannel his activity into a more acceptable area.

    c. To let him vent his aggressive feelings however he wishes.

    d. To punish him for any aggressive behavior.

12. Questions from a preschool child may become annoying. Adults should understand that:

    a. This is a period of rapid vocabulary growth.

    b. The child's "computer" is being programmed.

    c. Answers provide the child with a concept of adult attitudes and feelings.

    d. The child should always be given an answer.

        (1) a and c.

        (2) b, c, and d.

        (3) a, b, and d.

        (4) a and d.

        (5) All of the above.

13. A typical characteristic of a girl during the preschool stage of development is:

    a. Little curiosity about sex differences.

    b. Strong interest in and attraction to her father.

    c. Intense admiration of her peers.

    d. Interest in "gangs" with girls her age.

14. The so-called golden years of childhood are:

    a. 1 to 3.

    b. 3 to 6.

    c. 6 to 10.

    d. 10 through puberty.

    e. 14 to 20.

15. Family relations for the school child are characterized by:

    a. Identification with the parent of the same sex.

    b. Increasing independence.

    c. Importance of individual friendships.

    d. Resentment of rigid rules.

        (1) a and d.

        (2) b and c.

        (3) a, b, and c.

        (3) b and d.

        (5) All of the above.

16. A teacher finds a group of first graders involved in dramatizing a funeral. Which idea in regard to their play is likely to be most justified?

    a. Realistic play of this nature is unusual in children of this age.

    b. This play behavior is likely to be unrelated to the actual experience.

    c. The children should be gently guided to other types of play.

    d. Such play is an attempt to explore the reality of death.

17. The attitudes of a young girl toward menstruation usually reflect those of:

    a. Her best friend.

    b. The person who tells her about it.

    c. Her mother.

    d. Her family.

18. The major adjustments the adolescent has to make are:

    a. Physical adjustment to body changes.

    b. Social adjustment with peers.

    c. Sexual adjustment in boy-girl relationships.

    d. Moral adjustment so he or she will have a moral code to live by in the future.

        (1) a.

        (2) c.

        (3) b and c.

        (4) All of the above.

19. Usually the strictest behavioral control over the adolescent is exerted by:

    a. Parents.

    b. Church.

    c. Peers.

    d. School.

Basic Concepts of the Mind

LEARNING OBJECTIVES

Student will be able to:
1. Define *psychopathology.*
2. List three specific behaviors used to evaluate one's overall mental health.
3. Define the term *defense mechanism;* give two examples.
4. Define *neurosis* and *psychosis.*

THE MENTAL HEALTH CONTINUUM

If one successfully accomplishes the developmental tasks discussed in the preceding chapter, one can approach adulthood with the skills necessary to function as a mentally healthy, mature adult. Maturity and mental health are not dependent on the number of years lived but rather on an individual's problem-solving skills, ability to cope with life stresses, and ability to make good choices.

The emotionally healthy person is accepting of himself or herself and others and has developed the ability to give as well as receive. Such persons have an appropriate amount of self-confidence because they have realistically evaluated their own assets as well as liabilities and have found that they have the ability to cope with the challenges of life. They make decisions based on sound judgment and then accept responsibility for their actions.

Of course, one needs to remember that even the most emotionally competent and responsible individual sometimes acts in an immature or childish manner. It is only when one's behavior is frequently irresponsible or is significantly at odds with society's expectations that one begins to experience the maladjustments referred to as psychopathology.

Psychopathology is a term used to indicate that a person is emotionally unable to deal with the stress and strain of everyday life. Such a condition usually comes about when people's defense mechanisms are no longer able to defend them against the anxiety created by stress and strain, when they have not been able to develop defense mechanisms against such forces, or when they use defense mechanisms so excessively that reality is not accurately perceived. If individuals' defenses work adequately and they seem to be able to get along reasonably well in everyday life, they are said to be "adjusted." If they are not able to get along well and people see them as being strange or peculiar, or if their behavior is obviously inappropriate, they are said to be manifesting a significant degree of psychopathology.

To understand the difference between mental health and mental illness, it is helpful to think in terms of specific behaviors. For example, take the rather simple behavior of laughing. If people never laugh, we say they are depressed and do not have the capability of enjoying themselves. If they laugh all the time, we suspect that something is wrong with them, particularly if they laugh at inappropriate times. The point is, of course, that somewhere in between never laughing and laughing constantly, there is a range in which the behavior of laughing is both acceptable and expected. This demonstrates the idea of the mental health continuum. By looking at behaviors in terms of a mental health continuum, it is easy to see that most given behaviors have socially acceptable ranges of occurrence, and that either the absolute absence or the constant presence of those behaviors might be seen as abnormal. The drawing below demonstrates this idea.

```
     no laughter        appropriate laughter      constant laughter
|-----------------------|----------------------------|--------------------------|
```

With the idea, then, that most behaviors have an appropriate range that is both acceptable and expected, let us look at some of the specific things that may be used to judge one's overall mental health.

1. Thinking well of oneself; being fairly free of feelings of inadequacy and inferiority; being able to express or to communicate one's emotions.
2. The ability to trust oneself to make decisions and to act on those decisions after careful consideration of the consequences of one's actions.
3. A genuine feeling of well-being and a realistic degree of optimism (expectation that things will turn out well).
4. Accepting one's real limitations while developing one's assets.

5. Evaluating one's mistakes, determining their causes, and learning not to repeat the same behavior.
6. Being able to delay immediate gratification for future satisfaction (for example, putting off getting married until one's career preparation is finished).
7. The ability to form close and lasting relationships with persons of both sexes, being relatively satisfied with one's own sex, and having the ability to enjoy an active and satisfactory sex life.
8. An appropriate conscience that prevents the individual from getting into trouble by resisting behavior that is destructive either to the individual or to others; a conscience that also produces guilt when one behaves in an antisocial fashion.
9. The ability to accept authority (obey traffic laws, follow the rules of the organization for which one works, and so forth) in appropriate situations, but not to be afraid of authority and to contest authority if necessary.
10. The ability to meet one's needs in a socially acceptable manner while taking into consideration the needs of others.
11. The absence of petty jealousies and the need to exploit and manipulate others.
12. An ability to maintain a reasonably accurate perception of reality and of one's social and interpersonal interactions.
13. The ability to work alone and to work effectively with others; compromising and sharing when appropriate, but being able to compete and be aggressive when necessary; being organized and systematic in order to get things done; possessing an acceptable amount of cleanliness, promptness, orderliness, and neatness.
14. The ability to function in both dependent and independent roles; to follow or to lead, to take care of others or to be taken care of, depending on the circumstances.
15. Acceptance of the fact that stress and change are part of everyday life; being flexible enough to adapt to these continual changes without a great deal of psychologic discomfort.
16. A sense of humor; the ability to laugh at oneself and others when life situations are absurd.
17. The ability to maintain a balanced or integrated personality so that one can respond adaptively to life experiences.

It is difficult to define these factors accurately, to measure them, and to decide just how much of a behavior is acceptable and how much is not. Psychologists and psychiatrists attempt to make these decisions and often are asked to do so in court cases and competency hearings. Value judgments relative to these points should be avoided. For example, some societies reward their young men for stealing, and some subcultures in our country reward the young members of their gangs for stealing, running away from home, and going to juvenile detention centers. Often, the fact of having been in a juvenile detention center gives a young man a special status in his group and he is looked up to by the other members.

It seems that, in the final analysis, the degree to which a particular behavior is considered acceptable by individuals in our society is determined by how much of that particular behavior a society is willing to accept. Of course, what is acceptable to society changes from time to time. In 1950, it would probably have been quite upsetting to most people to have naked persons running around town; however, in the "streaking" fad of 1974, a great many young people were running around town wearing nothing but tennis shoes and a smile and were frequently applauded for their efforts. This particular fad even made its way to Hollywood, where perhaps the ultimate was reached when a daring young man streaked the televised 1974 Academy Awards presentation.

Had these behaviors occurred in 1950, it is likely that the streakers would have been jailed and that there would have been considerable public outrage; however, the permissiveness of the late 1960s and early 1970s made this behavior merely amusing to a great many Americans. Most of the legal cases involving streakers were dismissed from court, or the streakers were given minimal fines; however, even with the permissive attitudes prevalent in 1974, a "dirty old man" in the park wearing nothing but a raincoat and exposing himself to young girls as they passed by would not have met with a similar fate in court. He probably would have received a substantial sentence for indecent public exposure or, at least, been committed for psychiatric treatment. In 1992, rap musicians were jailed, fined, and otherwise harassed for the lyrics they performed onstage. Those opposing them felt harassed by the words they used and felt the music to be disgusting. In general, however, our courts have held that persons have a right to free speech and that poor taste is no excuse for taking away constitutional rights.

One further point should be made. Even though a person is seen as being well adjusted by most friends and peers, it is unlikely that anyone is totally adjusted. In fact, it has been said that the only totally adjusted person is a dead one. Every person who is active and who participates in his or her environment is continually subjected to conflicts that must be resolved. The young lady who meets a handsome young man and wants to go out with him but who also has a big exam the following day must confront the conflict and decide whether to go out with the young man or to study for the exam. A healthy response would be to decide to do one or the other. A less healthy response would be to do neither and to permit the conflict to remain unresolved.

Return, then, to the question of what happens when an individual becomes unable to manage anxieties and conflicts and thus becomes unable to function in a "well-adjusted" fashion. By and large, there are two major classifications for such maladjustments—the *neurotic maladjustment* and the *psychotic maladjustment*. Before these are discussed, however, it is necessary to know something about the psychologic defense mechanisms that help us function when we encounter highly stressful situations. The following section provides an overview of the defense mechanisms, including how they work and how they may be abused.

DEFENSE MECHANISMS

All of us have a basic image of ourselves (self-image) that is important to our general psychologic well-being. Basically, the self-image is the collection of ideas we have about what kind of person we are.

Sometimes people who have poor self-images try just as hard to maintain that poor self-image as other persons try to maintain a good self-image. Given that we frequently react to other people the way we react to ourselves, it is easy to see that the way in which we view ourselves is quite an important factor in our relationships with other people.

It is in this area of the self-image that the defense mechanisms work. In our efforts to maintain a constant way of viewing ourselves, we sometimes face situations that are threats to our worth or adequacy or to our cherished way of viewing ourselves. Such situations are stressful because they pressure us to change our ways of seeing ourselves and thus upset our feelings of "constancy."

The defense mechanisms are sometimes called adjustment or coping mechanisms. They are usually unconscious, although we sometimes become aware of their presence. At times, we may even use them consciously. These mechanisms are used daily by almost everyone. They are neither good nor bad. Whether they are healthy or unhealthy is probably best determined by whether they serve to help or hurt the individual using them. If they help one to meet one's personal and social goals in acceptable ways, they are healthy. If they cause us to distort reality unrealistically and to deceive ourselves, they are unhealthy. For example, if one always explains one's failures by blaming someone else or always rationalizes away one's inadequacies, one may never consider that one might be more successful if one learned to look for the real reasons for failures. A classic example that demonstrates this point occurs when a student fails an examination and blames the teacher for not giving a "fair" exam, for making the exam too difficult, or for not asking what he or she said would be asked on the exam. The student may be ignoring the fact of having studied for only an hour when 4 or 5 hours of study were needed for satisfactory performance on the exam.

To summarize, defense mechanisms are used by almost everyone. They are frequently used without one's conscious awareness, and they are used to help individuals maintain cherished beliefs about themselves and the world. The rest of this section lists specific defense mechanisms, with brief examples to show how they are used and how they might be abused.

REPRESSION

Repression is considered by many authorities to be the most common defense mechanism. Individuals use repression when they "forget" or exclude from conscious thought those things that they find too painful or anxiety provoking to remember. The repression of anxiety-producing situations is often incomplete, frequently resulting in vague feelings of worthlessness and insecurity. Sometimes people feel guilty almost constantly and are unable to discover why they have such feelings.

Perhaps one of the most classic and usual cases associated with repression occurs with sexual matters. A young female patient seen by one of the authors complained of not being able to "let go" sexually with her husband. She admitted that she wanted to like intercourse because she knew that it would please her husband; yet each time they started to have intercourse, she could feel herself "tighten up." The patient even "tightened up" talking about it to the therapist and became quite anxious. After several visits, the patient started to say something about an incident she dimly remembered but could not quite bring herself to talk about it. At the next therapy session, she began talking about an incident in which she and her brother, at ages 7 and 9, had been playing together and had become interested in how they were different from each other. Her mother discovered them while they were undressed and marveling at their differences. When the screaming, yelling, and whippings were over, the patient was confused, upset, and unaware of what she had done wrong. She was visibly uncomfortable talking about the incident, but after her recollection and further discussion and supportive therapy she began to respond to her husband sexually and, at last contact, was feeling much like a woman who had been, in her words, "set free." Of course, not all episodes of repression are so dramatic or have such an impact on one's behavior. Lesser incidents of repression occur daily. A young child receives an "F" on her report card and "forgets" to bring it home to be signed. A husband "forgets" his wife's birthday after a big fight. A businessman "forgets" the name of a customer whom he really does not like.

In any case, although it may help reduce anxiety temporarily, repression uses up valuable psychologic energy and may block one's efforts toward leading a "comfortable" existence. It is usually better to deal with the repressed material because doing so will help one to make a more healthy adjustment.

RATIONALIZATION

Rationalization is a favorite defense mechanism for many people. It allows us to do what we want to do when we know that we should not, and it helps us to accept ourselves when we do not live up to our goals or the expectations that we, and others, have for ourselves. It involves thinking up reasons for our behavior that are more acceptable than the "real" reason. A good rationalization may contain some elements of truth, and this, of course, makes it seem even more plausible. For example, a woman was about to be jailed for having written bad checks amounting to more than $9000. When asked why she had written the worthless checks, she said that her husband deserved to have some of the finer things in life and that all his hard work had not gotten him anything.

Other examples of rationalization include such statements as "If only I were taller, the girls would like me better" or "If I just had some new clothes, I would really knock them dead." Other examples are, "Yeah, if I were captain of the football team, I'd have 10 girl friends too," and "If I had his brains I could make A's too." One final example: "Everyone else cheats, so I have to; if I don't, I won't pass." The most serious consequence of rationalization is self-deception. Although it may be painful at times, one is probably better off accepting the truth about the motives for one's behavior. In doing so, one is more likely to benefit from experiences.

DENIAL OF REALITY

Denial of reality occurs when one simply refuses to see what is obvious to everyone else. The husband who refuses to recognize that his wife is "running around" on him when everyone else knows that she is doing so, represents a case in point. This mechanism is also frequently found among persons who have physical disabilities or who have lost limbs because of amputation. One young man was injured in an automobile accident and was paralyzed from the waist down. He was extremely attractive and bright. When asked what effect he thought the physical disability would have on his social life, he insisted that there would be little, if any, effect. He was denying the facts that he could not walk, that he had to be picked up and moved from a wheelchair to a car, or from a wheelchair to a bed, and that he had no control over his bowel and bladder functions.

A more common example of the use of denial as a defense mechanism is demonstrated by the insistence of a woman who wears a size 16 dress that she can wear a size 14 or 12; in fact, she buys the smaller dress. Someone who is ashamed of his very large feet may wear a pair of shoes one or two sizes too small and suffer the pain rather than admit that he has large feet. The old adage "Love is blind" also demonstrates a popular usage of the denial mechanism.

Of course, the major problem with denial is that if one is unable to recognize a legitimate problem, one is unlikely to react in a way that would lead to adequate personality development and to a higher level of maturity.

CONVERSION REACTIONS

In conversion reactions, the individual's emotional stress is unconsciously converted into physical complaints. This mechanism is so prevalent that the third revised edition of the American Psychiatric Association's *Diagnostic and Statistical Manual of Mental Disorders (DSM-III-R)* lists it as a diagnostic category (conversion disorder). In conversion reactions, the individual develops limitations related to physical factors for which no organic basis can be demonstrated. An extreme example is suggested by a young patient who attempted to get out of bed one morning and discovered that he could not walk. After several days of physical examinations, roentgenography, and neurologic examinations, no evidence of physical abnormality was found. The patient was referred for psychiatric treatment. In the course of treatment, it was discovered that the patient's sister had died from a muscular disease that had rendered her progressively less able to care for herself. The young man had been ignored during her illness while the parents took care of her. The patient came to resent his sister, and when she died, he felt guilty. He had apparently repressed most of his guilt feelings and seemed well for a while before becoming "paralyzed." Within 6 weeks, using behavior modification techniques, the patient was able to walk. There have been no recurrences of his paralysis.

A more common example of this particular defense mechanism occurs when we get "uptight," have a hard day, and subsequently develop a headache. Persons who have peptic ulcers also demonstrate the conversion mechanism.

Perhaps the greatest advantage of conversion is that it permits a great many people to blame their tiredness, headaches, and so forth on physical ailments. The disadvantage is that once such a satisfactory explanation is discovered, the individual may not try to discern the cause of his or her stresses or to do anything to make life more acceptable and more livable.

COMPENSATION

Compensation is a mechanism whereby one tries to cover up an area of weakness by showing a great deal of strength or excellence in another area. An example of this defense mechanism is the young man who is too frail or too small to play football but becomes an excellent student. A more direct example of compensation occurs in instances in which an individual loses the use of an arm and then uses the remaining arm to equal or surpass the performance that would have been possible using the lost arm.

Although the mechanism of compensation frequently produces desirable results, it may also produce undesirable results: for example, the young man from the "wrong side of the tracks" who feels that he is socially unacceptable and undertakes to become the meanest fighter on his block. Numerous television programs are built around the compensation theme, with a brilliant scientist being offended by his company or his country and subsequently developing weapons of tremendous capability for a competing power simply to "show" the people who rebuffed him. Positive examples of the use of this defense mechanism occur when an individual with a poor figure compensates by dressing in a particularly flattering manner, or when an overweight person develops an especially winning personality.

Compensation mechanisms frequently help persons to excel in some particular area when otherwise they might not have excelled in anything. The negative side of compensation may show up when the chosen areas of compensation are antisocial or detrimental to the individual. Perhaps Evel Knievel, the motorcycle exhibitionist, is an outstanding example of this latter point.

PROJECTION

Projection is a defense mechanism that enables one to justify one's own behavior and feelings by accusing others of having these same feelings, and by permitting one to blame shortcomings on other people or objects. One of the easiest ways to spot this mechanism is to recognize the "blaming" theme that is usually present. An example of this mechanism occurred in a state hospital. A court service worker who sometimes referred patients to the hospital always wrote letters describing the behavior of the referred patients. He never failed to mention the homosexual tendencies of the patients. In fact, he always found something to indicate the presence of homosexuality. In reality, few of the patients referred had homosexual tendencies. The worker's fear of his own homosexual impulses and characteristics was being projected onto other people. Another example of this mechanism is demonstrated by the tennis player who, after completely missing the ball, looks at the tennis racket as if it had a hole in it, in effect saying, "There must be something wrong with this racket; surely I couldn't have missed the whole dang ball." Frequently one blames many of life's troubles on bad luck, the stars, tarot cards, or the "fickle finger of fate."

The advantage obtained by the individual who uses projection is that one successfully avoids accepting the responsibility for one's own behaviors and is able to avoid some of the feelings of rejection that might come from having socially unacceptable thoughts and feelings. The major disadvantage is that such individuals may become constant "fault-finders" and do little or nothing to straighten out the internal problems that make the use of projection necessary.

FANTASY

Fantasy is a defense mechanism that practically everyone employs. In reasonable amounts, daydreaming can be fun and even productive. At one time or another, most people have daydreams about being a hero. In his daydreams, an adolescent boy may rescue the girl of his dreams from some terrible situation and thus become her hero and lover. A young girl imagines herself in a dazzling evening gown that causes the teacher upon whom she has a crush to be taken by surprise when he suddenly recognizes how mature and beautiful she really is. Other typical fantasy activity involves a small, skinny child who imagines himself beating up the school bully and thus becoming a hero, or a young man from a poor family seeing himself as becoming rich and powerful.

Perhaps the greatest benefit derived from fantasy is that it can permit temporary escape from painful environmental situations or it can help produce solutions to problems that might not otherwise be solved. On the other hand, fantasy can be overdone to the point that one begins to "live in one's head" and thus lose touch with reality.

When one begins to respond to fantasies as if they were real, one is in psychologic trouble. It is probably not too harmful for a young man to imagine himself as quite rich and important. It is something else, however, when he starts writing checks on his imaginary bank account.

INTROJECTION

Introjection is a defense mechanism whereby individuals incorporate into their own personality structures the attributes of persons or institutions in their environment. A good example of introjection occurs when a person is taken as a political prisoner and a year or two later is released and appears to have been "brainwashed" by the captors; that is, the person appears to have accepted their ideals and ideas. The expression "If you can't beat them, join them" is a popular concept that expresses the use of this defense mechanism. A young man who is beaten by a bully may subsequently become friends with him. Peer-group pressure is also an expression of this defense mechanism.

The basic idea in introjection is to protect oneself from threatening circumstances by attuning oneself to the ideas and characteristics of the environment so as to lessen the threat. The advantage in using this mechanism is that it allows one to survive in situations that might otherwise be destructive. Perhaps the greatest disadvantage is that if one is suddenly thrown into another culture or a different environment, those traits and behaviors that have been introjected may no longer be appropriate and may create adjustment problems.

REACTION FORMATION

Reaction formation is a defense mechanism whereby one denies unacceptable feelings and impulses by adopting conscious behaviors that, at least on the surface, appear to be contradictory to the thoughts, feelings, and impulses being defended against. A reformed alcoholic may become a teetotaler and spend a great deal of time and effort preaching against the evils of alcohol. The sexually promiscuous husband may spend hours lecturing his teenage daughter on the evils of sex. The "good Christian person" may be a malicious gossiper, and the businessman who always has a lecture ready about the poor morals of other businessmen may be found to shortchange customers in one way or another. It is interesting to note that there is some evidence to indicate that public censors who protect us from the evils of sex and violence in movies, magazines, and television have a hard time not enjoying their jobs. The Shakespearean quote from *Macbeth* aptly summarizes this defense mechanism: "The lady doth protest too much, methinks." It is one thing to be genuinely concerned about a particular issue. It is something else to be obsessed with it.

It is undoubtedly true that persons with reaction formations control some of their more unacceptable impulses. It is quite likely, however, that they would be much more comfortable with themselves and much more tolerant of other people if they could resolve the internal conflicts that make the use of reaction formation necessary.

REGRESSION

Regression is a defense against anxiety or threatening situations that permits one to go backward in development to a time when one felt more at ease and more capable of handling the environment. This, of course, permits escape from painful situations in the present and allows enjoyment of the relative peace and quiet of the stage of regression. Perhaps the most obvious case of regression is one in which an adult begins to behave in a childlike manner.

One of the more common examples occurs when a 3- or 4-year-old who has been toilet trained begins to wet himself or herself and to talk baby talk when a newborn baby is brought into the home. Other examples occur when older children or adults become highly dependent and demanding when they are threatened. Regression frequently occurs when patients are hospitalized.

Another form of regression is seen when individuals have grown up and entered the business world. They subsequently decide to "get out of the rat race" and go back to a more simple form of living. Frequently they go to rural areas and become farmers or, in some cases, live in communes. The idea of "getting back to nature" expresses the desire to return to a simpler time and to escape the complexities of a highly technologic world.

SUBLIMATION

Sublimation is a defense mechanism that allows an individual to divert unacceptable impulses and motives into socially acceptable channels. Rather than becoming a Peeping Tom or a simple voyeur, an individual may become a physician, an artist who draws nudes, or a photographer for the magazine *Playboy*. In fact, *Playboy*, at least in some circles, serves as a socially acceptable form of voyeurism. The popularity of sexually oriented scenes on television and in movies would seem to suggest that the need for the satisfaction of voyeuristic impulses is substantial.

Other examples of sublimation occur when individuals with strong, aggressive impulses become football or hockey players or participate in other physically violent activities that are sanctioned by society.

The advantages of sublimation are obvious in that they allow expression of questionable desires and impulses in socially acceptable ways. The disadvantage might come when the drives are so strong that even the sublimation is not sufficient to control the impulses and one nevertheless engages in the extreme behaviors.

RESTITUTION

The defense mechanism of restitution permits one to atone for behaviors that one feels are unacceptable. For example, the individual who acquired wealth by highly questionable means might become the greatest benefactor of an orphanage or otherwise contribute great sums of money to charity. This defense mechanism is sometimes referred to as "undoing," and its aim is to reduce the guilt and anxiety experienced by the individual for having engaged in behaviors that he or she now views as unacceptable.

DISPLACEMENT

Displacement is a defense mechanism by which an individual transfers hostile and aggressive feelings from one object to another object or person. A classic example of this mechanism occurs when a man comes home from work after having been "chewed out" by his boss and spies Fido lying in front of the door. Poor Fido gets a swift kick, gets yelled at, and slinks away wondering what in the world he did to deserve such treatment. Other examples, of course, include the wife or kids being yelled at as a result of some frustration the husband or father experienced in his work, or the husband getting yelled at because of the frustrating day his wife had.

The advantage of displacement, of course, is that one can stay on good terms with the offending person, thus avoiding the possibilities of being fired or otherwise facing the wrath of the offending person. On the other hand, if displacement becomes a way of life, alienation of friends or family members is probable.

The great effort at improving communications between people in business and other areas attests to the fact that it is important to learn to communicate feelings with the people involved in the interaction. It is discomforting to be yelled at and not know why.

NEUROSIS AND PSYCHOSIS

Now that we have covered the major defense mechanisms, the next step is to try to discover how these defense mechanisms are related to psychopathology. For all psychologic disorders that are functional in nature (that is, not related to physical or organic causes), we must presume that stressful situations are responsible for the maladaptive behavior. Most authorities have suggested that the concepts of threat, anxiety, and malfunctioning defense systems are closely related to the development of abnormal behavior. Therefore, when an individual tries to use defense mechanisms to ward off feelings of anxiety or threat, but cannot do so either because the defense mechanisms are not strong enough or are generally inadequate, there is an increase in both anxiety and the inappropriate use of defense mechanisms. If an individual is unable to deal with the anxiety-provoking problem through defense systems, that person is likely to develop more and more inappropriate and maladaptive behaviors that will result in the collapse of biologic, psychologic, and sociologic functioning. It is at this point that "symptom formation" begins to occur.

Depending on how well an individual's defense system is able to handle the threat and anxiety-generating stress on the individual's psychologic structure, the individual may experience either a mildly disruptive problem in an interpersonal relationship or severe personality decompensation to the point of losing contact with reality.

The difference between experiencing mild personality decompensation and severe personality decompensation is generally described by the terms *neurosis* and *psychosis*. In a *neurosis*, the individual experiences mild interference with social relationships, occupational pursuits, and sexual adjustment. Neurotics are rarely dangerous to themselves or to society. Neurotic patients usually maintain contact with reality, although there is often some distortion in the concept of reality. Neurotic patients usually realize that they have some emotional problems and may have some insight into the nature of the problems. Neurotics are usually well oriented in time, person, place, and so forth and do not have delusions or hallucinations. They do often show various symptoms, such as obsessions, compulsions, phobias, or hysterical paralyses. Except in severe cases, neurotic patients do not require hospitalization, and many neurotic patients go through life without obtaining any help for their problems.

On the other hand, in *psychosis*, patients frequently experience severe personality decompensation that interferes with vocational pursuits, and interpersonal relationships; and, of course, contact with reality is poor. In fact, in most cases of psychosis, there is a definite split between the reality of the world and reality for the patient. Patients frequently lose track of time, place, and person. Psychotic patients usually require hospitalization, and their behavior is sometimes injurious to themselves and others. Psychotic patients rarely have any insight whatsoever into the nature of their behavior; in fact, they frequently insist that nothing is wrong with them and that they

Table 3–1

CHARACTERISTICS OF NEUROSIS AND PSYCHOSIS

Factor	Neurosis	Psychosis
1. Description	A neurosis causes a loss of personal efficiency and a decrease in activity. Some personality disorganization may be present. Neurotics frequently have some insight into the fact that they have emotional problems.	A psychosis is characterized by serious personality disorganization. Impaired memory, perception, and judgment are often apparent. Patients may have difficulty recognizing that they are emotionally ill.
2. Symptoms	Patients have various complaints about nervousness, emotional upset, physical illnesses (with little organic basis), poor self-esteem, and feelings of worthlessness. Hallucinations do not occur.	Reality testing is impaired. Hallucinations, delusions, and bizarre bodily sensations occur frequently. A lack of reality contact is apparent.
3. Social elements	Social relationships are likely to show some deterioration but are not likely to be completely disrupted. Patients' behaviors are not likely to be injurious to themselves or others.	Social relationships are likely to be significantly impaired and in some cases totally disrupted. Patients may show behaviors injurious to themselves or others.
4. Orientation	Patients are usually oriented to time, place, and person. Patients' behaviors will probably not seem especially peculiar.	Patients are frequently disoriented as to time, place, and person. Patients' behaviors may appear to be quite odd or peculiar.
5. Therapeutic measures factor	Patients are usually treated in outpatient facilities, and many neurotic people receive no treatment at all. Only the most severe cases require hospitalization.	Patients frequently require hospitalization but may be maintained in outpatient facilities.

should be released. Table 3–1 summarizes the different characteristics of neurotic and psychotic patients.

This chapter has presented the concepts necessary for the formation of a framework within which to view the different types of mental illness. Chapters 5, 6, and 7 discuss specific diagnostic categories and some of the problems inherent in the diagnostic process.

ANNOTATED BIBLIOGRAPHY

Hazel, K.L., Herman S.E., and Mowbray, C.T.: *Characteristics of seriously mentally ill adults in a public mental health system.* Hospital and Community Psychiatry, 1991, 42(5):518–525.

> *A study exploring the sociodemographic and clinical information on mentally ill persons treated either in a hospital or community setting to aid in planning of mental health services.*

O'Connell, K.A.: *Why rational people do irrational things: The theory of psychological reversals.* Journal of Psychosocial Nursing and Mental Health Services, 1991, 29(1):11–14.

> *The reversal theory is applied to inconsistent and irrational behavior.*

Puntil, C.: *Integrating three approaches to counter resistance in a noncompliant elderly client.* Journal of Psychosocial Nursing and Mental Health Services, 1991, 29(2):26–30.

> *Discusses how resistance is used by the elderly patient and how nurses can work through the resistance.*

Riebschleger, J.L.: *Families of chronically mentally ill people: Siblings speak to social workers.* Health and Social Work, 1991, 16(2):94–103

> *A study exploring the emotional responses and needs of siblings of chronically mentally ill patients.*

Siegler, I.C., Zonderman, A.B., Barefoot, J.C., Williams, R.B., Costa, P.T., and McCrae, R.R.: *Predicting personality in adulthood from college MMPI scores: Implications for follow-up studies in psychosomatic medicine.* Psychosomatic Medicine, 1990, 52:644–652.

> *A study exploring the changes in personality from college age to adulthood.*

Matching. Match the defense mechanism listed in Column B with the appropriate statement listed in Column A. There is only one mechanism for each descriptive statement.

Column A

_____ 1. Denies unacceptable feelings and impulses by adopting conscious behaviors that are contradictory to the thoughts, feelings, and impulses.

_____ 2. Blames others for personal inadequacies or guilt feelings.

_____ 3. Refuses to see what is obvious to everyone else.

_____ 4. "Forgets" or excludes from conscious thought things too painful or anxiety provoking to remember.

_____ 5. Unacceptable impulses diverted into socially acceptable channels.

_____ 6. "Undoing."

_____ 7. Transference of hostile and aggressive feelings from one object to another object or person.

_____ 8. Going backwards in one's development.

Column B

a. repression
b. displacement
c. projection
d. restitution
e. denial
f. regression
g. reaction formation
h. introjection
i. sublimation
j. fantasy
k. suppression
l. identification
m. conversion

True or False. Circle your choice.

T F 1. The emotionally healthy person is accepting of himself or herself.

T F 2. The inability to accept authority or make decisions for oneself is a sign of good mental health.

T F 3. Our self-image is basically the ideas we have about what kind of person we are.

T F 4. Defense mechanisms are always healthy.

T F 5. To be effective, defense mechanisms must be consciously used.

T F 6. Psychotic patients rarely have insight into the nature of their behavior.

Fill in the Blanks. From the group of terms listed in Column B, select the letter of the most appropriate term(s) to complete the sentences in Column A.

<table>
<tr><td align="center">*Column A*</td><td align="center">*Column B*</td></tr>
</table>

1. _____ is a term used to indicate that a person is no longer emotionally able to deal with the stress and strain of everyday life.
2. A person whose defenses work adequately and who seems to get along reasonably well in everyday

   life is said to be _____.
3. There are two major classifications of

   maladjustments: _____ and

   _____ maladjustment.
4. Defense mechanisms are sometimes

   called _____ mechanisms.
5. _____ is sometimes called the granddaddy of all the defense mechanisms.

a. adjusted
b. neurotic
c. psychopathology
d. denial
e. coping
f. psychotic
g. repression
h. insane

Multiple Choice. Circle the letter or number that you think represents the best answer.

1. The mentally healthy individual has the capacity to:
   a. Accept his or her own strengths and weaknesses.
   b. Love others.
   c. Have an effective conscience.
   d. Tolerate stress and frustration.
      (1) a and b.
      (2) a and c.
      (3) a, b, and c.
      (4) All of the above.
2. When observing behavior, the nurse should remember that behavioral symptoms:
   a. Have meaning.
   b. Are purposeful.
   c. Are multidetermined.
   d. Can easily be understood.
      (1) b.
      (2) a and c.
      (3) a, b, and c.
      (4) All of the above.

Situation: Mrs. White is in the hospital for diagnostic tests. She says to you, "Yesterday my doctor told me he was referring me to a psychiatrist. There's nothing wrong with me that any psychiatrist can cure. I'm here to find out why I've been getting these backaches and that's all."

3. Mrs. White may be using the defense mechanism(s) of:
   a. Denial.
   b. Conversion reaction.
   c. Regression.
   d. a and b.
   e. b and c.

4. Your most therapeutic response to Mrs. White would be:
   a. "I can see why this would be upsetting, but don't worry. Everything will turn out all right."
   b. "I'm sure he had a good reason for suggesting this, so try not to be upset about it."
   c. "I have some time now. Could you tell me some of your feelings about seeing a psychiatrist?"
   d. "The x-rays of your back show nothing is wrong there."

5. Being referred to a psychiatrist may be perceived by Mrs. White as a threat to her:
   a. Self-esteem.
   b. Security.
   c. Identity.
   d. Independence.

6. Many people experience compulsions in everyday life. In the following examples, which actions would be fairly normal (not neurotic)?
   a. Habitually emptying ashtrays in the living room before retiring.
   b. Carrying soap and towel around and washing one's hand to the extent that no other activity is possible.
   c. Picking up every piece of paper one sees all day.
   d. Having a morning routine in order to get to work on time.
      (1) a.
      (2) b and c.
      (3) a and d.
      (4) All of the above.

7. Mental processes and behaviors that serve to protect our self-esteem by defending us against excessive anxiety are:
   a. The general adaptation syndrome.
   b. Psychologic adaptation processes.
   c. Defense mechanisms.

    d. Stressor factors.

    e. The fight-or-flight response.

8. Which of the following are true of defense mechanisms?

    a. They resolve intrapsychic conflicts.

    b. They minimize or eliminate anxiety.

    c. They may operate unconsciously.

    d. They may operate consciously.

    e. They are the same as mental mechanisms.

        (1) a, c, d, and e.

        (2) a, b, c, and d.

        (3) b, c, d, and e.

        (4) a, b, c, and e.

        (5) All of the above.

9. A patient has been told by her doctor that she needs to have surgery. This thought is very upsetting to her. She leaves the doctor's office and says to herself, "I won't think about it now. I'll do some shopping instead." She is utilizing which defense mechanism?

    a. Repression.

    b. Identification.

    c. Sublimation.

    d. Regression.

    e. Suppression.

10. A man is reprimanded by his boss. He comes home and proceeds to kick the family dog. This is an example of:

    a. Identification.

    b. Repression.

    c. Introjection.

    d. Suppression.

    e. Displacement.

11. Jane has done poorly on an exam. When asked about it, she replies, "I couldn't help it. I had planned to study all day Sunday and then my relatives came and stayed all day so I couldn't study." She is using the defense mechanism of:

    a. Compensation.

    b. Fantasy.

    c. Rationalization.

    d. Reaction formation.

12. Johnny was the shortest boy in the class and could never do well in athletics. However, he worked hard at his studies and achieved the honor roll. The defense mechanism here is:

    a. Substitution.

    b. Fixation.

    c. Displacement.

    d. Compensation.

13. Mrs. Green is a patient who is scheduled for shock treatment. Miss Jaynes, a new staff member, becomes very anxious and is unable to help with the treatment. She is using:

    a. Identification.

    b. Denial.

    c. Regression.

    d. Suppression.

14. A patient is angry because he was hit by a car and hospitalized for several weeks. His wife is working and taking care of their three small children at home. He directs his angry energy into pounding designs into leather wallets. He then sends the small amount of money home, thus making him feel better. This is an example of:

    a. Displacement.

    b. Identification.

    c. Sublimation.

    d. Regression.

    e. Suppression.

15. A person who consciously acts ill to avoid an unpleasant experience is referred to as a:

    a. Neurotic.

    b. Hypochondriac.

    c. Malingerer.

    d. Procrastinator.

16. Which of the following is true of neurosis?

    a. It involves profound withdrawal from people.

    b. It impairs but does not prevent occupational efficiency.

    c. It involves fragmentation of thought processes.

    d. It involves severe distortion in memory.

    e. It may cause short-term memory problems.

        (1) a, b, c, and e.

        (2) b and e.

        (3) b, c, and d.

        (4) c, d, and e.

17. Which of the following are true of psychosis?

    a. Possible illusions and hallucinations.

    b. No impairment in judgment.

    c. Awareness of personality disorder.

    d. Withdrawal from reality.

    e. Distorted affect.

        (1) All of the above.

        (2) b, d, and e.

(3) a, c, and e.

(4) a, d, and e.

(5) None of the above.

18. Psychotic patterns of response:
   a. Are not as severe as neurotic disturbance.
   b. Involve minor defects in reality testing.
   c. Are characterized only by hallucinating.
   d. Are disturbances in total personality functioning.

4

Legal and Ethical Considerations

Some experts call the present period in American history the "Age of the Consumer." For the past several years consumers have been insisting that they receive quality products and services for the money they pay. That fact has not been lost on the automobile industry, which, over the last decade, has lost much of the American market to Japanese and German automobile manufacturers. The same is true of the electronics industry. Now, in the 1990s, much of American industry is scrambling to catch up.

So what do consumers' rights and preferences have to do with the mentally ill? Consider for a moment the fact that patient care provided by a hospital or clinic is a service—and a costly one at that. Hospital room rates alone can run over $600 per day. These prices often do not include special treatments, medications, psychotherapy, or other "ancillaries." Because mentally ill patients frequently are hospitalized for weeks at a time, it is not difficult to understand why people are demanding the best care. In addition, we are operating in a highly competitive market, and a number of hospitals are closing because of insufficient demand. The lack of demand is not so much because the services are not needed as because many third-party payers are either refusing to pay for mental health care or are closely monitoring that care. Finally, many patients, or their families, will readily seek legal advice if the care they receive is not satisfactory.

The fear of a lawsuit, however, should not be the motivating factor in providing quality care to patients. Rather, the obligation to honor the trust of patients is the professional and ethical commitment. Honoring this trust, and communicating effectively with patients, would practically eliminate all lawsuits except those charging gross negligence.

A major responsibility of individual members of the mental health team is to help other team members create the type of environment that provides both physical and emotional safety and comfort for patients. One step toward the attainment of this type of environment is to treat all patients as unique individuals, taking measures to preserve their dignity and to respect the rights and privileges guaranteed them by law.

Most lawsuits involving members of the mental health team center around a negligent act (negligence being seen as willful neglect, abuse, harassment, or failure to attend adequately to a patient). For example, if a patient who is experiencing confusion following electroconvulsive therapy (ECT) is allowed to take a shower unattended and subsequently falls and breaks a hip, the patient would very likely win a negligence suit. The reasoning would be that the staff knew or should have known the patient was at risk due to treatment effects and should have attended the patient. If they neglected to do so, there may be an issue of liability.

The objective of this chapter is to provide basic guidelines to follow when working with mentally ill patients. These guidelines should help the mental health worker avoid legal entanglements that might otherwise arise when providing patient care. Mental health workers must become aware of the laws pertaining to the care of the mentally ill in the state in which they practice, because such laws vary considerably from state to state.

KNOW YOUR JOB RESPONSIBILITIES

Make sure you are familiar with the job description for your position. Know what you can legally do and then learn to perform those procedures in a correct and skillful manner. Ask questions, and tactfully refuse when asked to do any task for which you have not been prepared. Be sure to read carefully the rules and regulations of the hospital or clinic, and thoroughly commit to memory those that are specific to the unit in which you will be seeing patients. You should also familiarize yourself with the information in the procedures manual. Discuss with your supervisor any part of the procedures manual you do not understand completely. In many states you can be held legally responsible for any rules, regulations, and procedures that apply to patient care in your unit or in the hospital in general. This is true even if you do not "know" about a particular rule, regulation, or procedure. Make it your business to know. Be informed!

VOLUNTARY AND INVOLUNTARY ADMISSIONS

Familiarize yourself with the laws of your state regarding treatment of the mentally ill. In most states there are two main ways in which mentally ill patients are admitted for psychiatric care. When a person agrees that medical assistance is needed and agrees to be admitted to the hospital, it is said to be a *voluntary admission*. If an unwilling patient must be forced to enter the hospital, it is an *involuntary admission* (involuntary admission and involuntary commitment are considered to be interchangeable). Involuntary admissions require legal action. A judge, psychologist, or physician (it varies according to state law) who determines that a person is in danger of harming himself or herself, or others, has the responsibility of deciding whether or not to admit the person to a psychiatric hospital or mental health unit for treatment.

The main reason for being aware of the difference between these two procedures is best illustrated when one is faced with a patient who has decided to leave the hospital. In the case of voluntary admissions, patients should be allowed to leave if they have decided not to continue treatment. Most hospitals ask patients to put their intentions in writing and then wait 24 hours before leaving. Patients who refuse to do this are usually asked to sign a legal form that states that they know they are leaving against medical advice and that the hospital is not responsible for their actions. In most states, however, patients cannot be required to sign such a form. If the person in charge of the unit believes that such patients are likely to harm themselves or others if they leave, the person in charge may detain such patients against their will for a period of 24 hours. During this time legal procedures must be started in order to change the patient's admission status from voluntary to involuntary. Patients who have been involuntarily admitted should not be permitted to leave the hospital unless officially discharged by the attending physician (or psychologist in those states where psychologists have admitting privileges). Commitment is legally terminated on discharge.

CONFIDENTIALITY

The issue of confidentiality is one of the more perplexing problems in mental health. It is widely accepted that therapeutic effectiveness depends on patients' willingness to discuss those private thoughts and feelings that frequently underlie their emotional maladaptation. In the process of treatment patients sometimes reveal information about themselves or others that is incriminating and that, if made public, could result in disagreeable consequences to them. Generally speaking, mental health professionals are required to keep all information disclosed to them in confidence. Most patients realize that information given to one member of the mental health team will be shared with the entire team, but one should take great care not to imply to patients that what they say to you will be kept in complete confidence.

That lesson was learned the hard way by one of the authors in what might be called an "early career growth experience." A young patient, about 30 years old, had been doing quite well in therapy and was about ready to leave the hospital. The author was charting the patient's wonderful progress when the patient asked if she could say something that would be kept totally confidential. Perhaps distracted a bit by the charting activity and lulled into a false sense of security by the patient's apparent progress (please note the rationalizations), the author cheerfully said, "Sure." Big mistake! No sooner had the words left the author's mouth than the young woman said, "I've decided to kill myself; that's why I've been feeling so much better." That is what is called a therapeutic bomb! To make matters worse, when asked to be released from the commitment not to reveal the information about her suicidal intentions, the patient replied, "If you tell anyone, I will kill myself for certain." It is not difficult to see the bind. To break her confidence would risk the trust on which the therapeutic relationship was founded. Not to protect the patient against self-harm was unthinkable. The situation was resolved when the author was able to help the patient see the need to have the mental health team become aware of her decision so that appropriate therapeutic intervention could occur. The author has never made that error again.

DUTY TO WARN

Two other situations involving confidentiality require special attention. In addition to a responsibility to protect patients from themselves, caregivers have a "duty to warn." This responsibility was essentially established by a famous court case you might like to read if you have the opportunity. The case was *Tarasoff* v. *Regents of University of California* (1976). The essential elements of the case were that a patient told his therapist of his intent to kill his girlfriend. The therapist told the campus police of the patient's threat, but the patient was not arrested and the girlfriend was not warned. He later killed Ms. Tarasoff. Her family filed suit and won, establishing thoroughly the responsibility of therapists to warn potential victims of threats made against them.

A new crisis currently abounds in this area of duty to warn. What about the duty of caregivers to warn partners of AIDS victims; especially when the caregiver knows a patient is still sexually active and is not informing partners? This is a hotly debated issue, but Gray and Harding (1988) say: "We believe that it is at the expense of the uninformed sexual partner's safety to keep confidential the information that the client has the AIDS virus. In our opinion, a sexually active, seropositive individual places an uninformed sexual partner (or partners) at peril, and the situation therefore falls under the legal spirit of the *Tarasoff* case and the ethical tenets of 'clear and imminent danger.'"

DUTY TO REPORT CHILD ABUSE

The other situation requiring violation of confidentiality is that of child abuse. Most states require reporting of information involving the abuse of children, and there are legal penalties for not doing so. If a patient gives you information about child abuse, you should immediately inform your supervisor.

It may be helpful for you to know that there is a difference between a patient's right to confidentiality and "privileged communication." The right to confidentiality is a general understanding that information will not be disclosed without the patient's permission. However, this falls more under the rubric of ethics than legality, and there are many situations in which a court will order confidential information to be disclosed. Privileged communication, on the other hand, is a legislated and specific right, honored by the courts, granting an individual the ability to discuss matters with certain identified persons who cannot, by law, disclose that information without the individual's specific consent. Privileged communication is the right clients have in discussing information with their attorney. That right has been extended to physicians, psychologists, social workers, and nurses in some states. The right of privileged communication varies greatly from state to state, and you should learn whether it covers you in your state.

Court decisions generally seem to take the position that the protective rights of privileged communication and confidentiality end where public peril begins. It is almost always in everyone's interest to gain the patient's permission to reveal a confidence. Indeed, some patients appear to disclose information with the intent of having the caregiver intervene. Most mental health facilities have written policies informing patients of the circumstances under which their right to confidentiality or privileged communication may be abridged. If you have patients who make threats to hurt themselves or others, report this to your supervisor immediately. Failing voluntary disclosure by the patient, the supervisor will have to act on the information in accordance with procedure outlined by the agency or institution in which the patient resides.

THE PATIENT'S CIVIL RIGHTS

Our society values the rights of individuals and almost universally endorses the right of self-determination. It is important for all members of the psychiatric team to remember that patients admitted to the hospital on an involuntary basis do not necessarily lose any or all of their civil and legal rights. These patients do lose the right to leave the hospital without permission, but in most states they retain the right to vote, make contracts, drive a car, marry, divorce, write letters, and seek legal advice. As out-of-date laws are repealed in most states, the only way patients can lose civil and legal rights is to be declared *incompetent*. This is a special legal procedure and is not a routine matter for patients hospitalized on an involuntary basis. Once patients are declared incompetent, it takes another legal procedure to declare them restored to competency. Discharge from the hospital is not sufficient.

Since the early 1970s, more and more of the court suits filed by mental health patients have dealt with what they considered to be infringements on their basic human rights and freedoms as guaranteed to them by the Bill of Rights and the Civil Rights Amendments. Since hospitalized patients tend to be more vulnerable, they are more likely to have their rights violated.

Because of court rulings in the late 1960s and throughout the 1970s, thousands of patients have been released from state institutions and returned to a society ill prepared to meet their needs. This has led to conflict between society and the medical and legal professions. For example, many authorities attribute the substantial increase in the homeless population to the release of mental health patients and the refusal to hospitalize the ambulatory mentally ill. The laws governing mental health practices are in a state of flux, and many laws currently on the books are being challenged on the grounds that they are unconstitutional because they do not provide for due process.

ADEQUATE SUPERVISION OF PATIENTS

Be careful not to let your attention wander, not to be distracted, and not to be manipulated into ignoring your duties. Be especially careful when you are taking a patient or a group of patients off the unit or when a suicidal patient is under your supervision. A good rule to follow is that if you have more than one patient going off the unit, you should have more than one mental health worker with the group. Then, if something happens to a patient, one staff member can stay with the group while the other staff member goes for help. It is generally not a safe practice to try to manage patient groups larger than 10.

INFORMED CONSENT AND A PATIENT'S RIGHT TO REFUSE TREATMENT

Generally speaking, patients have a right to refuse treatment or to withdraw from treatment once it is started. The constitutional basis for this is the patient's fundamental right to privacy and personal autonomy. Today's mental health professionals walk a fine line between providing for patients' well-being and protecting their rights.

Except in extreme psychiatric emergencies, the mental health professional must explain all procedures and drugs to the patient in such a manner that the patient can make an intelligent, informed choice as to whether or not to allow it. The patient's agreement must be written. The patient should be given information regarding expected outcomes, potential risks, and alternative treatment modalities.

Informed consent is not valid if a patient is coerced, is under the influence of drugs or alcohol, or is in such a state of agitation that it prevents free choice. If the staff feels a patient cannot make rational decisions regarding care, the proper authorities should be notified and incompetency proceedings started.

If a patient is so out of control that he or she must be restrained or secluded, informed consent is, of course, not gained. If you must place a patient in seclusion, remember that seclusion is a protective device, not a punishment, and is used only when other methods (medication, talking, and so forth) fail. If such an order is given, make sure the patient is checked at least every 20 minutes. Stay with the patient yourself if at all possible, or try to find a staff member or a family member who can stay.

DUE CAUTION

Caregivers have a responsibility to exercise due caution and protect the patient from hazards. One should be constantly alert for potentially dangerous items on the unit. Remove the item when possible, and report any hazards to the supervisor. For example, one should pick up a nail file left by a visitor or report a torn screen to the head nurse. When repairpersons or other technical personnel have been on the unit, always check to be certain they have not left anything patients can use to harm themselves, staff members, or other patients.

ETHICS

Ethical responsibilities differ from legal responsibilities in that they do not carry the force of law. They do, however, carry the force of professional expectations and professional honor. Ethical responsibilities are guidelines that sometimes address legal issues, but from the position of expectation rather than law. It is very often the case that ethical positions become law as they become widely accepted. For example, sex between patients and caregivers progressed from being frowned upon, to being a violation of ethics, and now to being illegal in many states.

The Colorado Society of Clinical Specialist in Psychiatric Nursing adopted a set of guidelines in 1987, and a summary of the guidelines relating to respect for the rights of patients/clients was presented in the *Journal of Psychosocial Nursing and Mental Health Services* (1990). The eight ethical guidelines related to patient/client rights are as follows:

1. The right to informed self-determination, when the client is rational.
2. The right to protection of self from his or her own limitations of reasoning and judgment, when the client is psychotic.
3. The right to an opportunity for treatment, including equity in the quality of treatment relative to all other clients.
4. The right to attain and maintain a sense of human worth.
5. The right to privacy in terms of the body and in regard to the emotional, intellectual, and spiritual dimensions of self.
6. The right to protection from physical and verbal abuse or misuse, including abusive behavior that carries sexual and/or emotional implications.
7. The right to expect a high quality of psychiatric nursing care, even when the client is incompetent to assess the nursing care.
8. The right to expect that nursing care will be focused on each particular client's welfare to the greatest extent possible, even when such an individualized focus is in conflict with the welfare of the client's family, a group of clients, or society.

SUMMARY

Having reviewed some of the legal and ethical issues involved in treating the mentally ill, we hope it is clear that some of the important things to keep in mind include paying attention to patients, addressing their concerns and needs, being aware of state laws, not guessing at responsibilities but *knowing* what they are, honoring confidentiality, and appreciating the need to communicate with patients about their concerns. Ethical issues are also important and require that those of us working with the mentally ill be aware of ethical considerations as well as legal ones. In Chapter 8 we discuss some communication techniques that may help you manage your legal and ethical responsibilities.

ANNOTATED BIBLIOGRAPHY

Calfee, B.E.: *Protecting yourself*. Nursing, December 1991, pp. 34–39.

> *Presents ways in which nurses can protect themselves from being involved in a negligence lawsuit.*

Colorado Society of Clinical Specialists in Psychiatric Nursing: *Ethical guidelines for the Colorado Society of Clinical Specialists in Psychiatric Nursing*. Journal of Psychosocial Nursing and Mental Health Services, 1990, 28(2):38–40.

> *Features guidelines on confidentiality, accountability, and competence.*

Fiesta, J.: *Informed consent process—whose legal duty?* Nursing Management, January 1991, pp. 17–18.

> *Discusses informed consent and the liability involved for nursing staff.*

Gray, L.A., and Harding, A.K.: *Confidentiality limits with clients who have the AIDS virus*. Journal of Counseling and Development, 1988, 66:219–233.

> *Discusses the limits of confidentiality with AIDS patients who continue to be sexually active.*

Holden, R.J.: *Responsibility and autonomous nursing practice*. Journal of Advanced Nursing, 1991, 16:398–403.

> *Discusses personal and professional accountability in nursing practice.*

Kain, C.D.: *To breach or not to breach: Is that the question? A response to Gray and Harding*. Journal of Counseling and Development, 1988, 66:224–225.

> *Further examines the issues presented by Gray and Harding regarding patients who are HIV-positive and the duty to warn high-risk partners.*

Klop, R., Van Wijmen, F., and Philipsen, H.: *Patients' rights and the admission and discharge process*. Journal of Advanced Nursing, 1991, 16:408–412.

> *Discusses the information standard in regard to patient's rights, including concepts concerning informed consent, informed referral, and informed discharge.*

Leong, G.B., Eth, S., and Silva, J.A.: *The Tarasoff dilemma in criminal court.* Journal of Forensic Sciences, 1991, 36(3):728–735.

Legal, clinical and ethical issues associated with the Tarasoff *duty to warn.*

Smith, J.: *Privileged communication: Psychiatric/mental health nurses and the law.* Perspectives in Psychiatric Care, 1990, 26(4):26–29.

Examines the issues of confidentiality and privileged communication in mental health nursing and presents a discussion of statutory and case law.

Tingle, J.: *Nurses and the law: Ethical ways.* Nursing Times, 1990, 86(43):60–61.

Discusses ethical and legal issues in nursing practice and personal accountability for actions and performance.

Treadway, J.: *Tarasoff in the therapeutic setting.* Hospital and Community Psychiatry, 1990, 41(1):88–89.

Case example of the use of the Tarasoff *warning in a therapeutic setting.*

Weber, G., and Kjervik, D.K.: Legal and ethical issues. The Patient Self-Determination Act—The nurse's proactive role. Journal of Professional Nursing, 1992, 8(1):6.

Discusses a patient's right to die and the nurse's role in this process.

Judgment Exercises. The following situations provide an opportunity to apply the information learned in this chapter to situations that one is likely to face when assuming duties on a psychiatric unit. The five statements below describe actions taken by a mental health staff member. Some are appropriate and some are inappropriate. Mark an A by those believed to be appropriate and an I by those believed to be inappropriate.

_____ 1. A patient approaches the staff member, saying that he is tired of being "cooped up" and that he in going to leave the hospital. The staff member immediately notifies his supervisor, checks the patient's chart, and finds that the patient is a voluntary patient. The staff member then notifies the patient's physician, who asks the patient to sign a statement saying that he is leaving the hospital against medical advice. The patient signs the form and is permitted to leave.

_____ 2. Mr. Colbert is allowed to continue to carry his small pocket knife even though he had threatened to use it on a fellow patient. The team member assigned to caring for Mr. Colbert decided that the patient had just been angry and had not really meant what he said.

_____ 3. A patient, being very angry, screamed and yelled and called one of the staff several bad names. An hour later the patient became totally unmanageable and had to be restrained. In helping to apply the restraint, the staff member who had been verbally abused used more force than necessary to get the patient to settle down. Later, when the patient's arm began to swell, the staff member decided on his own to apply hot compresses to the area to reduce the swelling.

_____ 4. The staff member assigned to Mr. Goldstead, a patient who was confused as a result of a series of ECT treatments, was helping him bathe. Another staff member opened the door and asked the attendant to come help him move another patient, stating it would take only a minute or two. Mr. Goldstead's attendant asked the other staff member to find someone else to help.

_____ 5. A staff member who happened to be a be a very good bowler was demonstrating his bowling techniques to the 10 patients whom he had taken to the bowling alley. When a patient asked if he could return to the unit, he was permitted to do so in the company of another patient.

After responding to the above statements on your own, discuss what makes each statement appropriate or inappropriate with your classmates.

True or False. Circle your choice. (Some answers may vary according to the laws of your state. Have you read the laws of your state?)

T   F   1. Patients cannot be legally detained in the hospital if they admitted themselves voluntarily even though they are still very ill.

T   F   2. Involuntary admission and commitment are considered the same thing.

T   F   3. Patients under voluntary admissions can be held against their will for 72 hours.

T   F   4. When patients are admitted involuntarily, they automatically lose their civil and legal rights.

T   F   5. It is not necessary for patients admitted involuntarily to give their consent to special treatment or procedures.

T   F   6. A temporary commitment permits a patient to be hospitalized from 90 to 180 days.

T   F   7. Patients have the right to be present at the court hearing for their commitment.

T   F   8. Patients who are committed by court action retain all of their civil rights except the right to leave.

T   F   9. A legally committed patient has the right to conduct business.

T   F   10. A guardian is always assigned to a person who is declared legally incompetent.

T   F   11. Malpractice is a kind of negligence.

T   F   12. Communication between husband and wife is not considered privileged.

T   F   13. A patient who enters a psychiatric hospital retains all legal and civil rights except the right to leave.

T   F   14. The patient's nearest relatives may institute a commitment proceeding.

Matching. Select the appropriate term from Column B for each statement in Column A.

Column A	*Column B*
_____ 1. Violation of civil rights.	**a.** ECT
_____ 2. Does not have right to leave hospital without permission.	**b.** Restraining patients
_____ 3. Must have special signed consent form for voluntary patient.	**c.** Involuntary patient
_____ 4. May leave hospital without physician's permission.	**d.** Reading patient's mail
_____ 5. Special court procedure.	**e.** Incompetency hearing
	f. Voluntary patient

Short Answer. Answer the following questions as briefly and specifically as possible.

1. Negligence is defined as _____.
2. Define the difference between voluntary and involuntary admission.

_____

_____.

3. If you are unable to answer a patient's question correctly, the

   best thing to do is _____.

_____.

4. What would be the main reason for placing a patient in seclusion?

_____.

5. Most lawsuits involving members of the mental health team

   are usually centered around _____

_____.

PART II

Understanding the Patient's Diagnosis

Introduction to Diagnostic Considerations

A diagnosis is used primarily by members of the treatment team as a shorthand method of describing a group of behaviors that might be expected from a particular person. In general, in social conversation we often speak in shorthand and say we are upset, angry, sad, awful, hurt, stubborn, or some other such term that indicates a particular pattern of behavior. That is, one word or a few words are used to differentiate one behavioral or feeling state from another. We would expect a certain set of behaviors of persons who said they were hurt and a different set of behaviors from those who said they were happy. That same idea applies in the professional setting. When one describes a patient as "depressed," one simply uses that diagnosis to pass along the information that the patient is having trouble sleeping, has lost interest in life, has a poor appetite, may cry a great deal, is generally unhappy, chooses to be alone much of the time, finds little or no pleasure in life, and perhaps has undergone a recent loss. In mental health settings, diagnoses are necessary so that the insurance company can classify the particular disorder the patient has and determine if reimbursement can be made to treatment personnel and to the hospital or clinic. The advent of diagnostically related groups (DRGs) as a basis for third-party reimbursement has also affected the need for accurate diagnosis and assessment. All categories of mental illness fall within one of nine diagnostically related groups, and a fixed amount of money is paid for each illess depending on its DRG classification. In the "new" health care climate, that is, with the great emphasis on cost containment, treatment effectiveness, and alternative health care delivery systems, the newest trend is toward selecting specific providers who can demonstrate clear effectiveness with certain diagnostic groups through outcome data.

As of this writing, there is little solid data on outcomes of specific treatments in the mental health field, but there will be more in the near future. It is the authors' belief that within the next 5 to 10 years there will be prescribed, and fairly universal, treatment protocols for the treatment of specific mental disorders. This raises a hue and cry about "cookbook" medicine, but as the authors have seen in going around the country speaking and attending national conferences, there is evidence that protocols for treatment are being given a great deal of attention.

Interestingly, on the other hand, there is considerable sentiment in the mental health field for doing away with assigning diagnoses to patients. They are criticized as being inaccurate, misleading, and potentially damaging. In many cases, these criticisms are valid. There are incidents of patients treated over a period of years having as many as five or six diagnoses. Of course, it is possible that the diagnostic changes may have been warranted because patients do change in how they respond to life circumstances. However, the reason for different diagnoses is frequently that different professionals tend to have favorite diagnostic categories they prefer for certain classes of behavior. In some cases the professional doing the diagnosing simply pays special attention to a different set of factors or behavioral characteristics than did other persons who diagnosed the same patient. Except for some rather specific diagnoses, the consistency of diagnostic categories from one professional to another may be low. This is largely due to the inexact nature of the diagnostic process.

A notable attempt has been made by the American Psychiatric Association to reduce the inexactness of the diagnostic process. That attempt has been ongoing since the first *Diagnostic and Statistical Manual of Mental Disorders* was published in 1952. The third revised edition of the *Diagnostic and Statistical Manual of Mental Disorders (DSM-III-R)* of the American Psychiatric Association is the latest in the attempt to further reduce subjectivity in assigning diagnoses. Specific patient behaviors are given significant weight, while psychodynamic formulations are deemphasized. While this work has had a significant impact and has substantially improved the diagnostic process, there are still problems with reliability in assigning diagnoses.

Despite its limitations, the success of the *DSM-III-R* in improving the diagnostic process has led to the development of the fourth edition, *DSM-IV*, which is due to be published in the spring of 1994. The *DSM-IV* is intended to be based more on research data than on the consensus of expert committees, as was the case for previous editions of the *DSM* (Widiger et al., 1991). For the sake of consistency, the terminology used in this chapter to describe complexes of behavior is that suggested by the *DSM-III-R*.

DIAGNOSTIC CATEGORIES

The differences between the neurotic disorders and the psychotic disorders were presented in Table 3–1. Briefly, the difference between neurosis and psychosis is related to the degree of disorganization in the patient's thought processes, the degree of social disruption caused by the symptoms, the degree of reality testing (that is, the ability to distinguish between what is and is not real), and the kinds of treatment procedures needed to manage the symptoms.

NEUROTIC PATTERNS OF ABNORMALITY

The information listed in Table 3–1 is pertinent to the discussion of the specific diagnostic categories, in this and the next two chapters, within the broad categories of the neurotic and psychotic disorders. Of course, depending on one's theoretical persuasion, the origins of neurotic and psychotic behaviors are variable.

If we stick with the concept of the mental health continuum, with its emphasis on behavior, neurotic conditions have their basis in past events, the interpretation of those events, and past learning situations. Symptom formation provides neurotic persons with primary gain in that the symptoms provide a means of escaping the anxiety they feel and, in many cases, provides secondary gain, such as sympathy, sick leave, or financial benefits in the form of disability income or workers' compensation.

Frequently, in order to help patients conceptualize their emotional symptoms, the authors encourage them to look at their "neurotic behavior patterns" rather than their "neurosis" when they ask, "Am I neurotic?" We define neurotic behavior patterns as behavior patterns that are self-defeating in some way—that is, they cause isolation, loss of friends, loss of energy, loss of self-efficacy, and so forth. This allows patients to see their symptoms as more discreet and isolated and thus more managable. If patients see their symptoms as some huge, global, unmovable, unmanagable, insoluble mass of psychological ineptness, they are less likely to risk working on the symptoms because the task appears hopeless. Once they see their "neurosis" as maladaptive behavior patterns that can be isolated and defined, the task becomes managable and they become hopeful of ridding themselves of their discomfort.

As the saying goes, "nothing succeeds like success," and small successes in controlling maladaptive behavior patterns encourage patients to try even harder; they are almost always, in our experience, able to achieve a much more satisfactory lifestyle.

It is unlikely that *all* neurotic symptoms exhibited by a patient will fall into any one diagnostic category, and it is not particularly unusual for symptoms to change over time from one category to another. Also, different symptoms may be dominant at different times. However, there are recognizable symptom patterns or complexes that are identifiable. By identifiable, we mean that the behavioral elements of that symptom complex are often found together and represent a response or reaction to stressful conditions. We will now look at several of these identifiable symptom complexes that have been placed in diagnostic categories and labeled. We refer to these diagnostic categories individually as simply "the diagnosis." The numbers preceding the diagnostic label are the diagnostic codes in the *DSM-III-R*.

ANXIETY DISORDERS

The *DSM-III-R* lists nine different diagnostic categories for anxiety. The two that reflect general anxiety symptoms are:

(1)   302.02   Generalized anxiety disorder
(2)   300.00   Anxiety disorder, not otherwise specified

Persons suffering from the anxiety disorders are usually tense, anxious, and worried but are unable to say exactly why they feel that way. There is a sense of general apprehension or, as the *DSM-III-R* says, an "apprehensive expectation." Again, depending on one's theoretical orientation, the causes of anxiety disorders are varied, but they are almost always associated with either an internal (psychological, biological, or chemical) or external (environmental) stressor.

Anxiety patients frequently have a history of having been faced with childhood and other life situations that did not provide firm but supportive approval or disapproval of behavior. In addition, they have frequently found themselves in situations in which they were uncertain of what was expected of them. In other cases, individuals were given instructions and directives accompanied by such extreme inflexibility and drastic, or fear-inducing, consequences that they are unable to achieve any flexibility in how they respond. To respond any way other than the way they were taught would create so much stress that anxiety symptoms would appear and force compliance with the expected behavior. Compliance would reduce the stress, and the symptoms (anxiety) would go away.

Those of the psychodynamic persuasion often cast anxiety in terms of intrapersonal conflicts that occur among one's basic psychological drives and impulses and the threat of losing control of those impulses. Anxiety is also seen as stemming from a state of perpetual uncertainty. When one is uncertain of what is going to happen, a general fear of one's environment often develops, accompanied by a low frustration level and a tendency to view the world as a hostile, cruel place. These feelings frequently cause anxious neurotic patients to be uncertain of themselves, even in minor stress situations, and to have difficulty concentrating. We humans seem to need a fair degree of certainty in our lives—probably because knowing what is going to happen gives us the ability to predict our circumstances, and the ability to predict our circumstances gives us a comfortable degree of control. Perhaps that is why anxiety is often described as a disease of control—or, more to the point, a lack of control. In our practice, when presented with an anxious patient, we always look for the patient's perceived lack of control and aim our treatment at helping that patient gain or regain a sense of control through a combination of therapeutic techniques selected on the basis of the particulars of the patient's situation.

Let us look at a brief example. A young woman is engaged to be married. She is quite happy as she goes about planning her wedding, some 5 months away. One evening she notices that her fiancé is rather quiet and withdrawn. When she asks, he denies that anything is wrong and says he is just tired. A few days later, he does not call and is not at home when she calls him—all night. The next day she calls him at work and wants to know where he was last night. He does not answer and demands to know if she is checking up on him. Finally, he apologizes, says he was out with the "boys," and agrees to pick her up that night, which he does—3 hours late. At first she is angry, but when she sees he is not responding to her anger she suddenly feels hot all over and her hands get cold and her heart begins to beat faster. Her breathing becomes difficult and she feels nauseated. Finally, she asks the big question—"Do you still love me?" He says, "Yes, I guess I'm just not feeling too good myself." In various forms, this behavior pattern repeats itself for 3 more weeks. Now she is distraught, not sleeping well, and mistrustful of what her fiancé tells her. She cannot predict when he is going to show up for a date, cannot predict what kind of mood he will be in if he does show up, cannot predict how he will behave, has questions about whether he still loves her, and cannot predict whether the wedding will occur.

Within a month she is having daily headaches and intermittent nausea; she cannot go to sleep at night, cannot concentrate and attend to her job, and cannot seem to get anything done. She worries constantly and is losing weight. She also feels depressed, is extremely irritable, and is critical of others. She is short with her mother and father as well as her friends, and nothing pleases her. Her life feels out of control. Treatment will require helping her reestablish control by making some decisions about how she is going to deal with her fiancé's behavior. Is she going to tolerate his behavior and hope he will change before the wedding date, or is she going to confront him and risk losing whatever is left of the relationship? We all know what she "should" do, but how many of us have tolerated such situations much longer than we "should" have, hoping things would straighten themselves out?

As in the above situation, anxiety may affect practically all aspects of life. Frequently, in order to avoid anxiety-producing situations, neurotically anxious individuals will restrict daily activities so severely that they have very limited lives. They are usually unaware of their reasons for restricting activities; they only know they feel more comfortable in highly structured and familiar surroundings. In the process of reducing anxiety, however, they give up many of the satisfactions life has to offer through relationships with other people and with the environment in general.

As these individuals try to restrict their lives, they may experience strong anxiety reactions or anxiety attacks, which include sweating, difficulty breathing, and increased heart rate. Many anxious individuals become dizzy, experience dry mouths, and feel that they are dying. Frequently such patients come to the emergency room complaining of heart attacks. In such cases, hospital admission and treatment often ensue.

The *DSM-III-R* lists 18 symptoms related to a diagnosis of generalized anxiety disorder, at least 6 of which must be present to make the diagnosis. Those 18 symptoms are divided into three categories as follows:

Motor Tension

1. Trembling, twitching, or feeling shaky
2. Muscle tension, aches, or soreness
3. Restlessness
4. Easy fatigability

Autonomic Hyperactivity

5. Shortness of breath or smothering sensations
6. Palpitations or accelerated heart rate (tachycardia)
7. Sweating or clammy hands
8. Dry mouth
9. Dizziness or lightheadedness

10. Nausea, diarrhea, or other abdominal distress
11. Flushes (hot flashes) or chills
12. Frequent urination
13. Trouble swallowing or "lump in throat"

Vigilance and Scanning

14. Feeling keyed up or on edge
15. Exaggerated startle response
16. Difficulty concentrating or "mind going blank" because of anxiety
17. Trouble falling or staying asleep
18. Irritability

(Warning—it is not unusual for nursing students to have 10 or more of the above symptoms on test day!)

PHOBIC DISORDERS (PHOBIC NEUROSES)

Anxiety in phobic disorders is usually experienced when the individual with the phobia comes in contact with the feared situation, object, or condition. A *phobia* is usually described as a persistent and irrational fear of some object, place, or condition. Some of the more common phobias are related to high places, thunderstorms, closed places, being alone, crowds, darkness, and, recently, sexually transmitted diseases. Interestingly, fear of public speaking is the most frequently reported phobia.

In the psychodynamic view, the particular object of an individual's phobia is usually not itself the source of fear; rather the individual displaces anxiety from the original cause to the phobic object. The phobia helps the individual by allowing him or her to avoid the anxiety-provoking situation. For this reason, the phobia usually has symbolic significance to the individual. For example, a young man who is fearful of his hostile impulses that involve fantasies about shooting his father may develop a phobia for guns. He is not actually afraid of guns but displaces his fear of killing his father to guns. By avoiding all guns, he tries to avoid the anxiety associated with thoughts of killing his father. If untreated, a phobic person's fears may generalize to other related areas and may lead to increased isolation from relationships.

In all phobias, the basic elements involved are a persistent, strong, and irrational fear of some object or situation. Because of the tendency for a phobia to generalize or to become associated with objects other than the original phobic object, it is sometimes difficult to discover the symbolic significance of a particular phobic reaction. From a therapeutic standpoint, it should be recognized that phobias often generate feelings of dependency and helplessness in individuals and they are likely to need support and encouragement from the treatment team. It is also important to remember that phobias protect the individual from anxiety and that the individual does not understand the phobia any better than anybody else—and probably not as well as members of the treatment team. Except under controlled treatment conditions, using well-established cognitive-behavioral techniques, exposure to the phobia is not helpful to the patient. Reassurance, support, and acceptance of the patient, as well application of the aforementioned treatment procedures, are necessary for a return to adequate functioning by the patient.

The *DSM-III-R* lists five categories of phobic neurosis including panic disorder:

(1)   300.21   Panic disorder with agoraphobia
(2)   300.01   Panic disorder without agoraphobia
ʾ(3)   300.22   Agoraphobia without a history of panic disorder
(4)   300.23   Social phobia
(5)   300.29   Simple phobia

Briefly, panic disorder is a condition wherein the patient experiences the sudden onset of extreme anxiety during which many of the symptoms of anxiety already discussed appear in an exaggerated form. Although the symptoms may last from a few minutes to, in rare cases, hours, there is often a period of a minute or two in which the patient has an extreme fear of dying or "going crazy." Often there is intense fear of having another attack, which increases the discomfort and worry of the patient.

Agoraphobia, which can occur with or without panic symptoms, is a fear of being in a place, situation, or condition from which escape is felt by the patient to be difficult, impossible, or embarrassing. One of the most frequent of the symptoms reflecting agoraphobia is the refusal of some patients to leave their homes or to go into a crowded store or mall. Many patients restrict their lifestyle significantly and cannot go places unless someone accompanies them.

OBSESSIVE-COMPULSIVE DISORDERS

300.30   Obsessive-compulsive disorders (obsessive-compulsive neuroses)

Another group of diagnostic symptoms within the category of anxiety-related disorders is that of the obsessive-compulsive disorders. Patients experiencing an obsessive-compulsive disorder are unable to prevent thoughts or ideas that they do not wish to think about, or to keep from engaging in some repetitive behavioral act. The patients usually recognize that the thoughts or behaviors are irrational but are unable to prevent them. Importantly, these patients recognize that the obsessions or compulsions are a result of their own thought processes and thus do not ascribe them to something or someone outside themselves.

As with most other disorders, there are specific behavioral characteristics associated with obsessive-compulsive patients. They tend to be neat, perfectionistic, usually rather rigid, and sometimes obstinate. They very often have difficulty making up their minds and thus are unable to make decisions effectively. These patients may tend to blurt out particular statements or words and seem unable to control themselves. They may also show a strong need for structure or for doing things in a specific way, at a certain time, or in a certain position. Although obsessive thoughts can center on a wide range of subjects, the most common concerns are about bodily functions, right and wrong, religion, and suicide. A key feature of the obsessive thoughts is that they are unwanted but persistent, and the patient is frustrated by their presence.

In patients experiencing compulsive disorder, there is a strong desire to repeat some particular behavior or action or to repeat a series of behaviors. Frequently the patients believe something drastic will happen to them if they do not carry out their rituals, and the rituals are designed to prevent that occurrence. However, an objective observer would have difficulty understanding how the ritual could help prevent the occurrence of the dreaded event, since it does not appear to be realistically related to that event.

One patient had a particular series of behaviors that he felt he had to complete before going to bed each night. He believed that if he did not complete his routine, something terrible would happen to him, and his anxiety level would become so high he could not sleep. His ritual included crossing his left leg over his right leg twice, lacing his left shoelace inside his shoe, and placing the left shoestring across the laces of the shoe. He would also face the door and bow three times as well as recite a short poem he had learned. Eventually, with therapy, he was able to relinquish most of his ritual, but he maintained some of the behaviors and added others from time to time.

Of course, many of us engage in minor obsessive-compulsive behavior patterns when we are under stress or when we wish to accomplish a certain goal. As long as the obsessive-compulsive behavior patterns are relatively temporary and help us obtain our goal, there is probably no cause for great concern. However, when they begin to unduly restrict one's behavior, treatment is indicated.

In dealing with obsessive-compulsive patients in a treatment center, it is important to recognize that they are highly sensitive to stressful or threatening situations. One can expect these patients to try to rearrange their environment in an attempt to impose structure and rigidity so that they can control what happens. If they believe they can control their environment, they feel safer. The rituals and behaviors of obsessive-compulsive individuals are designed to help them adjust to the dangers and threats that they perceive as being all about them. Kindness, reassurance, and tolerance are necessary staff behaviors when treating these patients.

POST-TRAUMATIC STRESS DISORDER

309.89   Post-traumatic stress disorder

The last of the anxiety disorders is post-traumatic stress disorder. This complex of symptoms occurs in association with psychologically painful or distressing event. To meet *DSM-III-R* criteria, the event must be outside the normal range of human experience and would have to be stressful to almost anyone. The event associated with the development of the disorder is, by definition, traumatic and is usually accompanied by extreme fright, horror, or helplessness. Usual symptoms include the general anxiety symptoms discussed earlier; in addition, patients tend to reexperience the event repetitively through flashbacks (dissociative symptoms), nightmares or distressing dreams, or feelings of "reliving" the event or events. In extreme cases, patients may have illusions or hallucinations during which the experience is re-created and they feel they are actually back in the situation.

To qualify as a post-traumatic stress disorder, patients must experience the symptoms for more than a month. The disorder is not uncommon, to varying degrees, in persons who have been raped, nearly killed in some way, involved in terroristic actions, or involved in war-related events. Symptoms may occur almost immediately or may be delayed for years. Symptoms may come and go and may be rekindled by seeing similar events or symbols of the distressing event. The "anniversary" reactions refer to the exacerbation of symptoms around the time of the occurrence of the distressing event.

SOMATOFORM DISORDERS

The somatoform disorders are a group of five disorders that have the central feature of mimicking physical disorders but for which no physiological basis can be found. Two additional groups cover somatoform type disorders that do not fit into one of the five established categories. These disorders include the following:

(1) 300.11   Conversion disorder (hysterical neurosis, conversion type)
(2) 300.70* Body dysmorphic disorder
(3) 300.70* Hypochondriasis (hypochondriacal neurosis)
(4) 300.81   Somatization disorder
(5) 307.80   Somatoform pain disorder

(An asterisk [*] is used in the *DSM-III-R* to indicate that a code number has been used more than once to maintain compatibility with the ICD-9-CM [*International Classification of Diseases, Ninth Revision, Clinical Modification*]. An "x" is used to indicate a further refinement of the diagnostic category, such as mild or moderate severity, with or without psychosis, and so forth.)

CONVERSION DISORDER (HYSTERICAL NEUROSIS, CONVERSION TYPE)

At one point in our country's history, many people believed that being "struck" blind, dumb, or with a paralysis of some sort was due to the wrath of God or to demonic possession. However, as our society has become more educated, such reasons for the sudden onset of blindness, mutism, or paralysis have given way to more sophisticated explanations. Most people no longer believe that babies are "marked" at birth because the mother was frightened by a bear or scared by a "devil" or had evil thoughts during her pregnancy. But although such explanations for behavioral characteristics have changed, we still see many patients who suffer conversion disorders.

Conversion disorders are attempts by individuals to defend themselves from anxiety-provoking situations by unconsciously developing symptoms of a physical disorder that has no underlying organic, or physical, basis. Although the symptoms are psychogenic in origin, they are quite real to the patients. The basic characteristics of this disorder are that patients lose the ability to perform some physical function that they could perform before the onset of the disorder. The lost function is usually symbolically related to some situation which produces stress or anxiety for the individuals. Patients may lose sensitivity to some area of their bodies, be unable to hear or talk, have unusual sensations such as tingling or burning, or lose the ability to perform some motor function such as walking or the movement of an arm or a hand. "Primary gain" is achieved by keeping the anxiety-provoking need or conflict out of awareness, and "secondary gain" is sometimes achieved through the reception of sympathy from family or friends; in both cases, the symptoms are thus reinforced. Such persons are usually first seen by a physician, who can find no physical basis for the symptoms. They are often referred to a neurologist, whose tests are also negative. As a last resort, they are then referred to a psychologist or a psychiatrist.

To illustrate, one of the authors treated a young woman who had suddenly become paralyzed from the waist down and was unable to walk. The patient, who was 18 years old, had already been seen by her family physician and by a neurologist, neither of whom could discover any physical basis for the paralysis. In reviewing the patient's history, the psychologic factors leading to the paralysis became fairly clear-cut. The patient had a younger sister who had contracted polio at age 2 and was disabled by the disease. She died at age 15. Due to her disability, most of the family's efforts and attentions were focused on this child, and the older girl received little attention. Consequently, she developed some rather strong hostile feelings toward her sister. Of course, her hostility could not be expressed directly, and the patient suffered severe guilt feelings for the hostility that she felt.

A few months after her sister died, the patient was involved in an accident in which she was hit by a falling tree limb. The patient did not suffer any significant injury as a result of the accident, and no medical follow-up was required. However, several months later, the patient developed the paralysis. The patient's family, afraid that another tragedy had befallen one of their children, became quite concerned and showed a great deal of sympathy and attention to the patient. Several weeks of treatment were required for both the patient and her family before she was able to walk again.

Conversion disorders are not common. They constitute less than 5 percent of all neurotic reactions; unless one works in a hospital or clinic setting, one may never see a patient in this diagnostic category. Of course, a great many people have headaches, stomachaches, and minor aches and pains that may be related to emotionally stressful situations. It is only when they become severely debilitating, however, that they significantly affect a person's life.

Perhaps the most important aspect of conversion disorders is that they are caused by situations that individuals perceive as highly stressful and by their need to escape from the anxiety and stress created by that situation. The pain or the paralysis that may develop is real to the individuals, and the fact that it is psychogenic in origin does not diminish the effect of the condition.

Because there is no apparent organic dysfunction, people frequently assume that the patients are faking or that the paralysis or the pain is not real. However, the particular conversion reaction has meaning to the patients; whether or not members of the treatment team understand it, patients will not be helped by derogatory comments about their illness or by telling them that the illness is "all in the head."

BODY DYSMORPHIC DISORDER

Body dysmorphic disorder is a disorder in which individuals become preoccupied with the idea that something is wrong with their appearance but the imagined defect is not apparent to an objective observer. The complaints often are related to the face, skin, or other exposed body areas. Frequent trips to plastic surgeons are not uncommon. If the preoccupation with the imagined defect reaches delusional status, the diagnosis is delusional disorder, somatic subtype, since delusions are psychotic rather than neurotic in nature.

HYPOCHONDRIASIS (HYPOCHONDRIACAL NEUROSIS)

The hallmark of hypochondriacs is a preoccupation with the idea that they have some horrible or debilitating disease and nobody will help them. Despite complete medical clearance and reassurance from their physician, hypochondriacal patients are never quite comfortable that they have been adequately evaluated. If they had been properly evaluated, they reason, the physician would have found the disease process causing their concern. Such patients, under pressure, can usually admit that there is some possibility they are wrong and are misinterpreting the symptoms. Yet the appearance of any small symptom or sensation sets them off again, certain that this time their fears are justified. These patients often have a cupboard full of medicine and often see multiple physicians in their search for the disease process they are so certain is present. Patients sometimes have their anxiety focused in this particular way due to having had some true illness or by having a family member or friend with such an illness. These patients are often angered by any suggestion that they should seek mental health treatment.

SOMATIZATION DISORDER

The major difference between hypochondriasis and somatization disorder is that hypochondriacs tend to be preoccupied with having some *particular* disease process, while the somatization disorder patient focuses on a variety of symptoms without ascribing them to any particular disease process. Somatization disorder patients have a long history of multiple problems for which no suitable organic cause can be established. Symptoms usually begin before age 30. To qualify for this diagnosis, the patient must have complaints of at least 13 different physical symptoms. Their symptom list is often presented with drama and flair, and there is a long and involved medical history that can be overwhelming when one sits down to take a history. One has the feeling of not knowing where to start because so many things are wrong.

SOMATOFORM PAIN DISORDER

Somatoform pain disorder is characterized by patients' preoccupation with pain for 6 months or more for which no physical cause can be demonstrated. The concentration of attention on the pain is evident in that patients want to talk about little else and are often irritated that no one appreciates the intensity of their pain. Pain becomes the central focus of their existence and tends to govern much of their activity. The pain may not be consistent with any known pattern of physical pathology or may mimic known pain, such as angina or sciatica. There may be direct evidence of the role of psychological factors when development of the pain follows or is connected with some environmental event that causes an emotional conflict or need. If, for example, the pain intensifies each time the patient's wife tells him he needs to get out of the wheelchair and begin to use crutches, the pain may be serving the patient's dependency needs. Sometimes pain allows patients to avoid activities and situations to which they are averse, and sometimes other evidence for secondary gain is clear. In some cases there is no apparent psychogenic role. Care must be taken with somatoform pain patients to avoid unnecessary medication and medical procedures.

DISSOCIATIVE DISORDERS

Dissociative disorders (hysterical neurosis, dissociative type) form an interesting diagnostic group even though they, too, account for less than 5 percent of all neurotic reactions. The dissociative disorders are like the conversion disorders in that they frequently occur in the same personality type and both disorders serve to protect the individual from an especially stressful situation. Amnesia, fugue, depersonalization, and multiple personality are the major categories of dissociative reactions and reflect the major feature of this disorder, which is a disturbance in the proper integration of memory, consciousness, and identity. The four *DSM-III-R* categories are as follows:

(1)   300.14   Multiple personality disorder
(2)   300.13   Psychogenic fugue

(3) 300.12 Psychogenic amnesia
(4) 300.60 Depersonalization disorder (depersonalization neurosis)

MULTIPLE PERSONALITY DISORDER

Multiple personalities are perhaps the most famous of all dissociative disorders if you consider the number of television shows, movies, and novels about people who suffer from this disorder. In clinical practice there are few actual cases of true multiple personalities, although in the last few years many clinicians have come to believe it is not nearly so rare as once thought. The disorders appear almost always to originate in childhood and in association with a trauma of some kind, particularly physical and sexual abuse, and they are rarely discovered until adulthood. The number of personalities can range from two to over a hundred.

In multiple personalities, an individual usually shows evidence of having two or more identifiably different patterns or characteristic ways of responding to the environment. Each of these identifiable ways of responding is operationally defined as a different personality. Usually each individual "personality" within the patient is a complete personality system of its own, and the patient responds to the particular personality that is conscious at any given time by allowing that personality system to dominate his or her behavior or reactions to the environment. In many cases, but not all, some or all of the various personalities are aware of the others and may communicate internally. Some personalities are assigned roles such as "the worker," "the socializer," "the protector," and so forth, and different personalities may be in control at various times in the person's life. The personalities are often very different from each other and, astoundingly, research indicates that different personalities may have different physiologic characteristics (such as eyeglass prescriptions, asthma, and so forth) as well as different psychologic profiles.

One of the most frequent ways multiple personalities are discovered is that a patient will come to therapy for some reason other than multiple personalities and, in the course of therapy, the existence of alternative personalities is uncovered. Frequently, the tipoff comes when the therapist discovers time periods for which the patient has no memory. Another tipoff occurs when the therapist recalls something said by the patient but the patient has no recollection of it. This is a complex disorder to diagnose and to treat, and treatment should not be undertaken by persons without specific training in treating multiple personality disorder.

PSYCHOGENIC FUGUE

In psychogenic fugue, patients not only have amnesia but combine the amnesia with flight, leaving the area where they live or work. Fugue is usually precipitated by some socially or environmentally stressful situation from which patients attempt to remove themselves both mentally and physically. The removal, however, is unconscious rather than conscious in that patients are usually unaware of where they came from and are unable to recall their former identities. When an episode is over, the patient usually is unable to recall events occurring during the episode. A key feature in the diagnosis of fugue is that the travels of the person appear to be purposeful rather than aimless.

PSYCHOGENIC AMNESIA

Amnesia is the sudden and temporary forgetting of information about one's life or environment. There are four basic types of amnesia. They are (1) localized, (2) selective, (3) generalized, and (4) continuous. In localized amnesia, patients usually forget specific information for a specified but undetermined length of time. For example, patients may forget their names or a particular period of time, such as a traumatic event, a stressful operation, or an unhappy family situation. In selective amnesia patients cannot remember certain things that occurred during a specific time period. In generalized amnesia patients do not remember anything about their lives; this is also referred to as global amnesia. In continuous amnesia patients are unable to recall information from some particular time or event up to the present.

Amnesia is typically precipitated by a psychologically stressful event or situation, is usually fairly brief in duration, and often ends suddenly. Patients are usually able to regain all the lost information, and repeat experiences of amnesia are rare.

DEPERSONALIZATION DISORDER (DEPERSONALIZATION NEUROSIS)

The term *depersonalization* refers to a change in how one experiences one's own reality so that one's "mind" or consciousness seems separated from one's body. One feels outside oneself and feels as though one is merely an observer of what is happening to one's body or mental processes. Patients sometimes report feeling as though they had somehow escaped their bodies and were looking down from a corner of the room watching themselves. Patients are usually aware that something strange is happening, do not like it, and usually are able to maintain contact with reality. Some patients describe the experience as being in a dreamlike state.

MOOD DISORDERS

The *DSM-III-R* handles mood disorders differently from the other classifications of disorders in order to avoid duplication of diagnostic categories. Mood disorders include mood disturbances ranging from very depressed mood to elation, and they include disorders in which both extremes occur within the same individual. Mood disorders are divided into the two categories of bipolar disorder and depressive disorder.

BIPOLAR DISORDERS

(1) 296.6x Bipolar disorder, mixed
(2) 296.4x Bipolar disorder, manic
(3) 296.5x Bipolar disorder, depressed
(4) 301.13 Cyclothymia
(The x is a placeholder for indicating severity characteristics of the disorder, such as mild, moderate, with or without psychosis, and so forth.)

In the bipolar disorders, diagnoses are made depending on the nature of the moods experienced by the individual. In the "mixed" category, patients have had one or more manic episodes and one or more major depressive episodes. Manic episodes are characterized by strongly elevated mood, expansive mood, or irritability accompanied variously by inflated self-esteem or grandiosity, decreased need for sleep, pressured speech or being hyperverbal, racing thoughts, distractibility, increased psychomotor agitation, and/or behaviors carrying a high risk for harm or painful consequences. A common behavior in mania is the spending spree. Patients buy things they do not need and cannot use. They may give money away, believing they have an unlimited supply. They may sing and dance and preach and engage in promiscuous sexual behavior. And all the while they may believe they are managing everything just fine. However, there is marked impairment in social and occupational functioning, and manic patients are often hospitalized. Psychotic features also occur, usually in the form of delusions or hallucinations involving inflated worth, power, identity, or a special relationship with some famous person or deity. A less debilitating form of mania is hypomania; it is usually distinguished from mania by the fact that the symptoms are the same but not as severe and do not result in substantial impairment in social and occupational functioning.

In depressive episodes, patients show depressed mood characterized by feelings of sadness, sometimes irritability, and what are commonly called the "vegetative" signs of depression. These include a loss of appetite or overeating, inability to sleep or sleeping too much, decreased energy, anhedonia (inability to experience pleasure), loss of interest in activities, and weight loss or weight gain. In addition, depressed patients experience excessive guilt; have feelings of worthlessness, helplessness, and hopelessness; and have trouble maintaining attention and concentration. There is frequently a withdrawal from friends and acquaintances, and patients will sometimes lock themselves away from the world, refusing to answer the telephone or the door. Psychomotor retardation or agitation is also seen, along with indecisiveness. Suicidal ideation is also common and represents the most immediate and serious threat in depressed persons.

In cyclothymia, the symptoms described for mania and major depressive episodes occur but are of lesser intensity and meet the definition for hypomanic disorder rather than full mania. The symptoms involve both depressive episodes and hypomanic episodes. Some researchers maintain that cyclothymia is simply a mild form of bipolar disorder.

DEPRESSIVE DISORDERS

(1)	296.2x	Major depression, single episode
(2)	296.2x	Major depression, recurrent
(3)	300.40	Dysthymia (or depressive neurosis)
(4)	311.00	Depressive disorder, not otherwise specified

The above diagnostic categories describe those mood disorders that have only elements of depressed mood and do not include a history of manic or hypomanic episodes. In the "single episode" category are included patients who have never had either a manic, hypomanic, or previous depressive episode. If the patient has previously had a depressive episode, the "recurrent" category is used. Dysthymia bears much the same relationship to major depression that hypomania bears to mania. That is, the symptoms are of the same nature but are not as severe. This, of course, makes for difficulty in some cases in deciding if the person has dysthymia or a major depression. To make this diagnosis, the mood disturbance must have been present for 2 years (1 year for children and adolescents), with no more than 2 months of that time being symptom-free. The "not otherwise specified" category is for those patients with depressive symptoms who do not qualify for one of the other mood disorders.

In the next chapter we discuss the psychotic disorders. Questions for Chapters 5, 6, and 7 can be found at the end of Chapter 7.

ANNOTATED BIBLIOGRAPHY

American Psychiatric Association: *Diagnostic and Statistical Manual of Mental Disorders*, ed. 3, rev. APA, Washington, DC, 1987.

Barth, F.D.: *Obsessional thinking as "paradoxical action."* Bulletin of the Menninger Clinic, 1990, 54:449–511.

> *Uses Schafer's theory of obsessional thinking as paradoxical action and case examples to illustrate the treatment and the resistance to treatment of persons suffering from obsessive-compulsive disorder.*

Kaplan, A.S.: *Biomedical variables in the eating disorders.* Canadian Journal of Psychiatry, 1990, 35:745–753.

> *Focuses on the medical and nutritional assessment and management of patients with eating disorders and the medical complications that may arise.*

Meyer, J.K., and Levin, F.M.: *Sadism and masochism in neurosis and symptom formation.* Presented at the Fall Meeting of the American Psychoanalytic Association, New York, December 17, 1988. Scientific Proceedings, 1988, pp. 789–804.

> *Presents several theories on the development of sadism and masochism and provides case examples for further study.*

Pollack, L.E.: *Improving relationships: Groups for inpatients with bipolar disorder.* Journal of Psychosocial Nursing and Mental Health Services, 1990, 28(5):17–22.

> *Discusses the use of group therapy to improve social skills in patients with bipolar disorder.*

Rogers, B.: *Socio-economic status, employment and neurosis.* Social Psychiatry and Psychiatric Epidemiology, 1991, 26:104–114.

> *Explores the social, occupational, and educational status of persons suffering from neurosis.*

Simoni, P.S.: *Obsessive-compulsive disorder: The effect of research on nursing care.* Journal of Psychosocial Nursing and Mental Health Services, 1991, 29(4):19–23.

> *Defines obsessive-compulsive disorder and presents concepts for nursing care and intervention.*

Whitley, G.G.: *Ritualistic behavior: Breaking the cycle.* Journal of Psychosocial Nursing and Mental Health Services, 1991, 29(10):31–35.

Presents treatment strategies for working with patients with obsessive-compulsive disorders.

Widiger, T., Frances, A., Pincus, H., Davis, W., and First, M.: *Toward an empirical classification for the* DSM-IV. Journal of Abnormal Psychology, 1991, 100(3):280–288.

The empirical basis for the DSM-IV *is discussed, and a historical perspective of the past editions of the* DSM *is presented.*

6

The Psychotic Diagnostic Categories

LEARNING OBJECTIVES

Students will be able to:
1. Discuss three different categories of psychosis.
2. Identify several characteristics of persons suffering from psychoses.
3. Identify the largest single group of psychotic patients.
4. Name several different types of psychotic mental disorders.

The psychoses are generally divided into two categories, the organic psychoses and the functional psychoses. Organic psychoses are those caused by some disorder of the brain for which physical pathology can be demonstrated. The functional psychoses are psychotic disorders that are caused by psychologic stress. That is, they occur in response to psychologic stresses and in the absence of demonstrated neurologic pathology. In both categories, patients exhibit bizarre behavior and are obviously ill. One is much more likely to notice the bizarre quality of a psychotic person's behavior than to notice a patient with a neurosis. This is largely due to the fact that the psychotic patient's behavior differs a great deal from the so-called normal behavior of human beings.

A third category of psychotic reactions is sometimes used when mental health teams wish to separate psychotic reactions caused by toxic substances. These are called toxic psychoses and are generally caused by the ingestion of drugs or poisons of some type.

In psychotic reactions, as opposed to neurotic reactions, it is important to realize that patients are not dealing with objective reality. The reality that these individuals experience is unique to them and is not the same reality that a healthy person experiences. To psychotic patients, the spiders they see on their arms are real and the persons to whom they are talking, but who are unseen by others, are also real. The voices that psychotic patients hear are real to them, and they are sincerely convinced that they are Jesus Christ or Napoleon or a prophet or an FBI agent or that their food or water is being poisoned. Arguing with patients or trying to demonstrate logically that their perceptions of reality are in error is of very little benefit. This is primarily true because "logical" arguments by staff members appeal to a reality that does not exist for the patients. They just do not see the world in the same way that staff members do.

Contrary to what many people in the general population believe, a very large percentage of patients admitted to hospitals with a psychotic disorder recover and are able to once again function effectively. After a sufficient period of recovery, many patients suffering from psychotic disorders are able to resume their lives and to make a good adjustment subsequent to hospitalization. However, far too many, for reasons we do not yet understand, become chronic and live with a reality that is incompatible with adequate social and occupational productivity.

Since the differences between neuroses and psychoses have been discussed previously, what follows is a description of the different functionally (nonorganic) based psychotic categories of the third revised edition of the *Diagnostic and Statistical Manual of Mental Disorders (DSM-III-R)*. They are presented in order that one may develop some familiarity with the major diagnostic classifications of nonorganic psychotic disorders.

SCHIZOPHRENIC DISORDERS

(1) 295.2x   Schizophrenia, catatonic
(2) 295.3x   Schizophrenia, paranoid
(3) 295.1x   Schizophrenia, disorganized
(4) 295.9x   Schizophrenia, undifferentiated

In general, most authorities are uncertain about why people develop schizophrenia. Hereditary factors have been linked to schizophrenia, and research suggests that individuals may be predisposed to develop schizophrenia under stressful environmental conditions. Factors such as family behavioral patterns and other sociologic and cultural differences have been designated as causative factors of schizophrenia. It seems more likely, however, that schizophrenia is the result of a complex combination of biologic, psychologic, and sociologic factors.

Schizophrenic reactions may occur suddenly, in which case they are referred to as being acute schizophrenic reactions. They may also be of long duration and may develop slowly over a rather lengthy period of time. In this latter case, they are called chronic schizophrenic reactions.

Schizophrenia comprises the largest single diagnostic group of psychotic patients. Approximately 1 percent of the people in the United States suffer from schizophrenia as it is now defined by the *DSM-III-R*. As is obvious from the list above, there are many different classifications of schizophrenia. However, the overriding characteristic in the schizophrenias is the bizarre nature of the thought content and processes. The thought content of schizophrenics tends to include both delusions and hallucinations that are so patently strange or bizarre as to defy all logic. Patients believe the television is giving them messages from God or the president or the CIA. A patient of one of the authors believed he was receiving messages from aliens in outer space through the filling in his teeth, and still another patient thought he was dead. Patients sometimes believe thoughts are being inserted into their heads against their will, that others can read their thoughts or are stealing their thoughts, and that they are being controlled by or are controlling forces outside themselves. They may think that some force, such as x-rays or radio waves, has somehow disturbed their body and is causing it to rot or some other equally illogical outcome.

Disturbances in the thought processes of schizophrenics show up in how verbalizations are processed and organized. This disturbance in cognitive processing is called a formal thought disorder. Patients demonstrating a formal thought disorder may have an extremely tangential relationship with reality and be unable to answer questions in a relevant way. Their associations may be quite loose (thoughts are not logically related or expressed, and they jump from one subject to another), they may show flight of ideas, be incoherent and use neologisms (words that are made up and have no real meaning in the language), talk all around an issue and give so many nonessential details that they have trouble getting to the point they wish to make (circumstantiality), or demonstrate echolalia (echoing what is said to them), mutism, thought blocking, posturing, poor abstraction abilities, and a supreme lack of awareness that they are communicating poorly. Their perceptions are often bizarre and include delusions and hallucinations. Affect (emotional tone) is often flat or inappropriate, with giggling or unpredictable laughing or crying. There is often a loss of a sense of personal individuality, with patients being unsure of their relationship to the world and their place in it. Some patients become preoccupied with questions about the meaning of life and other esoteric concerns. Schizophrenic patients often have difficulty with impulse control, especially while acutely ill, and lack the ability to appreciate the social consequences of their behavior. Most schizophrenic patients show very limited insight and may show very poor judgment. There is impairment in social relationships and impairment in the ability to get organized to perform tasks and accomplish goals. Suicide is also a serious risk in schizophrenic patients.

CATATONIC SCHIZOPHRENIA

The catatonic schizophrenic is quite striking because of the extreme nature of the person's withdrawal. Catatonic patients may refuse to eat, will not speak, and may remain motionless for hours or days. The two phases of catatonia are the stuporous phase, wherein the patient is motionless, and catatonic excitement, wherein the patient is over-reactive, shouts, talks, paces, and appears quite manic. Patients may alternate between these phases, sometimes quite rapidly, but most seem to show a preference for one or the other. One particularly interesting and clear diagnostic indicator of catatonia is that of posturing, or catatonic rigidity. In this condition, patients refuse to allow their body position to be altered. In waxy flexibility, when a patient's hand or some other body part is placed in some particular position, even an uncomfortable one, the patient tends to maintain that position. It is as if they were made of soft warm wax and can be molded into almost any position. Catatonia is fairly rare but dramatic in its presentation, and when you see these conditions you will likely recognize them right away.

PARANOID SCHIZOPHRENIA

The paranoid schizophrenic often shows much hostility and suspiciousness and may show a great deal of overt aggression. The "glaring" intensity of many paranoid schizophrenic patients has sometimes led people to refer to the "paranoid stare" as a characteristic. These patients sometimes relate in an intense, overbearing way, and one can often feel the anger and hostility as they talk and interrelate with others. Paranoid schizophrenic patients tend to be rather well organized in their delusions and hallucinations, and those phenomena are usually organized around a single idea or theme. They do not seem as "strange" or bizarre as the other types of schizophrenic patients, and therapists often speak of these patients' ability to "reconstitute" quickly. That is, they can sometimes pull themselves together very quickly; with only brief exposure to these patients, if you did not know about their illness, you might find yourself wondering why they were in treatment. Sometimes these patients appear so well organized and their delusional material so logical that one finds it necessary to talk to family or others who know them in order to verify what is and is not fact. However, after being around these patients for a while, you will recognize their preoccupation with whatever is the central theme to their illness.

DISORGANIZED SCHIZOPHRENIA

In disorganized schizophrenia, patients may appear manic and have bizarre mannerisms. They often laugh and giggle inappropriately and are preoccupied with trivial things. They represent one of the most severely disorganized personality structures in the schizophrenic group. Delusions and hallucinatory phenomena, when they occur, tend to be random and very poorly presented. In talking with such patients, one recognizes right away that something is tremendously wrong, and it is usually difficult to make any emotional contact with disorganized schizophrenics. The withdrawal is extreme, and one is never sure that any emotional contact has been made with them. These patients suffer the most social isolation over time because they tend not to have significant remissions and their course is often quite chronic.

UNDIFFERENTIATED SCHIZOPHRENIA

In undifferentiated schizophrenia, there are prominent delusions or hallucinations, incoherence, or other evidence of grossly disorganized behavior that does not meet the criteria for other types of schizophrenia or meets the criteria for more than one.

SCHIZOAFFECTIVE DISORDER

295.70   Schizoaffective disorder

The authors have chosen to include this diagnostic entity here probably more out of obstinacy than anything else. The *DSM-III-R* classifies it under "Psychotic Disorders Not Elsewhere Classified." We have disagreed with the deletion of this category from the schizophrenic disorders, but it was deleted because mood disorders have been thought to be distinguishable from thought disorders.

In schizoaffective schizophrenia, a significant thought disorder is apparent, along with a significant mood variation. These patients may at first appear to be merely depressed or manic, but further inquiry reveals a basic personality disorganization. The framers of the *DSM-III-R* require that this disorder be diagnosed only when there have been times when the patient presented with symptoms of both a mood disorder and a schizophrenic disturbance and there have also been times when the patient presented with a psychotic disturbance but no mood disturbance. The authors have found this diagnosis very useful with a select group of patients who seem clearly to have disorders that cannot be classified purely as a mood disorder or as a schizophrenic disorder but have elements of both.

DELUSIONAL (PARANOID) DISORDER

297.10   Delusional (paranoid) disorder

The *DSM-III-R* uses the term *delusional* disorder for this diagnostic category in order to escape the multiple implications inherent in the term *paranoid*. This disorder is separate from that of paranoid schizophrenia and is differentiated largely on the basis of the lack of bizarreness and the mental disorganization seen in the paranoid schizophrenic. Auditory or visual hallucinations are not usually a part of the clinical picture for patients with delusional disorder, and they are not often seen as eccentric or strange.

There are five general themes that make up the bulk of the delusional material in this disorder:

1. *Erotomanic type.* This is the category of delusion we so often see played out on the nightly news, sometimes referred to as "fan obsessions." Movie and television stars often find themselves the targets of delusional people who are convinced the star needs them for one reason or another or that the star loves them but just does not realize it. Any persons of public prominence may be targets of persons with erotomanic delusions simply because of their public stature, but star status is not a requirement to become a target. Targets may be a boss or a neighbor or even a stranger. The person suffering the delusion may try to contact the target in a number of ways, including calling, writing, stalking, and other such tactics. Such experiences are often rather frightening for the target and have sometimes resulted in the death of the target (as in the case of Rebecca Schaffer from the television program "My Sister Sam"), but the motivation is not usually sexual gratification. For whatever reason, perhaps because of social conditioning, men more often pursue their delusions to the point of contact with police than do women.

2. *Grandiose type.* Persons suffering from grandiose delusions usually act on a strong belief that they are somehow special or have been assigned a special project by some very important figure. They sometimes believe they have been entrusted with a secret that will save the world or humanity, or have invented some marvelous new device with fantastic potential, or have developed special knowledge or ability of great value. If they believe themselves to be some living person of great importance, they believe that the actual person is a fraud or imposter and may go to some lengths to try to prove it. One

area that seems particularly attractive for delusional persons is religion and, if one is adept enough at managing such a delusion, one can attract a lot of followers. Some years ago Jim Jones not only convinced many of his followers to go with him to a foreign country but convinced them to participate in a mass suicidal destruction of his entire following. The adults gave poisoned Kool-Aid to their children, then drank it themselves.

3. *Jealous type.* In this delusion patients come to believe that their spouse or lover is engaging in a relationship with another person. To make this diagnosis, there cannot be objective cause for the concerns. The authors have seen instances in which the patient's spouse is rarely out of sight but the patient persists in believing that the spouse is unfaithful. Patients find small cues and "evidence," which is taken as proof that the imagined relationship is occurring. This "evidence" often throws patients into an angry outrage, and they may become physically abusive and violent toward the spouse or lover. Patients will often play "detective" and follow the object of their concern in an effort to prove the validity of their beliefs—and when one looks that hard, one often finds some tiny bit of information that can be construed as being consistent with the delusional belief.

4. *Persecutory type.* These patients are often disliked by staff members, other patients, their family, and everyone in general because they are so very difficult to get along with and are frequently quite hostile. They are resentful and usually mistrust the motives of almost everyone. Frequently they are overly concerned with issues of right and wrong and are quite rigid in their beliefs and expectations. They will go to ridiculous extremes to right an imagined wrong or to avenge an imagined slight and thus are frequently threatening to take legal action. Delusions will often include such things as being poisoned, plotted against, ignored, having their ideas stolen, or being in some way deprived of something that is rightfully theirs. Persons with persecutory delusions can be frightening at times and do sometimes act out violently against those they believe responsible for their torment.

5. *Somatic type.* The *DSM-III-R* recounts that the most frequent manifestation of paranoid somatic delusions is that patients believe that some part of their body is emitting a foul odor, that they have some type of parasite living in their bodies, or that they have some type of infection. There may also be a perception, with no objective evidence, that some part of their body is malformed or misfunctioning. Such patients usually are discovered when they visit a family doctor or other specialist for attention to their somatic complaint.

A major difference between delusional (paranoid) patients and paranoid schizophrenics is that paranoid patients usually have better intellectual control and are able to make more appropriate intellectual and social responses. Compared with paranoid schizophrenics, paranoid patients are usually more reality oriented. Except in the area of their delusions, their intellectual capacities are much better organized, and they are able to present their feelings in a much more effective manner.

Among the most important things for a mental health worker to recognize are that paranoid patients have significant difficulty recognizing their own hostilities and anger and that they tend to project their anger onto others. The defense mechanism of projection is used heavily by paranoid patients, helping to prevent them from having to recognize their own anger and hostility. Paranoid patients will frequently do something deliberately to anger a staff member or a fellow patient in order to confirm their delusion that other people do not like them or are angry at them. If the staff member or fellow patient responds in an angry fashion, paranoid patients feel that their original belief was correct and justified. In general, paranoid patients are often difficult to manage. However, they represent a very small percentage of psychiatric patients, probably accounting for less than 1 percent of all psychiatric admissions.

In the next chapter we discuss the personality disorders and sexual disorders. Questions for Chapters 5, 6, and 7 can be found at the end of Chapter 7.

ANNOTATED BIBLIOGRAPHY

American Psychiatric Association: *Diagnostic and Statistical Manual of Mental Disorders*, ed. 3, rev. APA, Washington, DC, 1987.

Chapman, T.: *The nurse's role in neuroleptic medications.* Journal of Psychosocial Nursing and Mental Health Services, 1991, 29(6):6–8.

> *Neuroleptic medications for the treatment of schizophrenia often have adverse side effects. Patients were allowed to express their attitudes concerning the need for these medications.*

Dauner, A., and Blair, D.: *Akathisia: When treatment creates a problem.* Journal of Psychosocial Nursing and Mental Health Services, 1990, 23(10):13–17.

> *Explains the symptoms and dangers of akathisia (a side effect of antipsychotic medications) and gives several case examples of patients suffering from these symptoms.*

Dzurec, L.C.: *How do they see themselves? Self-perceptions and functioning for people with chronic schizophrenia.* Journal of Psychosocial Nursing and Mental Health Services, 1990, 28(8):10–14.

Research study describing the relationship between the self-perceptions of schizophrenic patients and their level of daily functioning.

Koontz, E.: *Schizophrenia: Current diagnostic concepts and implications for nursing care.* Journal of Psychosocial Nursing and Mental Health Services, 1982, 20(9):44–48.

Explores schizophrenia from the DSM-III multiaxial approach. Describes the various types of schizophrenia: disorganized, paranoid, catatonic, undifferentiated, and residual.

Malone, J.A.: *Schizophrenia research update: Implications for nursing.* Journal of Psychosocial Nursing and Mental Health Services, 1990, 28(8):4–9.

Discusses the scientific advances made in the understanding and treatment of schizophrenia, what areas need to be further explored, and the implications for nursing practice.

Yaktin, U.S., and Labban, S.: *Traumatic war stress and schizophrenia.* Journal of Psychosocial Nursing and Mental Health Services, 1992, 30(6):29–33.

Research study examining the correlation between traumatic war stress and the onset of schizophrenia.

The Personality Disorders and the Sexual Disorders

LEARNING OBJECTIVES

Students will be able to:
1. Discuss the significance of personality disorders to the lives of people who have them.
2. Identify four characteristics of persons having personality disorders.
3. Understand and express the reasons persons with personality disorders are often shunned by treatment personnel.
4. Name several different types of personality disorders.
5. Name two major categories of sexual disorders.
6. Identify several characteristics of persons who experience sexual disorders.

PERSONALITY DISORDERS

The personality disorders include patterns of behavior that are neither psychotic nor neurotic but that are nonetheless substantially maladaptive. There are few data about the cause of personality disorders, but, as usual, we suspect a role for such factors as genetics, environment, culture, and maturation. Personality disorders involve behavior patterns that are usually longstanding and are frequently apparent from early adolescence. Because personality disorders are often not seen as being as "serious" as neurotic or psychotic conditions, and perhaps because they are so prevalent in our society, their significance is often overlooked.

Perry and Vaillant (1989, p. 1352), have made the point that a number of "saints, artists, revolutionary heroes and true innovators" had personality disorders. They have also pointed out that a large percentage of prison inmates, welfare recipients, and persons "known in lay terms as bad, deviant, sinning, cranky, or n'er-do-well [sic]"

95

are among those with personality disorders. They enumerate four characteristics shared by persons with personality disorders:

1. An inflexible and maladaptive response to stress.
2. A disability in working and loving that is generally more serious and always more pervasive than that found in neurosis.
3. Elicitation of problematic responses by interpersonal conflict.
4. A particular capacity to "get under the skin" of and distress others.

Personality disorders are differentiated from personality "traits" primarily on the basis of the degree of maladaptation and personal discomfort created by the personality characteristics. Patients with personality disorders have difficulty managing emotionally intense situations, have trouble managing anger, and want others to adapt to their demands rather than adapting themselves to the demands of others. They tend to view people as difficult to live with, have trouble seeing their own faults and problems, and tend to blame others when things go wrong. Individuals with personality disorders tend to ask what is wrong with the world rather than what is wrong with themselves.

Because of the foregoing characteristics, persons with personality disorders tend to be shunned by treatment personnel. They are difficult to treat, reject efforts to help, do not see the need for change, and are irreverent and sometimes openly contemptuous toward the caregiver. These characteristics are not endearing, and these persons' resistance to change regardless of what mode of therapy is used often makes them less than favorites as patients. There is often a perception that personality disorders are untreatable, but it would be unreasonable to assume that an enduring personality adaptation would remit as readily as, say, a phobia, which creates a great deal of discomfort for the affected person. Patients with personality disorders often see their personality characteristics as consistent with getting their needs met and as necessary to dealing with an uncaring world. Given that mind-set, it is not surprising that they are reluctant to change.

Personality disorders are divided into three clusters in the third revised edition of the *Diagnostic and Statistical Manual of Mental Disorders (DSM-III-R)*. They are as follows:

Cluster A—The odd and the eccentric

(1) 301.00   Paranoid personality disorder
(2) 301.20   Schizoid personality disorder
(3) 301.22   Schizotypal personality disorder

Cluster B—The dramatic, emotional, and erratic

(1) 301.70   Antisocial personality disorder
(2) 301.83   Borderline personality disorder
(3) 301.50   Histrionic personality disorder
(4) 301.81   Narcissistic personality disorder

Cluster C—The anxious, fearful, and introverted

(1) 301.82   Avoidant personality disorder
(2) 301.60   Dependent personality disorder
(3) 301.40   Obsessive-compulsive personality disorder
(4) 301.84   Passive-aggressive personality disorder

PARANOID PERSONALITY DISORDER

Paranoid personalities are decidedly unlikable for the most part. They are angry, are prone to misinterpret the actions and intentions of almost everyone, hold grudges (seemingly forever), are quick to blame others for everything, and seldom accept responsibility for the circumstances they have created. They tend to react with rage and vindictiveness when they feel that they have been wronged and are quick to resort to threats of legal action. They are quite vigilant and seem afraid of anything "foreign" or poorly understood. Paranoid personalities have difficulty finding humor in the world, especially if it is at their own expense. These patients have great difficulty with love and intimacy but, curiously, perceive that they are desired by those they fear will hurt them. One must always be sensitive to their lack of trust, insistence on being treated with dignity and honor, and propensity for misinterpreting friendly overtures that infringe too much on their need for emotional distance. Paranoid personalities are quite aware of the roles people are supposed to play and may react strongly when someone begins to play "one-up" or to assume more responsibility than his or her assigned role would dictate. Finally, these patients are always looking for evidence that they have been slighted, ignored, taken advantage of, or otherwise exploited—and they usually find such evidence. One would do well to be aware that patients with paranoid personality traits are likely to take very personally any event that seems to them to be demeaning, and almost anything can be interpreted in that fashion by these patients.

SCHIZOID PERSONALITY DISORDER

The hallmark of the schizoid personality is a rather marked withdrawal from social contact. Such withdrawal encompasses most aspects of these patients' lives and severely limits their social interactions—

which tend to be meager or nonexistent. These patients are usually seen as quiet, strange, lonely, and alienated. They seem not to desire social contact and to shun social gatherings, preferring instead the fantasy and self-involvement that seems more controllable and safe. These patients have a difficult time handling anger, rarely showing it in other than passive ways. They often prefer jobs that take them away from society and may be seen as "the strong, silent type," although they are seldom romantic figures because they are too nerdish to carry off the role. They sometimes revel in "deep and meaningful" issues, which translates into obscure and unusual interests. They have difficulty forming close, warm, and intimate relationships and usually function poorly sexually. On the positive side, these patients are well organized intellectually and emotionally and often have much success in occupational endeavors—even though their occupational efforts usually involve solitary jobs.

SCHIZOTYPAL PERSONALITY DISORDER

Individuals with schizotypal personality disorder differ from schizophrenics in that, although clearly odd and eccentric, they do not show the florid bizarreness of the schizophrenic, nor have they ever experienced an episode of outright psychosis. Instead, schizotypal patients show more subtle forms of perceptual distortion, such as magical thinking, depersonalization, or thinking that they have special abilities such as clairvoyance or a sixth sense or are capable of mental telepathy. Schizotypal patients may have myriad social fears and preoccupations and may have many strikingly odd beliefs and experiences. They often show ritualistic or repetitive mannerisms and may hold many unconventional attitudes and beliefs. Their speech often contains unusual use of language, and one must be careful to understand the context in which the schizotypal patient uses the language. These patients are usually more comfortable with their own thoughts and feelings than in interactions with others. Some authorities consider such people as palm readers, astrologers, and religious cult leaders to be among those suffering from schizotypal personality disorder.

ANTISOCIAL (SOCIOPATHIC) PERSONALITY DISORDER

Although many factors are important in determining one's personality structure, persons with antisocial personality disorder (previously called sociopathic) often have a history of a chaotic family life and of not being required to live within defined limits—including not having to face the consequences of their behavior. There is usually a history of a distant parent-child relationship that lacked warmth, intimacy, and genuine emotion, or a history of parental deprivation resulting in inadequate exposure to social controls. Severe conflicts between parents may also lead to the development of antisocial behavior, because such conflicts leave the growing child with no choice but to learn to manipulate in order to avoid being rejected by one or both parents.

This personality type is thought to make up as much as 3 percent of the male population and 1 percent of the female population. It is characterized primarily by a lack of responsiveness to social norms and rules. Such individuals fail to develop a concern for the welfare of others and use relationships to get their own needs met. They have little or no concern for what effect their behavior might have on others, and they seldom feel remorse or guilt.

Persons with antisocial personality disorder are frequently friendly, outgoing, likable, intelligent people who can be quite charming. Their relationships with others, however, tend to be quite superficial because they lack the capacity for deep emotional responsiveness. Sexual activity is usually for the sake of sex and is not used as a means of expressing affection or intimacy. Sexual activity is carried out with many different people and usually with little regard for the partner's satisfaction.

Other characteristics worthy of mention include the use of physical intimidation and aggression, physical fighting, lying, stealing, arson, inability to maintain employment, extreme conflict with any kind of authority, blatant exploitation of relationships (including spouse and child abuse), lack of forethought, engaging in high-risk behaviors, lack of regard for the rights of others, and continual justification or rationalization of their actions. Persons with antisocial personality disorder refuse to accept responsibility for their actions and always perceive undesirable outcomes as someone else's fault. They have great difficulty learning or profiting from experience. They are unreliable, untruthful, undependable, and insincere. Because they do not feel "responsible," they are often impulsive and seek immediate gratification of wants and perceived needs. They give little thought to delaying gratification of immediate needs, wants, or wishes, even though it might be beneficial in the long run to do so.

A large number of people in our society have antisocial traits that, as with most other personality characteristics, vary in number and severity. Individuals with antisocial personality disorder are found in all professions, although most manage to contain their acting-out behaviors because they are intelligent enough to be aware of the external controls placed on them by society. They avoid acting out not because of internal values or controls but because they do not wish to be punished. It is also true that the more intelligent an individual with antisocial personality disorder, the better able he or she is to find socially acceptable ways to meet needs and wants.

Antisocial personalities generally have a very low frustration tolerance and find it difficult to work at any task for a prolonged period. They are easily bored and continually seek excitement. When they are unable to manipulate their environment to meet their wishes, they may threaten suicide. Many persons with antisocial personality disorder die by accident as a result of a manipulative suicidal gesture. Such a case occurred when a young girl broke up with her boyfriend. He tried to get her to come back to him; when she refused, he impulsively told her he was going to kill himself. He jumped into his car and, in full view of the girl, headed straight for a high bank at the edge of a large lake. Although he tried to swerve away before he got to the edge, the car turned over and rolled over the bank into the water. He was trapped inside the car and drowned before he could be rescued.

Individuals with antisocial personalities usually come to treatment as a result of having been "caught" in some fashion. They may have committed either a minor or a major crime, in which case they will have been sent for evaluation by the court. They may have attempted suicide or may have been required to seek treatment by an employer or a family member. They can be expected to continue their manipulative ways with the clinic or hospital staff and to show little positive change. Antisocial behavior patterns are difficult to alter and show poor response to one-on-one therapeutic intervention. External control of these individuals' acting-out behavior is necessary and often represents the only means of effectively altering their behavior. Examples of external control are incarceration, probation, and hospitalization. The lack of adequate socialization often prevents the normal use of guilt and the desire for approval from being effective internal controlling mechanisms.

In summary, patients with antisocial personality disorder are often well liked by staff members but extremely difficult to treat. They are often helpful and friendly and provide the staff with a lot of verbal reinforcement. They learn to speak the language of psychology and can often report personality dynamics as thoroughly as the therapist can. They can make great promises and build great dreams, but when the time comes to face reality, they can usually be found going merrily on their charming way, never giving a thought to the lies told, the hearts broken, or the misery created in their wake. These individuals are said to "burn out" at about age 40, if they live that long, and may become depressed. They seldom present voluntarily for treatment before this time, and they present themselves for treatment of their depressive symptoms—not of their antisocial symptoms.

BORDERLINE PERSONALITY DISORDER

Patients with borderline personality disorder are another group who are difficult to treat. These patients have recently received a lot of attention in such movies as *Fatal Attraction* and *Basic Instinct*. This disorder occurs much more frequently in women than in men— estimates range from 2:1 to 5:1. It seems to have its genesis in a poor ability to handle strong emotion. This deficit leads the person to have difficulty in responding effectively and consistently to stressful environmental events and results in behavior that appears unstable to the casual observer.

It is this extreme affective instability—which includes an unstable identity, unstable relationships, and difficulty in maintaining a stable mood—that defines borderline personality disorder. Probably the characteristic about these patients that is most easily recognized is their poorly controlled anger, which they often vent indiscriminately and aggressively. The unrelenting anger is often directed at themselves in the form of repeated suicide attempts, drug abuse, and self-mutilation. It is sometimes directed at others in the form of screaming, shouting, hitting, or even more physically damaging attacks—with various weapons in extreme cases. The angry outbursts and other affective displays are unpredictable and often outrageous.

The unstable identities of patients with borderline personalities are demonstrated in their inability to make solid progress toward career goals, their inability to define what they wish to do with their lives, and their difficulty identifying their sexual orientation. In discussing such issues with these patients, a caregiver often feels overwhelmed and has a sense of not knowing where to start in the face of such a broad range of emotional difficulty. Should one start by discussing anger management or by addressing the deep loneliness and emptiness expressed by these patients, or should one start with the extreme fear of rejection and abandonment so painfully felt by them?

Patients with borderline personalities, much more than other diagnostic groups, use the defense mechanism of splitting. *Splitting* refers to the idea of splitting people into totally good and totally bad groups, according to how they are experienced by the observer. Because of the peculiarities of their perceptual processes, these patients tend to see people as all good or all bad and thus have difficulty appreciating the complexities of human relationships. Just because a person does one or two things we disagree with does not mean that the person is all bad. We all have good and not so good, or even "bad," characteristics, and most of us learn to integrate those characteristics into a healthy, well-functioning personality. To patients with borderline personality disorder, however, we are either all good or all bad, depending on how they experience our ability to meet their dependency needs and how we fit into their fantasies about rejection, nurturance, and abandonment. They tend either to overidealize us and thus see us as impossible to reach, or to devalue us and thus reject us as bad.

Treatment for borderline personality disorder is difficult because of the extreme demands these patients place on a therapist. Their anger, often directed at the therapist, is difficult to manage, as is their often repeated attempts at self-mutilation, seduction, and self-destruction. They show brief periods of psychosis; deep depressions and dissociative episodes are not infrequent. Borderline personality patients often drop out of treatment because they are angered by confrontation and cannot tolerate the structure and expectations for change inherent in the therapeutic process. Long-term therapy offers the only likelihood for substantial change.

HISTRIONIC PERSONALITY DISORDER

In many ways, persons with histrionic personality disorder are captured by the drama, or perhaps melodrama, of life. Emotions are much more important to them than thought processes. They live for and by their feelings, and their needs for attention and excitement are often exaggerated. Some of our best entertainers, writers, and artists have histrionic personality disorder and some of the liveliest and most likable people have to varying degrees histrionic personalities. They pay great attention to physical attractiveness, like to be the center of attention, and do not do well when out of the limelight. Histrionic personalities manipulate others with emotional displays and often are unaware of their hidden agenda having to do with getting dependency needs met or avoiding painful affect.

A characteristic of histrionic personalities is the amount of attention given to how they dress and how they present themselves to the public. While not outrightly lying, they often embellish reality just enough to enhance their status with others. They are dramatic, often exhibitionistic, and often overtly seductive in their approach to others. When confronted with these behaviors or asked to acknowledge them, however, they protest that they meant no such thing by their actions and express resentment for such an interpretation of their intentions. Even so, these patients live for approval and acceptance and will go to great lengths to attain them. As with all diagnostic categories, histrionic types vary from mildly to severely histrionic, and the degree of disturbance in social relationships depends on the degree of histrionic symptoms. At the more severe end of the spectrum, one can expect a lot of anger over the fact that their demands to be the center of attention are frustrated; they demand constant reassurance of their worth and constantly seek praise, even when it is unwarranted. Histrionic personalities do not like introspection. They would much rather bask in the light of someone else's flattering impression of them than deal with the reality of their needs when they are alone.

NARCISSISTIC PERSONALITY DISORDER

While histrionic personality disorder is more prevalent in women, narcissistic personality disorder is more prevalent in men. Both of these categories of personality disorder reflect a need for attention and approval from others as well as a need for admiration. Narcissistic personalities are convinced that they are special and are upset when their "specialness" is questioned. They are not plagued by self-doubt; rather, they suffer from a sense of entitlement. Entitlement refers to the idea that whatever good things one wants should come to one just because one is there. No effort should be required because it is enough that one's wonderful presence is available to receive that which one wishes to have.

Having such a wonderful view of oneself would understandably create problems for persons when they are criticized or demeaned in any fashion. Narcissistic personalities often react to criticism with extreme anger, frustration, and depression. They have a very unstable sense of self-worth and overreact to any suggestion that they may not be as wonderful as first thought. We all have a need to be wonderful, but persons with narcissistic personality disorder need to be wonderful all the time. The paradox is that when narcissistic personalities receive praise, they have a difficult time allowing it to become a part of how they see themselves and thus do not accept it as being true. That puts them on a treadmill of always having to do more and more to prove how wonderful they are. Underneath the superficial shell of self-confidence and invulnerability is a person struggling with a deep sense of worthlessness and strongly held feelings of inferiority.

At its worst, narcissistic personality disorder can create strong problems for its host. These individuals tend to be accused of being willing to "sell their soul for that promotion"; having little regard for the rights of those around them; taking credit for other people's ideas; believing their needs are special and deserve special consideration; being consumed with thoughts of success, status, image, and power; and lacking empathy, as shown by their difficulty in understanding why other people do not like them. They often envy the accomplishments of others and have great difficulty tolerating the success of others, especially when it exceeds their own.

Treatment usually focuses on helping narcissistic personalities to stabilize self-esteem and learn to accept reasonable limitations in themselves and others. As with all other behaviors, certain aspects of narcissistic personality disorder can be helpful; those having the less damaging of those behaviors will do well because they believe in themselves and epitomize the phrase "them that say it can't be done should get out of the way of them who are doing it."

AVOIDANT PERSONALITY DISORDER

Persons afflicted with avoidant personality disorder rarely come to anyone's attention because they stay as far away from people and social events as their life demands will allow. They are quite uncomfortable in new and unfamiliar situations and have little sense of adventure. They avoid social relationships out of a fear of rejection and lack of acceptance, and feeling comfortable only with family and friends they have known for a long time. These patients are often overly concerned about saying or doing something that would result in embarrassment for themselves and are overly concerned with what others think of them. They are easily hurt by criticism and quick to anticipate disapproval. They tend to overestimate the probability of various happenings and use that overestimation to justify not doing what could otherwise be done. They often put themselves down and are eager to please others in an effort to fend off the anticipated rejection. Anxiety about rejection causes a refusal to make their needs known, and thus their needs often go unmet because no one knows about them. Intimacy is difficult due to fear of becoming vulnerable with exposure. Anticipation of rejection often leads to the perception of rejection by others when none was intended. Work achievement is made difficult by the shyness and introverted social style. Treatment usually centers around establishing a good relationship with the therapist, gaining group support, and assertiveness training. A great deal of role playing may be desirable in order to reduce the likelihood of failure when these patients try to exercise assertiveness skills.

DEPENDENT PERSONALITY DISORDER

Persons with dependent personality disorder are very much a mixed blessing for those around them. On the one hand, they are devoted and often sacrifice everything in order to satisfy the needs of their families, lovers, or friends. They will always let others make decisions and rarely disagree with what others want to do. They tend to be thoughtful and considerate of others and try to change anything for which they are criticized. On the other hand, they have great difficulty being alone, are often easily frightened, try to get others to make decisions for them, feel unable to manage even mundane tasks outside the home, and never take leadership positions. In fact, they try never to make a decision for which they could be criticized. They will go along with a decision with which they privately disagree but cannot say so for fear of rejection. These patients may agree to take on jobs or duties that others shun because those jobs or duties are dirty, demeaning, or otherwise undesirable. This is done in an effort to win acceptance and approval. Dependent personalities have trouble with social relationships because they put so much into them and rely on them so much that when they end, the dependent person is crushed and feels overwhelmed with the task of finding someone else on whom to depend. These patients tend to be pessimistic, filled with apprehension, misgivings, and self-doubt; they are skeptical about their ability ever to function except in the shadow of some person they perceive to be competent. They become so invested in doing things for others that they may have great difficulty doing things only for themselves. In therapeutic relationships with these patients, one would do well to remember that, no matter how clear it is to the caregiver that these patients' tolerance for abusive behavior is destructive, great care must be taken to appreciate the patients' attachment issues. Dependent patients fear a loss of attachment more than anything else, and in that context "even a bad love is better than no love at all."

OBSESSIVE-COMPULSIVE PERSONALITY DISORDER

Most successful people have elements of the personality style associated with obsessive-compulsive personality disorder. In its less pathologic manifestation, it is the heart of achievement. It allows its host to stick to the job until it is completed and completed correctly. Attention to detail is assured, and order and organization will always result in finishing a task on time. So what if rigid adherence to the rules and "doing it the right way" took all the fun out of it? Life is not meant to be fun, anyway. Life is much too serious to be fun—and so is everything else. There is no room for pleasure—pleasure is for the no-goods out in the world who will never accomplish anything. The rules are what are important, along with bathroom habits, lists of what needs to be done today, keeping everything clean, neat, and orderly, and being on time. And, of course, setting unreasonable goals is only proper. If one does not set unreasonable goals, then one will never achieve what one achieves while reaching for unreachable goals. In addition, one must always check and double-check every detail, because to make a mistake, even a small one, would be intolerable. Great attention must be given to every detail, and when discussing situations or decisions, every aspect of those situations or decisions must be beaten to death. Even then a decision must be made with caution—premature commitment might result in a wrong decision. New information may come along at any time and render the decision inadequate—along with the person responsible for the decision. Somewhere there is a "right" solution, and persons with obsessive-compulsive personalities are determined to find it and relieve their anxiety. To the obsessive-compulsive patient, the preoccupation with being right and perfect is only "right," considering that perfection is a fact and must be discovered.

The foregoing paragraph has actually been a test. For those reading it and thinking that the authors have taken too great a license with the presentation of serious professional material, we now pronounce you official members of the OCPD club!

For those charter members of the OCPD club, we offer the following. Patients with obsessive-compulsive personality disorder are highly perfectionistic, are preoccupied with details, insist that everything be done the right way, forsake social and personal pleasure to ensure occupational success, are indecisive because of the fear of being wrong and thus of being rejected, tend to be overly rigid in their thought processes and expectations of others, have a difficult time expressing affection, finding pleasure, laughing, playing, or otherwise having a good time, tend to be stingy and are "pack rats" (that is, they never throw anything away).

Treatment usually centers on getting patients away from thinking processes, because they are already overly introspective and "think" everything into oblivion. The problem is that they are unable to access their emotions and do not manage them well when they do discover them. Obsessive-compulsive patients are prone to power struggles and are control addicts. One should try to avoid these struggles by focusing on how the patient feels. The patient will always win the power struggle.

PASSIVE-AGGRESSIVE PERSONALITY DISORDER

Passive-aggressive personality disorder involves a set of behaviors that people generally find annoying in others but sometimes engage in themselves. These behaviors are usually associated with social or occupational roles and expectations, but they tend to be pervasive and resistant to change without direct intervention. Passive-aggressive patients have a lot of resentment and anger and find themselves in the bind of not being able to express that resentment and anger in a direct manner for fear of rejection, punishment, or disapproval. Instead, the anger and resentment are expressed through passive resistance to demands and expectations. These individuals are always late for deadlines but always have good "reasons" or are apologetic to the point of eliciting acceptance of the behavior.

At other times passive-aggressive patients will sulk or pout or "drag their heels" or perform poorly when asked to do something they do not want to do. They frequently display a chronic anger toward authority by ridiculing or speaking derogatorily of persons in authority. They are often chronic complainers who find something wrong with everything. They feel that they are required to do more with less than anybody else in the world and are certain that they could do their boss's job better than the boss. They rarely offer solutions for problems but can find more problems than anybody can possibly solve. When efforts are made to solve problems, it soon becomes apparent that no matter what is done nothing will satisfy the complainer. The passive-aggressive person is tied to resentments in such a way that he or she knows no other way to respond. This individual sometimes becomes a scapegoat because others recognize the resistance but nonetheless are victims of the passive-aggressive behaviors. They reject the patient by ignoring him or her or by making jokes about the patient's behavior. These patients sometimes feel a need for revenge but, in keeping with their style, exact that revenge more by passive resistance than by acting out their frustrations. Treatment is difficult due to the fact that these patients wish to become dependent on the caregiver and resent frustration of that need. They experience encouragement toward independence as rejection; but to support their dependency need also supports the very behaviors for which they are seeking treatment. These patients insist on their right to do as they please. Trying to change that will start a battle that is difficult to finish.

SEXUAL DISORDERS

The diagnosis of a sexual deviation is reserved for those persons who fail to develop what society deems appropriate patterns of sexual behavior. What is appropriate is determined by the society in which one lives, and there is usually some distinction between the relatively nonaggressive forms of sexual deviations, such as voyeurism, and the highly aggressive and dangerous forms of sexual deviations, such as masochism and sadism.

Many sexual behavior patterns that were considered deviant in the past are not now considered deviant by most people in our society. Masturbation, the manual or mechanical stimulation of one's genitals for the purpose of obtaining sexual pleasure, is one of the most notable examples of this change. Masturbation is not considered abnormal unless it is used to totally replace sexual activity with another person. Homosexuality, being sexually attracted to a person of the same sex, is another example of sexual behavior that was at one time considered deviant but is now generally understood to be the nonpathologic expression of sexual preference.

Many people have the misconception that violent, unrestrained behavior is characteristic of sexual deviants. Actually, much of the research indicates that most persons with sexual disorders are rather reserved and timid and have a great deal of difficulty interacting effectively with people of either sex. The more serious and the more persistent the sexual deviations, the more difficulty the individual is likely to experience in other areas of his or her life. The major deviations are defined below. If more in-depth information is desired, a good text on abnormal psychology should be consulted.

The usual term for disorders considered by the general public to be sexual disorders is *paraphilia*. These disorders involve sexual activity and arousal patterns not common to the general population. The other main category of problems in the sexual arena is that of *sexual dysfunctions*. This second category involves problems with adequacy of desire or problems in carrying through the usual sexual-response cycle from attraction, to desire, to arousal, to intercourse, to orgasm. The sexual dysfunctions category is reserved for disorders that are within the usual pattern of sexual arousal and functioning. The paraphilias, on the other hand, include those disorders that involve arousal patterns and activities outside those common to most adults in our society.

The sexual disorders are listed in the *DSM-III-R* as follows:

(1) 302.30   Transvestic fetishism
(2) 302.40   Exhibitionism
(3) 302.84   Sexual sadism
(4) 302.83   Sexual masochism
(5) 302.82   Voyeurism
(6) 302.81   Fetishism
(7) 302.20   Pedophilia
(8) 302.89   Frotteurism

TRANSVESTIC FETISHISM

In transvestic fetishism, sexual gratification is obtained by wearing clothing of the opposite sex (cross-dressing). Transvestic fetishism is sometimes associated with transsexualism. Transsexualism, which is coded as a gender identity disorder in the *DSM-III-R*, involves a more drastic form of changing one's sexual identity—that of actually changing one's anatomic structure to that of the opposite sex.

EXHIBITIONISM

Exhibitionism involves the attainment of sexual gratification by exposing one's genitals to another person. Male exhibitionism involves the display of the male genitals primarily to women and children. There are few reported cases of female exhibitionism. However, females who are exhibitionists may find a socially appropriate outlet for exhibiting themselves, such as becoming a stripper.

SEXUAL SADISM

Sexual sadism occurs when one is able to obtain sexual gratification only by inflicting physical or mental pain on another individual. The most deviant example of this category is the person who can receive sexual pleasure only by drawing blood from a tortured individual or even by causing the death of an individual. Sadism is often practiced with a masochistic partner, although in many cases the sadist only gains satisfaction when the partner is fearful of the impending sadistic acts. Manifestations of this disorder can range from fairly mild behavior such as spanking or paddling, to low-level bondage, to stabbing, to strangulation, and to other forms of mutilation to the point of death.

SEXUAL MASOCHISM

Sexual masochism refers to the attainment of sexual satisfaction by being physically or mentally abused. Inflicted pain becomes a source of pleasure and sexual excitement and is sometimes self-inflicted. Masochism may range from something as simple as needing a "cave man" approach to sexual activity to the need for severe punishment and/or humiliation before sexual gratification can be achieved. It is diagnosed only when such punishment is necessary for sexual fulfillment.

VOYEURISM

Voyeurism occurs when sexual gratification is obtained from observing the sexual organs of others or as a result of watching others engage in sexual intercourse or other sexual behavior. Many people enjoy viewing the nude bodies of members of the opposite sex; and this is not voyeurism unless the voyeuristic desires exceed the individual's desire for intercourse.

FETISHISM

Fetishism occurs when a material object—usually some article of clothing such as bras, shoes, or other objects belonging to members of the opposite sex, or in some cases the same sex—produces sexual gratification and fulfillment for an individual. Masturbation is commonly associated with the object, and the object is used as a primary means of sexual arousal.

PEDOPHILIA

Pedophilia occurs when an adult, usually male, has some form of sexual relationship with a child. This sexual activity may be either heterosexual or homosexual; it is said to occur frequently among persons who are unable to obtain sexual gratification with adults because of fears of inadequacy or impotence. There are two subtypes of pedophiles, the exclusive type and nonexclusive type. Exclusive types are attracted only to children, while the nonexclusive types are attracted to both children and adults. The children may be victimized with a wide range of sexual activities, from behaviors that would be normal if both partners were adults to behaviors related to sexual sadism to the point of death. In some cases the child molestation is limited to members of the perpetrator's family. In such cases, the diagnosis specifies that the pedophilia is limited to incest.

FROTTEURISM

Frotteurism is a disorder in which sexual arousal occurs in response to rubbing against or touching someone who does not consent to the touching. The individual usually chooses a crowded, public place where the frottage can take place in such a manner as to confuse the victim about who is doing the touching or from which the perpetrator can escape or can claim it was an accident if he is caught. The frotteur usually engages in strong fantasy activity while pressing his penis against the victim and experiences an instantaneous erection. Frotteurs can often reach excitement to the point of ejaculation within 60 to 90 seconds. If ejaculation occurs, the frotteur quickly disengages. Otherwise, he may try again.

ANNOTATED BIBLIOGRAPHY

Caccaro, E.F., and Kavoussi, R.J.: *Biological and pharmacological aspects of borderline personality disorder*. Hospital and Community Psychiatry, 1991, 42(10):1029–1033.

> *Discusses the use of medication in the treatment of certain symptoms of borderline personality disorder that may have a biologic basis. These symp-*

toms include affective instability, transient.psychotic phenomena, and impulsive aggressive behavior.

Kroessler, D.: *Personality disorder in the elderly.* Hospital and Community Psychiatry, 1990, 41(12):1325–1329.

A review of the literature on the prevalence of personality disorders in the elderly.

Oldham, J.M.: *Borderline personality disorder: An introduction.* Hospital and Community Psychiatry, 1991, 42(10):1014.

Discusses the addition of borderline personality disorder to the DSM-III-R, as well as the prevalence and symptoms associated with this disorder.

Meyer, J.K., and Levin, F.M.: Sadism and masochism in neurosis and symptom formation. *Scientific Proceedings, Fall Meeting of the American Psychoanalytic Association,* New York, December 17, 1988. American Psychoanalytic Association, New York, 1988, pp. 789–804.

Presents several theories on the development of sadism and masochism and provides case examples for further study.

Widiger, T.A., and Weissman, M.M.: *Epidemiology of borderline personality disorder.* Hospital and Community Psychiatry, 1991, 42(10):1015–1020.

Presents information on the prevalence, incidence, and sex ratio of patients diagnosed with borderline personality disorder. Also provides information on further testing designs that can be used.

The Quality Assurance Project: *Treatment outlines for paranoid schizotypal and schizoid personality disorders.* Australian and New Zealand Journal of Psychiatry, 1990, 24:339–350.

Presents treatment outlines for paranoid, schizotypal, and schizoid personality disorders, using advice from expert committees, a review of the literature, and the opinions of practicing psychiatrists.

REFERENCES

American Psychiatric Association: *Diagnostic and Statistical Manual of Mental Disorders,* ed. 3, rev. APA, Washington, DC, 1987.

Perry, J.C., and Vaillant, G.E.: *Personality disorders.* In Kaplan, H.I., and Saddock, B.J. (eds.): Comprehensive Textbook of Psychology, ed. 5. Vol. 2. Williams & Wilkins, Baltimore, 1989, p. 1352.

This post-test corresponds to the material covered in Chapters 5, 6, and 7.

Matching. Match the diagnoses listed in Column B with the appropriate symptoms listed in Column A.

Column A	*Column B*
_____ 1. Person feels tense, anxious, or worried but is unable to pinpoint exactly why.	**a.** Obsessive-compulsive
_____ 2. Person engages in repetitive behavioral acts.	**b.** Paranoid disorder
_____ 3. Adult engages in sexual relationship with a child.	**c.** Conversion disorder
_____ 4. Abnormal continuous grief over a lost one.	**d.** Anxiety disorder
_____ 5. General symptoms exhibited are inappropriate affect, autism, and inability to deal with reality.	**e.** Dysthymia **f.** Schizophrenia **g.** Dissociative disorder
_____ 6. Person is able to obtain sexual gratification only by inflicting pain on others.	**h.** Pedophilia **i.** Sexual sadism
_____ 7. Person shows signs of grandiosity and persecution.	
_____ 8. Loss of hearing with no physical basis.	
_____ 9. Sometimes called "split" personality by laypersons.	

True or False. Circle your choice.

T   F   1. Diagnostic categories are helpful only for insurance purposes.

T   F   2. Diagnosis is necessary because from that diagnosis the mental health worker is able to predict the exact behavior that will be exhibited by the patient.

T   F   3. Anxiety disorders constitute approximately 30 to 40 percent of all neurotic disorders.

T   F   4. Obsessive-compulsive persons feel that if they are not allowed to carry out their rituals, something drastic will happen to them.

T   F   5. The patient with a diagnosis of organic psychosis usually will exhibit more bizarre behavior than the patient with a functional psychosis.

T   F   6. Arguing with psychotic patients in order to make them realize that their thinking is not logical is a major role of the mental health worker in caring for psychotic patients.

T   F   7. Schizophrenia basically means "split personality."

T   F   8. Paranoid patients are usually disliked by everyone.

T   F   9. Paranoid patients are usually the easiest of all psychiatric patients to accept and manage.

T   F   10. Some authorities feel that the manic phase of a bipolar disorder is a defense against anxiety.

T   F   11. Sexual deviants tend to be violent and unable to control their behavior.

T   F   12. Sexual sadism is often performed with a masochistic partner.

T   F   13. Paraphilia refers to individuals who obtain sexual gratification only with children.

Short Answer. Answer the following questions as briefly and specifically as possible.

1. Phobias are usually described as _____.

2. Give three of the basic behavioral characteristics associated with the obsessive-compulsive patient.

   a. _____.

   b. _____.

   c. _____.

3. List three of the personal traits one would expect to see in a patient with a diagnosis of dysthymic disorder.

   a. _____.

   b. _____.

   c. _____.

4. One of the most important things a mental health worker can do in caring for the patient with a diagnosis of dysthymic disorder is

   _____.

5. What is the basic difference between an organic and a functional psychosis? _____

   _____.

6. Briefly discuss the difference between sexual disorders and sexual dysfunctions.

_____

_____

_____ .

Multiple Choice. Circle the letter or number that you think represents the best answer.

1. The person diagnosed as paranoid schizophrenic will present all the following symptoms except:
   a. Waxy flexibility.
   b. Extreme suspiciousness.
   c. Delusions of persecution.
   d. Hallucinations.
2. The most common characteristics of schizophrenia are:
   a. Apathy and autistic thinking.
   b. Flat affect, autistic thinking, ambivalence, and associative looseness.
   c. Ambivalence, ideas of reference, autistic thinking, and associative looseness.
   d. Confabulation and intuition.
3. All of the following statements are generally true of schizotypal personality disorder except:
   a. Patients are often eccentric.
   b. Delusions and hallucinations are rare.
   c. Patients often become vagrants, wandering from place to place picking up menial jobs.
   d. The onset is sudden.
4. All of the following are considered possible causes of schizophrenia except:
   a. Disturbed mother-infant relationship.
   b. A poorly adjusted family situation.
   c. The precipitating factor may be a situation calling for close interaction with another human being.
   d. Abnormalities in the way the brain is formed.
5. Fifty percent of the resident population of long-term mental hospitals is comprised of patients with a diagnosis of:
   a. Senile brain disease and cerebral arteriosclerosis.
   b. Schizophrenia.
   c. Alcohol intoxication or addiction.
   d. Personality disorders.
   e. Psychosis.

6. Antisocial individuals usually:
   a. Profit from their mistakes.
   b. Assume responsibility for their own conduct.
   c. Do not feel shame for their conduct.
   d. Are responding to hallucinations.
7. In relating to an antisocial patient, the mental health worker should anticipate that rapport will be established:
   a. Without difficulty and within a few days.
   b. With difficulty and over a long period of time.
   c. With difficulty and within a few days.
   d. Without difficulty and within a few hours.
8. Mr Green is a 24-year-old patient who has been diagnosed as an antisocial personality. Your primary responsibility for him will most likely be to:
   a. Set firm and consistent limits on his behavior.
   b. Help him to develop insight.
   c. Encourage him to get involved in ward activities.
   d. Arrange opportunities for him to develop stronger superego controls.
9. Mrs. M., a 23-year-old newlywed, was admitted to a psychiatric hospital after a month of unusual behavior that included eating and sleeping very little, talking or singing constantly, charging hundreds of dollars worth of furniture to her father-in-law, and picking up dates on the street. In the hospital, Mrs. M. monopolized conversation, insisted on unusual privileges, and frequently became demanding, bossy, and sarcastic. She had periods of great overactivity and sometimes became destructive. She frequently used vulgar and profane language. Mrs. M. had formerly been witty, gay, and the "life of the party." Her many friends say she was ladylike in spite òf her fun-loving ways and was a kind, sympathetic person. The symptoms that Mrs. M. exhibited are suggestive of which of the following diagnostic entities:
   a. Manic bipolar disorder.
   b. Schizophrenic disorder.
   c. Paranoid disorder.
   d. Major depression.
10. Exaggerated mood swings from deep depression to wild excitement are seen in:
    a. Anxiety disorders.
    b. Schizophrenic disorders.
    c. Mixed bipolar disorders.
    d. Paranoid disorders.

11. Which of the following are characteristic of obsessive-compulsive disorder:
    a. Flexibility.
    b. Enjoyment of people.
    c. Excessive conformity to standards.
    d. Ability to relax easily.
    e. Difficulty "finding just the right words" in expressing self.
       (1) a, c, and e.
       (2) c, d, and e.
       (3) b and d.
       (4) c and e.
       (5) None of the above.
12. One of the major personality characteristics of an obsessive-compulsive patient is:
    a. Dependency.
    b. Self-deprecation.
    c. Impulsiveness.
    d. Orderliness.
13. The symptom that characterizes paranoia in its true form is:
    a. Bizarre hallucinations.
    b. Inappropriate affect.
    c. Severe depression.
    d. Systemized delusions.
14. The major defense mechanism used in paranoid thinking is:
    a. Reaction formation.
    b. Rationalization.
    c. Compensation.
    d. Sublimation.
    e. Projection.
15. Malingering differs most significantly from a conversion disorder in that the malingerer:
    a. Unconsciously simulates illness to avoid an unpleasant situation.
    b. Converts anxiety arising from some conflictual situation into somatic symptoms.
    c. Seems unconcerned and shows no anxiety about his or her disabling symptoms.
    d. Simulates illness on a conscious level to avoid intolerable alternatives.
16. The term that best describes the reaction of an individual who makes an emotional response through an organic illness is:
    a. Neurotic reaction.
    b. Organic reaction.
    c. Psychosomatic reaction.
    d. Psychotic reaction.

17. A problem from which neurotic patients suffer is:
    a. Memory loss.
    b. Indecision.
    c. Disorientation.
    d. Hallucinations.
18. People suffering from neuroses usually complain of:
    a. Hallucinations, delusions, and fatigue.
    b. Fatigue, fears, and physical problems.
    c. Fatigue, rejection, and dissociation.
    d. Flight of ideas, illusions, and disorientation.
19. Which of the following is (are) characteristic of pedophiles:
    a. They are attracted only to children of the opposite sex.
    b. They never engage in sexual activity with children in their
       own family.
    c. They never engage in sexual activity with adults.
    d. They are often unable to engage in sexual activity with adults
       due to fear of inadequacy or impotence.
    e. They are also sadistic.
       (1) a, b, and c.
       (2) a and d.
       (3) d.
       (4) c.
20. Obtaining sexual gratification by rubbing or touching individuals
    who do not consent and who are often unaware of who is touching
    them is known as:
    a. Voyeurism.
    b. Fetishism.
    c. Paraphilia.
    d. Frotteurism.
21. Needing severe punishment and/or humiliation to achieve sexual
    fulfillment is known as:
    a. Sexual sadism.
    b. Sexual masochism.
    c. Frotteurism.
    d. Fetishism.
22. Obtaining sexual gratification by dressing up in clothing of the
    opposite sex is known as:
    a. Transvestic fetishism.
    b. Homosexuality.
    c. Frotteurism.
    d. Exhibitionism.

Therapeutic Treatment Activities

Communication Skills

Communication, a key factor in the development of any therapeutic relationship, occurs on both a verbal and a nonverbal basis. *Verbal communications* are transmitted through the spoken or written word, and *nonverbal communications* are transmitted through behavior. Regardless of the mode of transmission, the aim of all forms of communication is to provide information, receive information, or exchange information.

WRITTEN COMMUNICATION

When using written communication, the writer provides information without the benefit of feedback; therefore, if the one to whom the message is written does not understand the message, successful communication has not been achieved. For example, if a staff member charts that a patient is "hostile" and Dr. Jones reads the chart after that staff member has gone off duty, he really does not know what happened and probably will not have a clear understanding of what the staff member meant by "hostile." This is especially true if Dr. Jones sees the patient sitting calmly in the day room visiting and chatting with other patients. In order to discuss the behavior with the patient, Dr. Jones must understand what the staff member meant by "hostile."

One means of clarifying and making written communication more explicit is to use *description*. Instead of saying that the patient is "hostile," it would be better to write exactly what the patient said or did. For example, "The patient is walking up and down the hall cursing" or "When other patients walk by, Mr. Brown screams at them and tries to hit them." This tells the doctor exactly what the patient has been doing. Since unclear written communications are likely to result in either no information or misinformation, the use of descriptive writing is extremely important.

VERBAL COMMUNICATION

Most people know how to communicate verbally because we all converse daily. Unfortunately, we frequently do not think before we talk and are unaware of what we are communicating to other people. Verbal communication, however, is largely effective because it is easy to talk and because feedback can alert one to the possibility that the desired message is not being communicated. For example, a person listening to a speaker may question what has been said, may challenge a statement, may ask for clarification of a point, or may add to a statement, thus facilitating effective communication.

A frequent error made by people when communicating verbally occurs when they say things they do not mean. A mother says to her son who has misbehaved, "I'm not going to love you anymore." Obviously the message being sent is not true. A mother is not going to stop loving her child because he misbehaved. The message she wanted to communicate was, "I do not like the way you are behaving. I love you, but I want you to change your behavior." When we say things we do not mean, the messages we send are misunderstood and may cause problems in interpersonal relationships. Communications such as these, if consistent over a long enough period, may contribute to mental illness by further isolating people from one another.

NONVERBAL COMMUNICATION

Some authorities believe that nonverbal communication is the most accurate of all forms of communication. People communicate nonverbally via their behavior and their body posture. Persons who are depressed may slump, walk with their heads down, and have a gloomy look on their faces. These behaviors send a message to all those who come in contact with them. The message is, "I don't feel well; I'm depressed." Remember the song that says, "If you're happy and you know it, then your face will surely show it"? Well, it is true that when people are happy, their faces generally show it. They also express their feeling of well-being when they walk at a brisk pace with their head up and shoulders thrown back. One's behavior thus often indicates one's state of mind, and mentally ill patients are no exception. Their behavior implies a great deal about their feelings. When a nurse walks into Mr. Brown's room and says, "How are you feeling this morning?", the patient may respond by saying that he feels fine. If, however, while stating this, he is lying in a fetal position with the covers drawn up to his shoulders and refuses to have his room light turned on, his nonverbal behaviors would indicate that he is not feeling well.

Why would Mr. Brown respond to you with "I'm feeling fine" when he is obviously not? There are several possibilities. Perhaps Mr. Brown is afraid if he says that he is not feeling well, the doctor will not let him go home on Friday as planned. Mr. Brown may have heard a nurse standing outside his door complaining to another staff member about the floor being overloaded with patients, thus causing the staff to be overworked. Therefore Mr. Brown is afraid to say he feels bad because that might put another burden on the nurses.

We have all said things that we did not mean, and patients are no exception. Since nonverbal communication conveys attitudes, feelings, and reactions much more clearly than verbal communication, it is generally more accurate. We must, therefore, always be alert to nonverbal clues, which may actually be a better indication of patients' true feelings than what they say.

STAFF-PATIENT RELATIONSHIPS

In establishing a therapeutic relationship, the first step is to make initial contact with the patient. Obviously, in talking to a patient for the first time, one cannot expect that patient to relate his or her life history. People are generally cautious about meeting someone new. They are not sure what the new person's attitude will be toward them and are uncomfortable if the new person is too pushy, overly friendly, or too inquisitive. Mentally ill people are often very sensitive individuals who have been hurt by their interpersonal relationships many, many times. The people they have trusted may have often let them down. They may have shared their personal problems with individuals who seemed to care but ultimately responded in a way that caused the patients to feel they had been laughed at, ridiculed, degraded, or otherwise treated unkindly. They may not trust people because their experiences have taught them that people cannot be trusted.

It follows, then, that a primary objective of early staff-patient contacts is to establish a relationship that promotes mutual trust. A step is made in that direction when a staff member is honest and straightforward with patients. For example, if staff members do not know the answer to patients' questions, they should tell the patients they do not know the answer but that they will try to find the answer for them. When a staff member makes such a promise, care should be taken to be certain that adequate follow-up is made. Staff members should consider carefully what they tell patients they will do for them. Casual remarks and half-hearted offers are often taken seriously. Since one can never be sure what the events of the day will bring, a thoughtful response to make to a patient who asks to go for a walk might be, "It looks as though my schedule is free this afternoon and unless something unusual interferes, I'll go for a walk with you around 4:00." If something does interfere, one might say to the patient, for example, "I'm really sorry, but Dr. Jones is making rounds and I can't leave the unit now" or "I've been called to a staff meeting so we can't go for a walk this afternoon; I'll be back around 5:00" or "Is there something special you wanted to talk about with me? If not, we'll really try to take that walk tomorrow."

When a staff member is beginning to develop a trusting and therapeutic relationship with a patient, it is often best to have frequent contacts of short duration. At the first meeting, one should introduce oneself and tell the patient one's title (nurse, nursing assistant, social worker, and so forth), then explain one's purpose for approaching the patient. A mental health worker on a hospital unit might say: "I'm Jane Doe, a mental health technician. I work the 3-to-11 shift and I'm assigned to take care of you this evening. If you need anything, or want to talk, or have any questions, I'll be happy to help." Then engage the patient in a discussion of some neutral topic. If the patient had been watching television or reading the newspaper, one could make some comment about the program or some very neutral comment about a sporting event or weather forecast reported in the paper. Try to have a short, pleasant conversation and then leave the patient for a while. Later, try to interest the patient in some social activity, such as playing cards or checkers or having a cup of coffee with another person.

Staff members should work toward helping all patients realize that the staff are sincerely interested in them and their problems. Patients need to feel important, and there are two key approaches to helping make them feel that way. First, the very fact that a staff member would want to spend time with them helps patients to feel important. Mental health workers are often seen as authority figures and as special persons by patients. Thus, many patients are surprised when a staff member says, "I would like to sit and talk with you for a while." Their self-esteem is frequently so poor that they may have a difficult time believing someone as important as a staff member would want to talk with them or could really be concerned about their problems.

As a staff member, another way to help patients feel important is to make sure one's time with them is not spent in talking about one's own personal life. Talking about oneself or unloading one's own personal problems on a patient says to that patient that the staff member is not really interested in anyone but himself or herself.

There are other reasons, of course, that staff members should not talk about their own personal lives. Mentally ill patients sometimes use the personal information given them to justify ill feelings toward the very staff member who shared the information with them. They may also use the information to gossip with other patients. If one tells depressed patients one's own burdens in an attempt to help them understand that they are not the only person with problems, it may make them even more depressed. They may even feel that they should not add to the staff member's load by discussing their own problems.

It is not a good idea to tell a patient one's address or telephone number, even if the patient insists. When a patient makes such personal inquiries, one might respond by saying, "What makes you ask?" and then attempt to involve the patient in a discussion directed toward his or her own problems. One might also say, "This time is for you to talk about your problems" or "It would be more helpful if you would talk about yourself." This is especially important in the first few patient-staff contacts, when the patient may be unclear about the relationship and the purpose of the discussions. If all else fails, one may simply say that one is not permitted to discuss personal information.

Dating patients is also an unwise practice for staff members, even after patients have been discharged from the hospital. One never knows when a patient might need to return to the hospital, and it is extremely difficult, and often unethical, to mix personal and professional relationships. If a patient's efforts to establish a social relationship persist, one might need to respond in the following manner: "I'm sorry, but it's hospital policy that staff members not see patients socially." A hospital is an impersonal object, and a patient may ventilate anger toward it without causing any great harm.

Because spending time with patients is one of the most therapeutic activities in which a staff member can engage, it is important to make the most of each opportunity. A 5-minute visit may seem much longer to the patient if the staff member seems relaxed, unhurried, and discusses topics that are important to the patient.

When talking with patients, one should pull a chair close or sit beside them on the sofa. One should pay attention to what the patient is saying. One should not fidget in the chair, tap one's feet, or wring one's hands. One should adopt a pleasant, sincere, interested attitude that says to the patient, "I'm here to talk to you, and I'm interested in what you have to say." Try never to stand over a patient. To do so makes one appear rushed, and the patient may become anxious and uncomfortable. If one is in a hurry, let the patient know when there will be time to talk.

Since time with patients is limited, it is important that one's verbal communication be as effective as possible. The use of *goals* can help. Such goals are determined by the purpose of one's contact with a patient and may be further influenced by the amount of time one has to spend, the nature of the information to be communicated, and one's attitude toward the patient. For example, if a staff member is to tell Mr. Jones about a test he is going to have the next day, then the goal of the conversation is to familiarize Mr. Jones with that test. Mr. Jones will need to be told when the test is scheduled and whether he has to have any special preparations for the test. He should then be allowed to ask questions for clarification and to express any feelings or concerns he might have about the procedure.

The goals of the conversation described above would be quite different from the goals of a conversation one might have with a patient who is depressed and just wants someone to sit and listen. In this situation, the staff member's goals would probably be aimed toward supporting the patient while allowing the patient an opportunity to talk.

COMMUNICATION TECHNIQUES

Often when patients try to tell their doctor, nurse, social worker, or mental health worker about their problems, their illness or inexperience in effective communication causes them to leave out important details and/or to skip from one subject to another before completing their original thought. Listed below are some techniques that staff members may find useful in helping mentally ill patients communicate more effectively.

1. The high anxiety level experienced by many mentally ill patients, plus their preoccupation with the things that are upsetting them and making them anxious, greatly decreases and narrows their attention span. They may appear confused and may hear very little of what is said to them. It may be necessary to repeat one's name several times or to reintroduce oneself each time the patient is approached. Staff members, therefore, should watch for behavioral or verbal clues which would indicate that a patient has not understood the intended message and thus cannot respond appropriately. On the other hand, some patients are acutely aware of all that is happening

in their environment and would feel greatly insulted if a staff member kept repeating things over and over again.

2. It is important for staff members to use simple, direct statements and questions. Long, involved sentences and explanations may just confuse patients. Use the simplest language possible to convey the message. Avoid the use of abstract statements, such as "It's raining cats and dogs outside." If this was said to a psychotic patient, the patient might take it literally and respond inappropriately.

3. Do not use indefinite pronouns such as *she, he, they*, and so forth. Be specific about the person being discussed. Encourage the patients to do the same. Ask for clarification about the identity of the person the patient is discussing. For example, a patient might say, "She always belittles me; I can never do anything right." The staff member might respond by saying, "Who is she" or "Who is it that you feel belittles you?"

4. Psychiatric patients sometimes have difficulty trying to describe or explain things that happen to them. Since their interpretation of their experiences may be very different from what actually occurred, it is helpful to such patients if a staff member can help them more objectively describe their experience and then consider alternatives that were previously overlooked. If Mr. Green is unfriendly one morning, Mr. Jones may become upset because he believes Mr. Green is angry with him. If a staff member helps Mr. Jones see that Mr. Green is upset about a personal problem, Mr. Jones may be able to relax and feel less anxious.

5. It is often necessary for staff members to help patients maintain an orientation to the here and now. Patients sometimes try to escape a problem by denying its existence or by talking about getting out of the hospital, Aunt Bee's new hat, or the possibility that a rich uncle may die and leave them a fortune. It is usually more beneficial for patients to deal with their real problems in an open manner than to smooth over them with wishes, dreams, and fantasies.

6. Open-ended questions should be used when one wishes to engage a patient in conversation or obtain general information. If one asks a patient, "Are you married?" the probable response would be "yes." The question is answered, but the conversation is over. On the other hand, if one uses an open-ended statement, such as "Mr. Jones, tell me about your family," the patient cannot answer with a simple "yes" or "no." He will have to elaborate on his response, and one can begin a conversation that may lead to further discussion of related topics. Questions such as "Tell me about yourself," "What happened to bring you to the hospital?", or "What have you done today?" are all examples of open-ended questions. The open-ended question also allows the patient some freedom in choosing what to discuss. Mr.

Brown may choose a neutral topic when asked, "What has happened since we talked last week?" He may say that he got a nice birthday card from his mother, or that he had a date, or that it was a nice weekend, all very safe subjects. On the other hand, he may choose to tell you that he had a terrible fight with his girlfriend. In either case, Mr. Brown chose the topic and is, therefore, less likely to feel that the staff member is prying or pushing him to discuss something that he is not ready to discuss.

7. Mentally ill patients may use mental health staff members as role models and pattern much of their behavior after that of the staff. Likewise, they may pattern their communication style after the style of the person with whom they are working. Therefore it is important to be a good role model when communicating with patients as well as with other staff members.

8. Because patients sometimes take cues about a staff member's expectations of them from the way a statement is phrased, words such as *can, could,* and *would* may create problems. A sentence beginning with *can* or *would* may lead patients to believe that they have some choice in the matter when they really do not. If one says to a patient, "Can you get up?" or "Would you come with me?", the patient may say "no." If a patient must go somewhere for a treatment; it is probably best to say, "It is time for your treatment; please come with me." From that statement, it is obvious that the patient is expected to cooperate. Most authorities agree that it is better not to offer a patient a choice when there is none. Offering a nonexistent choice may only anger the patient and create animosity.

9. Whenever possible, the patient should be consulted when the staff is developing the patient's care plan. If Mr. Jones likes to take his bath in the evening and there are no valid staff objections, his preference should be honored. This consideration helps Mr. Jones feel that the staff sees him as an individual and that his personal concerns are important. As a general rule, no one is more interested in patients' well-being than the patients themselves. Most patients feel better when they have some say in, and control over, their own lives, even when they are sick.

10. Mentally ill patients sometimes have difficulty focusing on one topic at a time or may skip from one subject to another without ever finishing a thought. This may occur because their anxiety level is high, making it difficult for them to concentrate. Skipping from subject to subject may also allow patients to avoid talking about particular topics that make them feel anxious. It is important to help patients improve their ability to discuss one topic at a time, especially if the topic involves an area of conflict. If such a topic can be discussed

fully, the patient may gain a better understanding of it and may even uncover some of the reasons behind the conflict.

11. It is helpful to realize that patients often relate to mental health staff members as authority figures and, therefore, may want staff members to make many or all of their decisions for them. One should be careful not to allow that to happen. Having someone else make decisions for them does not help patients learn to deal more effectively with their problems, nor does it help them learn to be more responsible for their lives. Also, if patients do not like the suggestions made to them by a staff member, the staff member will likely receive the blame.

12. Silences often provoke anxiety, and both patients and staff members are likely to feel uncomfortable when they occur. It is helpful to remember that both patients and staff members sometimes need a brief period of silence in order to collect their thoughts. For example, Mr. Green, a patient who is anxious, may need time to organize what he is going to say or to decide exactly how he feels about something. Mental health workers need to be good observers in order to determine whether patients are silent because they are out of contact with reality, are uncomfortable with the subject matter, or simply need to collect their thoughts.

13. A good technique to use when working with patients who are communicating nonverbally is to help them identify their feelings. A staff member might say something like the following to a patient: "Are you feeling anxious?" If the patient responds, "No, what makes you ask?", one might say, "Well, I noticed you were swinging your foot and you've smoked six cigarettes in the last 20 minutes." Helping the patient to become aware of nonverbal cues of anxiety may lead to the patient's becoming able to discuss such feelings verbally. It is also necessary to remember that just as staff members observe patients for their nonverbal communication, patients also notice the nonverbal communication of staff members. If, during a conversation, the staff member swings a leg or twiddles a piece of clothing, the patient may believe that the staff member is bored, is in a hurry, or wishes that the patient would get on with the topic of discussion.

14. When they discuss painful or embarrassing subjects, patients need support and encouragement. If one looks at the patient in a helpful, interested, concerned manner, the patient is encouraged to continue. In addition, one might occasionally say, "I see" or "Go on" or "I can understand that." Such statements also encourage the patient to continue talking and let the patient know that the staff member is listening and attentive to what is being said.

15. If one does not understand something that was said by a patient, it may be that the patient is not clear about the subject either.

Ask for clarification: "I'm sorry, but I didn't hear the last thing you said" or "I don't understand what you mean; please explain it to me." Do not make statements such as "You talk so low I can't understand what you are saying" or "The last statement you made was mean." Statements such as these run the risk of causing patients to feel intimidated and inferior, thus lowering their self-esteem and, therefore, possibly blocking further attempts to communicate.

16. Mental health workers should avoid using emotionally charged words and incriminating statements. Statements such as "You know smoking can cause lung cancer" may cause a patient to become unduly upset. One should also avoid leading questions, such as "It doesn't hurt when you bend over, does it?" Such questions imply that a particular answer is expected and predispose the patient to admit or deny symptoms.

Communication is something we have practiced all our lives. Some of us just happen to be better at it than others. Fortunately, it is a skill that can be improved if one takes time to learn and practice a few basic techniques such as the ones discussed in this chapter.

REPORTING AND RECORDING

One of the most important uses for good communication skills is in the reporting and recording of information concerning patients. Pertinent information is kept in a legal document called the patient's record or the patient's chart. Each patient's record should contain everything of significance pertaining to that patient. Accurate and complete charting and verbal reporting of observations encourage continuity of patient care by providing useful information about the patient to other team members.

The suggestions about effective communication techniques in this chapter, along with the specific instructions regarding charting listed below, should be helpful when reporting or charting one's observations about patients.

1. Write or print legibly in ink. Be sure that notations are made on the correct patient's chart and that all notations are dated and signed.
2. Do not erase. If a mistake is made, draw one line through it and print the word *error* above the line.
3. Be concise, yet make the meaning of each sentence clear.
4. Be objective by providing a description of what the patient has said or done. Try to avoid interpreting the patient's behavior. Remember that behaviors taken out of context may seem bizarre but, when described in the situations

in which they actually happened, may be quite normal and appropriate.

5. Use only the abbreviations approved by one's institution.
6. Chart medications and treatments after they are given, not before. If a patient refuses to participate in an activity, take a medication, or allow a treatment, be sure to chart the refusal. Whenever possible, the patient's reason for the refusal should also be noted.
7. Report and record any sudden change in the patient's behavior.
8. Always record the time of occurrence of the event being recorded. It is a good idea to record events as soon after they happen as possible because important details may be forgotten if one waits several hours to write the report.
9. Accidents should be reported and recorded according to the policy of one's institution. Thoroughness in writing such reports is extremely important because legal action may later require detailed information about the accident.

The following charts are provided as a guide to some of the factors that need to be observed and recorded when working with mentally ill patients. Many hospitals and clinics routinely use similar charts.

BEHAVIORS TO BE OBSERVED

Appearance	Personal hygiene: clean ____ dirty ____ body odor ____ bathes self ____ requires help with bath ____ Dress: appropriate ____ inappropriate ____ neat ____ unkempt ____ dresses self ____ requires help dressing ____
General Behavior	cooperative ____ helpful ____ dependable ____ quiet ____ loud ____ excitable ____ overactive ____ depressed ____ listless ____ irritable ____ verbally aggressive ____ anxious (specify: _____) complaints (specify: _____) physically aggressive ____ temper tantrums ____ bites nails ____ uses obscene language ____ shows fear of others ____

BEHAVIORS TO BE OBSERVED—*Continued*

pacing ___ seems overtly nervous ___ masturbates ___ sexually interested in staff ___ sexually interested in other patients ___ expresses suicidal impulses ___ expresses homicidal impulses ___

Body Behavior

staring into space ___ rigid, stiff movements ___ obviously tense ___ jerking, spastic movements (tics) ___ frequent startled responses ___ holds one position for prolonged periods ___ seems to be in a trance ___ coordinated motor behavior ___ staggers ___ falls ___ slumps when sitting ___ good general posture ___ poor general posture ___

Verbal Behavior

Speech: slow ___ rapid ___ slurred ___ otherwise impaired ___ unintelligible ___ rambling ___ dramatic ___ talks to self ___ repeats words or phrases over and over ___ talks compulsively or constantly ___ talks very little ___ does not talk at all ___

Thought Processes

Answers to questions: relevant ___ irrelevant ___ rambling ___ incoherent ___

Hears voices: threatening ___ ordering ___ accusing ___

Has visual hallucinations (specify) _____

Has visions (specify) _____

Has peculiar bodily sensations (specify) _____

BEHAVIORS TO BE OBSERVED—*Continued*

Has delusions (specify) _____

Ideas of: reference ____ persecution ____
conspiracy ____ people
controlling ____ outside forces
controlling ____ body
destruction ____ famous
people ____ having unusual
powers ____ having a divine
mission ____

Orientation

Oriented to: time ____ place ____ person ____
date ____ month ____ year ____
Able to recognize: staff ____ other
patients ____ own room ____
Short-term memory: good ____ poor ____
bad ____
Long-term memory: good ____ poor ____
bad ____ frequently
forgets who he(she)
is ____

PHYSICAL SYMPTOMS

Vital Signs

Temperature ____ Pulse ____ Respiration ____
BP ____ Weight ____

Neck, Face, and Skin

Appearance: pale ____ rosy ____
clammy ____ hot ____
cold ____ sweaty ____
acne ____ scars ____ red
spots ____ bruises or
lacerations ____ smooth
texture ____ rough
texture ____

Mouth

Teeth: Natural ____ dentures ____ clean ____
good hygiene ____ poor hygiene ____

PHYSICAL SYMPTOMS—*Continued*

	Gums: good color ___ smooth ___ irritated or inflamed ___ wet ___ dry ___ chewed or bitten ___ Breath: clean ___ sour ___ fruity ___
Urine	Color: pale yellow ___ bloody ___ pus ___ dark ___ Odor: essentially odorless ___ foul odor ___
Urinary habits	Voiding: voids easily ___ trouble voiding ___ voids too often ___ incontinent for urine ___
Stool	Consistency: liquefied ___ soft ___ hard ___ normal ___ Color: (brown, etc.) _____ Unusual odor ___ blood ___ mucus ___
Pain	Area (leg, etc.) _____ sharp ___ dull ___ stabbing ___ throbbing ___ intense ___ mild ___ occasional ___ frequent ___ continuous ___ first noticed (time) ___ How long has patient had the pain (days, hours, etc.) _____
Vomiting	Time (1:00 A.M., etc.) _____ Color (yellow, etc.) _____ Amount: little ___ moderate ___ much ___ Consistency: watery ___ average ___ thick ___ bloody ___ Material vomited (breakfast, etc.) _____
Cough	When: continuously ___ moderately ___ occasionally ___ mostly A.M. ___ mostly P.M. ___ day ___ night ___ Type: dry ___ sputum produced ___ blood ___ loud ___ soft ___ hacking ___ whooping ___ hoarse ___

PHYSICAL SYMPTOMS—*Continued*

Sleep

Amount (7 hr, etc.) _____
day ____ night ____ sound ____ moderate ____
light ____ fitful ____ disturbed ____
restless ____ up a lot ____ sleeps
easily ____ sleeps with difficulty ____ needs
sleep medication ____

Eating habits

Appetite: very good ____ good ____ fair ____
      poor ____
eats without assistance ____ needs
assistance ____ throws food ____
Table manners: good ____ fair ____ poor ____

Medicines

Takes meds without complaints ____ "cheeks"
meds ____ hoards meds ____ refuses
meds ____ no side effects noted ____ side
effects (specify) _____

BEHAVIORS AND PROBLEMS FREQUENTLY SEEN

Anxiety Disorders

1. Increased heart rate, palpitations, increased blood pressure
2. Muscular tension, parasympathetic responses
3. Increased respirations to the point of hyperventilation
4. Weakness
5. Dilated pupils
6. Constipation
7. Dry mouth
8. Anorexia
9. Urinary frequency, diarrhea
10. Headaches
11. Nausea and vomiting
12. Decreased sexual functioning
13. Restlessness
14. Tremors
15. Accident proneness

Dysthymic Disorders or Major Depression

1. Poor personal hygiene
2. Decreased motor activity

3. Fatigue
4. Anxiety, restlessness
5. Low self-esteem
6. Decreased mental processes
7. Constipation
8. Increased or decreased appetite
9. Sleeping disturbances—increased or decreased sleep, early morning awakening
10. Suicidal verbalization or gestures

Manic Disorders

1. Increased agitation
2. Hyperactivity
3. Loose associations
4. Insomnia
5. Hostility
6. Acting out
7. Hallucinations
8. Delusions
9. Sexual acting out
10. Rapid speech

Psychotic Disorders

1. Hallucinations
2. Delusions
3. Inappropriate affect
4. Regressive behaviors
5. Withdrawn behaviors
6. Sleep disturbances
7. Disorganized, illogical thinking
8. Acting out
9. Aggressive or destructive behaviors
10. Suicidal verbalization or gestures
11. Poor personal hygiene

Neurologic Disorders

1. Short attention span
2. Disorientation
3. Confusion
4. Confabulation
5. Poor immediate recall
6. Inappropriate or dramatic changes in social behavior
7. Poor judgment
8. Anger, hostility, or combativeness
9. Withdrawal
10. Inability to complete a task
11. Impaired ability to take care of activities of daily living

ANNOTATED BIBLIOGRAPHY

Crowther, D.J.: *Metacommunication: A missed opportunity?* Journal of Psychosocial Nursing and Mental Health Services, 1991, 29(4):13–16.

> *Presents communication as a multilevel phenomenon and discusses the importance of obtaining the transcending or underlying meaning when working with patients.*

Garvin, B.J., and Kennedy, C.W.: *Interpersonal communication between nurses and patients.* Annual Review of Nursing Research, 1990, 8:213–234.

> *Discusses the use of empathy, self-disclosure, support, and confirmation in forming the nurse-patient relationship.*

Haselfeld, D.: *Patient assessment: Conducting an effective interview.* ARON Journal, 1990, 52(3):551–557.

> *Illustrates the importance of interviewing to the nursing process and provides guidelines for more effective interviewing techniques.*

Oliver, S., and Redfern, S.J.: *Interpersonal communication between nurses and elderly patients: Refinement of an observation schedule.* Journal of Advanced Nursing, 1991, 16:30–38.

> *Research study focusing on the amount and type of nurse-patient interpersonal communication. Discusses the importance of touch as a means of communication.*

Stevenson, S.: *Heading off violence with verbal de-escalation.* Journal of Psychosocial Nursing and Mental Health Services, 1991, 29(9):6–15.

> *Presents therapeutic communication as a means of altering the course of the aggression cycle before the patient's behavior becomes violent.*

Tofp, M., and Dambacher, B.: *Teaching interpersonal skills: A model for facilitation optional interpersonal relations.* Journal of Psychosocial Nursing and Mental Health Services, 1981, 19(12):29–33.

> *On the basis of several recent research studies, this article explores three principles of interpersonal communication including interpersonal complementarity, interpersonal versatility, and interpersonal influence.*

True or False. Circle your choice.

T F 1. The two basic forms of communication are verbal and nonverbal.

T F 2. A common problem associated with verbal communication is the sending of messages one does not really mean.

T F 3. Some authorities believe that nonverbal communication is the most accurate of all forms of communication.

T F 4. In establishing a therapeutic relationship with a patient, the first step is to read the patient's chart very carefully.

T F 5. People communicate nonverbally via their behavior and their body posture.

T F 6. Nonverbal clues may be a better indication of a patient's true feelings than what the patient actually says.

T F 7. Patients who are highly anxious are usually better listeners than ones who are relatively calm.

T F 8. One should not offer patients a choice if in reality they do not have a choice.

T F 9. If patients appear to be having difficulty making decisions, a staff member should make them for them.

T F 10. Patients should be involved as much as possible in planning their own care and treatment plans.

Multiple Choice. Circle the letter or number that you think represents the best answer.

1. The manner in which questions are asked can be improved by all of the following except:
   a. Listening before asking.
   b. Phrasing questions clearly and concisely.
   c. Asking only questions pertinent to the subject at hand.
   d. Phrasing questions so that a "yes" or "no" will suffice for the answer.

2. If verbal communication is difficult, it is sometimes helpful and therapeutic to:
   a. Digress from focusing on the patient's problems and mention similar problems of your own.
   b. Ask the patient direct questions that require concrete answers.
   c. Ask several nonproductive questions that will not make the patient feel threatened.
   d. Engage in a social activity with the patient so that he or she will feel more comfortable.

3. The mental health worker's ability to effectively interpret communication is most dependent on:
   a. Sources available for validation of communication content.
   b. The immediacy with which the staff member attempts interpretation.
   c. The staff member's understanding of psychiatric terminology.
   d. How well the staff member listens and observes.

4. When observing behavior, the staff member should remember that behavioral symptoms:
   a. Have meaning.
   b. Are purposeful.
   c. Are multidetermined.
   d. All of the above.

5. Accurate recording of observations made in psychiatric settings includes:
   a. Employing psychiatric terminology whenever possible.
   b. Recording data as soon as possible.
   c. Expressing personal opinions and interpreting behavior.
   d. Using common, everyday, descriptive language.
      (1) d.
      (2) a and c.
      (3) b and d.
      (4) a, b, and c.
      (5) All of the above.

6. The main purpose for record keeping (charting) in the psychiatric setting is to:
   a. Provide a subjective report of the patient's behavior.
   b. Provide an objective report of the patient's behavior.
   c. Provide a description of the patient's environment.
   d. Note behavior signs of a specific illness.

7. If a patient becomes silent for a few seconds during an interaction, the staff member should probably:
   a. Interpret this as an indication that the patient is ready for the staff member to depart.
   b. Ask the patient a simple, nonthreatening question to get the conversation going again.
   c. Remind the patient that you can best be helpful if he or she shares feelings with you.
   d. Remain with the patient and be quietly attentive.

8. The therapeutic relationship is enhanced when a staff member uses verbal and nonverbal communication to:
   a. Give attention and recognition to the patient.
   b. Foster a patient's self-esteem.

    c. Indicate understanding.

    d. Communicate a feeling of acceptance and security.

        (1) d.

        (2) b and c.

        (3) a and d.

        (4) a, b, and d.

        (5) All of the above.

9. Ms. Long, a social worker, approaches one of her patients and starts a conversation. The patient says, "I don't want to talk today." What response by Ms. Long would indicate that she understood and accepted her patient's behavior?

    a. "You say you don't want to talk?"

    b. "I'll sit here with you for a while."

    c. "There is no need for you to talk."

    d. "Why don't you want to talk today?"

10. Mrs. Adams tells a staff member that she is feeling depressed about the recent death of her father. Which of the following responses would communicate understanding and acceptance?

    a. "I know just how you feel."

    b. "Everyone gets depressed when they lose a loved one."

    c. "This must be very difficult for you."

    d. "Try to think positive. He was ill only a short time and didn't have to suffer long."

11. Which of the following responses could prevent effective communication?

    a. "What you should do is . . . "

    b. "In my opinion . . ."

    c. "Try not to worry; everything will be all right."

    d. "Why did you do that?"

        (1) d.

        (2) a, b, and d.

        (3) a, b, and c.

        (4) All of the above.

12. While communicating with a schizophrenic patient, the mental health worker should:

    a. Sit quietly and not encourage the patient to verbalize.

    b. Talk with the patient as one would a normal person.

    c. Allow the patient to do all the talking.

    d. Use very simple, concrete language in speaking to the patient.

13. When talking to a patient for the first time, the staff member must realize:

    a. That hostile behavior in a patient indicates that the staff member's initial approach has been inadequate.

b. That the case history should be read before talking with the patient.

c. That the patient's physical appearance provides an accurate index as to whether or not the patient will be receptive.

d. That the patient is a stranger to the staff member and the staff member is a stranger to the patient.

9

Drug Therapy

In the mid-1950s, the development of a group of drugs known as phenothiazines revolutionized the care of the mentally ill. It was first thought that these drugs might actually "cure" mental illness, but this did not prove to be the case. However, these drugs did calm patients, decreasing the severity of symptoms to the point that they could be responsive to other forms of therapy. Patients receiving phenothiazines became more aware of their surroundings, began to participate in daily activities, were more cooperative with hospital routines, and, most important, began to communicate. These drastic changes in patient behavior allowed staff to begin to help them establish interpersonal relationships and to cope more effectively with their environment.

Since this major breakthrough in drug therapy, many other drugs effective in the treatment of various psychiatric disorders have been developed. The two major classifications of the psychotropic drugs (drugs active in decreasing symptoms of mental illness) are the tranquilizers, which are further divided into major and minor groups, and the antidepressants. We also discuss the anticonvulsants, sedatives, hypnotics, and antiparkinsons, since they are also used in the treatment of psychiatric patients.

THE ROLE OF THE NURSE

Although one purpose of this chapter is to focus on the use of medication in the treatment of psychiatric patients, another is to emphasize the nurse's role in drug therapy.

The nurse uses knowledge about medications, knowledge of the patient, and his or her relationship with the patient in helping to evaluate and establish baselines to monitor the effectiveness of drug interventions. This requires use of all the skills nurses have in building a therapeutic relationship plus the assumption of the critical responsibility of consistently and knowledgeably administering and monitoring the effects, side effects, and overall response of the patient to the medication given.

It also places the nurse in the important role of teacher to the patient. Because it is the nurse's responsibility to help patients understand how to responsibly administer their own medications after discharge, this role cannot be underestimated or overlooked because it is critical to patients' health and safety.

MAJOR TRANQUILIZERS

The word *tranquilize* means to make tranquil, that is, calm and basically free from agitation or disturbance. This is exactly the effect tranquilizers are intended to have on disturbed patients. Drugs designated as major tranquilizers not only calm patients but also help control severe agitation and reduce the frequency of hallucinations, delusions, thought disorders, and the type of withdrawal symptoms seen in catatonic schizophrenia. In other words, these drugs cause patients to exhibit more normal behavior. It may take several days of drug therapy before the symptoms mentioned begin to subside, but during this time patients usually become less fearful and hostile and are less upset by any disturbance in sensory perceptions. As their disturbed thinking and behavior improve, patients become more receptive to psychotherapy and other forms of treatment.

The phenothiazine derivatives are the largest group of antipsychotic drugs. All the drugs in this group have essentially the same type of action on the body, but they vary according to strength and the type and severity of their side effects. Phenothiazines produce several side effects that, although rarely serious, can cause discomfort. Patients should be observed carefully on a regular basis for the possible occurrence of the side effects discussed below. Since early detection is important, it is desirable for all members of the treatment team to become thoroughly familiar with these major side effects.

SIDE EFFECTS

Extrapyramidal Symptoms. There are three major types of extrapyramidal symptoms: (1) pseudoparkinsonism—restlessness, masklike facial expression, drooling, and tremors; (2) akathisia—inability to sit still, complaints of fatigue and weakness, and continuous movement of the hands, mouth, and body; and (3) dyskinesia—lack of control over voluntary movements. For example, the patient might want to reach for something but be unable to do so. The patient may have a protruding tongue and a drooping head and may become very frightened if stiffness of the neck and swallowing difficulties develop. Immediate action must be taken to combat extrapyramidal side effects; administration of antiparkinson drugs usually produces a dramatic reduction in symptoms.

Autonomic Reactions. This group of side effects includes dry mouth, constipation, excessive weight gain, and edema. Strict attention must be paid to patients' personal hygiene, and they should be informed of the possibility of these side effects and given suggestions about how to combat them. Increasing patients' intake of fluids, especially water, helps the mouth dryness and also triggers the body's mechanism to reduce water retention, thus reducing the edema. A drug called Urecholine is also now being used to decrease mouth dryness. Since excessive weight gain is a potential problem, patients should be cautioned to lessen their intake of fattening foods and increase their intake of salads, fruits, and so forth. This will also help reduce constipation problems.

Postural Hypotension. This is a drop in blood pressure that occurs when a patient moves from lying flat in bed to a standing position. Symptoms include dizziness, heart pounding, and a feeling of faintness. Because patients could faint and injure themselves when first getting up, they should be cautioned to sit on the side of the bed first and dangle their feet a while before standing. Patients receiving a high dose of a phenothiazine drug should have their blood pressure checked on a regular basis. Any patient who is given a large oral or intramuscular (IM) dose of one of the phenothiazines should lie in bed for about an hour.

Allergic Reactions. These are rare but serious when they do occur. If the patient develops dermatosis, jaundice, or ulcerative lesions in the mouth or throat, the drug will usually need to be discontinued.

Thus, if a patient complains of a sore throat or other signs of infection, the physician should be notified immediately.

Sedation. If a patient receiving phenothiazines is lethargic and wants to sleep a great deal, the dose of medicine may be too high and may need adjustment.

Decreased Sexual Interest. The possibility of this side effect needs to be explained so that the patient will know what is happening if sexual interest diminishes. Women patients may exhibit some of the signs and symptoms of pregnancy, such as absence of the menstrual cycle, false-positive pregnancy tests, and weight gain. If the patient is checked further and there are no positive signs of pregnancy, she should be assured that the medication is the causative factor.

Photosensitivity. If this side effect occurs, the patient will become especially sensitive to light and prone to sunburn and may complain of visual problems. Therefore lengthy periods of direct sunlight should be avoided or protective clothing and glasses should be worn.

Other Side Effects. Patients on phenothiazines often experience blurred vision and drowsiness and should not drive or use dangerous equipment. Patients on phenothiazine therapy should be cautioned about taking other medications without their physicians' permission because phenothiazines may increase the action of other drugs, especially pain medications.

If any of the side effects discussed above cause the patient an unusual amount of difficulty or serious hazards, the physician may try one of the following three remedies: (1) the drug dosage may be decreased; (2) if symptoms persist, the medication may be completely withdrawn for 24 hours, then be restarted with a gradual buildup of the dosage; or (3) the drug may be changed to another phenothiazine derivative known to be less likely to produce the troublesome side effects.

Table 9–1 lists some of the major phenothiazine-type tranquilizers. Knowing these trade names will alert you to the fact that a patient is taking a phenothiazine drug and should be carefully observed for side effects.

PATIENT TEACHING

Since hospitals stays are shorter and shorter, an important responsibility of the nurse is to teach patients how to care for themselves at home. One of the most important aspects of caring for patients on medication is to teach them about the prescribed medications. Before you can teach the patient, it is important for you to understand how the medication works, the expected action of the medication on the body, the importance of compliance with the treatment regimen,

Table 9–1.

MAJOR TRANQUILIZERS (PHENOTHIAZINE DERIVATIVES)

Antipsychotics (major tranquilizers, neuroleptics, anti-emetics)

Chemical Classification	Route*	Generic Name (Trade Name)	Average Dosage for Daily Administration†
Butyrophenones	PO, IM, IV	Haloperidol (Haldol)	1–100 mg
Dibenzoxazepines	PO, IM, IV	Loxapine (Loxitane)	25–250 mg
Dihydroindolones	PO, IV	Molindone (Moban)	10–200 mg
Phenothiazines		Acetophenazine (Tindal)	50–150 mg
	PO	Butaperazine (Repoise)	30–100 mg
	IM, PO, IV suppository	Chlorpromazine (Thorazine)	50–1500 mg
	IM	Fluphenazine (Permitil, Prolixin) (Prolixin D)	25–50 mg
	IM	Mesoridazine (Serentil)	25–400 mg
	PO, IM	Perphenazine (Trilafon)	10–60 mg
	IM, PO, suppository	Prochlorperazine (Compazine)	10–150 mg
	IM	Promazine (Sparine)	100–1000 mg
	PO	Thioridazine (Mellaril)	150–500 mg
	IM, suppository	Triflupromazine (Vesprin)	50–350 mg
	PO	Piperacetazine (Quide)	25–100 mg
	PO, IM	Trifluoperazine (Stelazine)	20–100 mg

*Abbreviations: PO = per os, by mouth; IM = intramuscularly; IV = intravenously.
†Please be aware that in some instances, the dosage range for a trade name drug may vary slightly from that of its corresponding generic drug.

how to recognize if the medication is effective, and how to recognize side effects. After you have learned this information, it should then be shared with patients so that they can administer the medicine appropriately at home.

It is important to teach patients the reason the antipsychotic medication is given—that it will help reduce their symptoms of agitation or anxiety and will help control their behavior. Make sure the patient understands that it may take up to 3 weeks for a therapeutic response and that it is important to take the medication as the physician has ordered. If the patient misses a dose but remembers within 1 hour of the prescribed time, he or she should take the medicine. If it has been longer than 1 hour, the patient should wait until the time for the next prescribed dose. However, remind the patient to take only a single dose, not twice the dose, at the next scheduled time. Teach the patient to identify adverse side effects and to whom to report the side effects if they occur.

Teach patients not to take over-the-counter drugs when they are on major tranquilizers, especially antacids that prevent or interfere with absorption.

Explain the importance of not reducing or stopping a drug once the drug has taken effect. Sometimes, when patients feel their symptoms less intensely, they have a tendency to quit taking the drug. Patients should see their therapists before discontinuing use.

MINOR TRANQUILIZERS

Minor tranquilizers reduce anxiety and the muscle tension associated with it. They are primarily useful in treating patients with psychoneurotic and psychosomatic disorders. When given in small doses, they are relatively safe and have few side effects. Unlike the major tranquilizers, however, some of the minor tranquilizers tend to be habit forming. If the drug is discontinued, the patient may experience severe withdrawal symptoms, which may even include delirium and convulsions.

SIDE EFFECTS

Patients are occasionally hypersensitive to the minor tranquilizers and may have rashes, chills, fever, nausea, and vomiting. Minor tranquilizers may also cause headaches, poor muscle coordination, some inability to concentrate, and dizziness. Patients taking these drugs should be cautioned against driving or performing any task that requires mental alertness and careful attention to detail. Excessive amounts of these drugs may lead to coma and death; however, death

Table 9-2.

MINOR TRANQUILIZERS

Chemical Classification	Route*	Generic Name (Trade Name)	Adult Dosage for Daily Administration†
Antihistamines	PO, IM	Hydroxyzine (Vistaril, Atarax)	50–400 mg
Benzodiazepines	PO	Alprazolam (Xanax)	0.5–4 mg
	PO	Lorazepam (Ativan)	2–10 mg
	PO	Chlordiazepoxide (Librium)	25–300 mg
		Chlorazepate dipotassium (Tranxene)	10–45 mg
	PO, IM, IV	Diazepam (Valium)	5–40 mg
	PO	Halazepam (Paxipam)	50–150 mg
	PO	Oxazepam (Serax)	25–125 mg
	PO	Prazepam (Centrax)	25–45 mg
Propanediols	PO	Meprobamate (Equanil, Miltown)	200–1200 mg

*Abbreviations: PO = per os, by mouth; IM = intramuscularly; IV = intravenously.
†Please be aware that in some instances, the dosage range for a trade name drug may vary slightly from that of its corresponding generic drug.

is much less likely to occur with an overdose of a minor tranquilizer than with an overdose of barbiturates.

Table 9–2 lists many of the minor tranquilizers commonly used.

PATIENT TEACHING

Provide patients with information about the specific drug, including the medication name, action, dose, onset of effects, possible side effects, and interactions. Explain that this drug is primarily to help them relax. Patients should continue to see their physicians while taking the drug because it usually should not be taken for more than a few months because it is habit forming. Patients should not discontinue the drug without seeing their physicians.

Explain to patients the importance of taking the drug as prescribed and not to take more of it, take it more often, or take it longer than prescribed. Teach patients not to take this medication with other medicines, such as pain medication, sleeping pills, over-the-counter antihistamines, or any other drugs that cause drowsiness. Explain that they should not take this drug with alcohol.

If patients forget a dose but remember within 1 hour of the scheduled time, tell them to take it. If they remember after 1 hour, they should skip that dose and resume taking the medication at the next scheduled time; they should not double the dose.

Explain to patients that this drug may make them feel dizzy, drowsy, or sleepy and to be certain they are sufficiently alert to participate in any activities requiring alertness, such as driving or operating mechanical or electrical equipment.

ANTIDEPRESSANTS

Historically, two types of antidepressants have been prescribed: monoamine oxidase (MAO) inhibitors and tricyclics. However, several types of new antidepressants have been introduced recently despite the fact that little is known about the specific actions of these drugs. It is important to understand that antidepressants work biochemically to elevate the patient's mood. They also help decrease the patient's preoccupation with feelings of worthlessness, inadequacy, and hopelessness.

MAO INHIBITORS

The value of the MAO inhibitors is being questioned by many authorities in the field of psychiatry because they tend to produce a number of severe side effects. Many of these side effects have led to fatalities or prolonged and serious medical problems. Because these drugs are primarily used to treat depressed patients, who often have suicidal tendencies, another drawback exists. It takes 1 to 2 weeks of drug therapy before MAO inhibitors effect behavior change. The suicidal patient needs faster-acting medicine.

Hypertension (high blood pressure) crises have occurred after patients receiving MAO inhibitors have consumed certain foods (such as cheese, bananas, and avocados) or beverages (such as beer and Chianti wine). Patients taking MAO inhibitors must also avoid certain other drugs used for relieving colds, hay fever, and nausea. Hypertension crises may cause severe headaches and intracranial bleeding. Nausea and vomiting, chills and fever, neck stiffness, sensitivity to light, chest pain, and heart arrhythmias may also occur. If any of these symptoms appear, they should be reported immediately and the drug should be discontinued by the physician.

MAO inhibitors are contraindicated if the patient suffers from any severe major medical problem and especially if there is a history of impaired kidney function. An MAO inhibitor should not be mixed with other MAO inhibitors and should not be given if the patient is

Table 9–3.

DRUGS COMMONLY USED FOR DEPRESSION

Chemical Classification	Route*	Generic Name (Trade Name)	Average Dosage for Daily Administration†
Bicyclics	PO	Fluoxetine (Prozac)	25–75 mg
	PO	Trazodone (Desyrel)	150–400 mg
Monoamine oxidase inhibitors (MAOs)	PO	Isocarboxazid (Marplan)	10–25 mg
		Phenelzine (Nardil)	50–100 mg
	PO	Tranylcypromine (Parnate)	10–50 mg
Tetracyclics		Maprotiline (Ludiomil)	75–200 mg
Tricyclics	PO, IM	Amitriptyline (Elavil)	50–300 mg
	PO	Amoxapine (Asendin)	100–300 mg
	PO	Desipramine (Norpramin)	50–300 mg
	PO	Doxepin (Adapin, Sinequan)	25–300 mg
	PO, IM	Imipramine (Tofranil)	50–200 mg
	PO	Nortriptyline (Aventyl, Pamelor)	50–100 mg
	PO	Protriptyline (Vivactil)	10–50 mg
	PO	Trimipramine (Surmontil)	50–200 mg

Abbreviations: PO = *per os,* by mouth; IM = intramuscularly.
†Please be aware that in some instances, the dosage range for a trade name drug may vary slightly from that of its corresponding generic drug.

taking alcohol, barbiturates, or morphinelike drugs because they potentiate the action of these drugs.

Table 9–3 lists some commonly used MAO inhibitors.

CYCLIC ANTIDEPRESSANTS

These antidepressants are used to elevate the patient's mood and to stimulate the patient's activity level. As with the MAO inhibitors, it tends to take 1 to 4 weeks of drug therapy before drugs in this group effect significant changes in the patient's outlook. Antidepressants are sometimes given in large doses in the afternoon or evening because their sedating effect may facilitate the patient's ability to sleep. Since these drugs sometimes excite patients rather than sedate them, patients must be observed closely for individual reactions.

Common side effects include dry mouth, fatigue, weakness, blurring of vision, constipation, parkinsonian syndrome, and increased perspiration. Most, if not all, of these symptoms can be controlled by lowering the dosage of the medication. Table 9–3 also lists some commonly used tricyclic antidepressants.

PATIENT TEACHING

Provide information to patients about the specific drug, including the medication name, action, dose, onset of effects, and possible side effects to watch for. It is particularly important to caution patients to be alert to certain food and drug interactions while using these drugs.

MAO Inhibitors

1. Teach patients not to take them with excessive caffeine and foods containing tyramine or tryptophan, such as bananas. (If possible, have a dietitian visit patients to give a full explanation of food-drug interaction.) Remind patients not to take them with other over-the-counter drugs and many other prescription drugs, such as insulin and oral antidiabetic medications.
2. Teach patients not to take them with sleeping pills.
3. Teach patients not to take them with alcohol.
4. Teach patients that the medication may require 2 to 3 weeks to reach therapeutic effectiveness.

Cyclic Antidepressants

1. Explain to patients that maximum therapeutic effectiveness may not occur for 2 to 3 weeks.
2. Help their families understand that patients' potential for suicide sometimes increases when their mood increases enough for them to have enough energy to carry out the process.
3. Teach patients the importance of good oral hygiene because of these drugs' drying effect on the mouth and the importance of a high-fiber diet because of the constipating effects of these drugs.

The nurse should teach patients to take medication with food or after a meal in order to decrease gastric irritation and, as with major tranquilizers and other medications, stress the importance of taking medication as prescribed. Explain to patients the importance of reporting the use of this medication before any type of surgery, including dental surgery.

SEDATIVES AND HYPNOTICS

The barbiturate hypnotics, nonbarbiturate hypnotics, and other sedatives are similar in effect to the minor tranquilizers in that they act to reduce anxiety. A main difference in their action is that these drugs tend to cause the patient to be more sleepy than do the tranquilizers. Barbiturates are also much more dangerous because an overdose, whether accidental or planned, can cause death. In addition, barbiturates are highly addictive and greatly potentiate the action of drugs such as alcohol and narcotics. Since these drugs, along with the minor tranquilizers, are often used by depressed patients, one should observe the patient closely for suicidal intentions. When suicidal potential exists, only small amounts of these drugs should be given in order to avoid the deliberate taking of a massive overdose (especially if the patient is an outpatient). It may even be necessary to check the hospitalized patient's mouth carefully to make sure the medication has been swallowed and is not being saved until enough is collected to constitute a deadly overdose. Never leave the medication with patients to take when they are "ready."

Compared with barbiturate hypnotics, the nonbarbiturate hypnotics have less toxic effects if an overdose occurs, are less habit forming, and result in fewer "hangovers." They are also less likely to cause paradoxic excitement (rather than calm) in patients who have unusual reactions to drugs. Patients can also develop tolerance or allergic reaction to barbiturates, thus making them ineffective. When this occurs, nonbarbiturate hypnotics can be safely substituted.

After the administration of these drugs, patients should be observed closely for any reactions. If they fall into a deep sleep, they should not be awakened for the next dose. If patients seem unusually unresponsive, the next dose of medication should be withheld and their physician notified at once. It is also important to remember that elderly patients, especially if cerebral vascular disease is present, may react to sedatives and hypnotics in a manner opposite to the desired effect. They may become excited and confused and even try to get up. Safety must be maintained; this may require staying with patients, talking in a quiet, calm manner, repeating their name, and telling them where they are in order to reorient them to their environment.

Barbiturates and sedatives, when abused, can cause a certain degree of euphoria; therefore patients with a history of alcoholism or drug abuse should be carefully observed when taking any of these drugs over a long period. Staff members might suggest and help

Table 9–4.

SEDATIVES AND HYPNOTICS

Chemical Classification	Route*	Generic Name (Trade Name)	Average Dosage for Daily Administration†
Barbiturates	PO, IV, suppository	Pentobarbital (Nembutal)	25–200 mg
	PO, IM, IV, suppository	Secobarbital (Seconal)	25–200 mg
	PO, IV	Amobarbital (Amytal)	50–300 mg
	PO	Aprobarbital (Alurate)	40–160 mg
	PO	Butobarbital (Butisol)	50–100 mg
	PO, IM, IV	Phenobarbital (Luminal)	50–300 mg
Other sedatives and hypnotics	PO	Buspirone (BuSpar)	5–60 mg
	PO	Chloral hydrate (Noctec, Somnos)	500–1000 mg
	PO	Ethchlorvynol (Placidyl)	500–1000 mg
	PO	Glutethimide (Doriden)	250–500 mg

*Abbreviations: PO = per os, by mouth; IM = intramuscularly; IV = intravenously.
†Please be aware that in some instances, the dosage range for a trade name drug may vary slightly from that of its corresponding generic drug.

patients learn alternative methods of handling nervousness, such as listening to music, taking a warm bath at bedtime, or developing a hobby in order to help them gradually give up sedatives and tranquilizers. Table 9–4 lists frequently used sedatives and hypnotics.

ANTICONVULSANTS

Anticonvulsants are used to treat various kinds of convulsive seizures. Phenobarbital and Dilantin are the most commonly used of all anticonvulsant drugs. Phenobarbital often has to be given in doses so large that it produces sleepiness and lethargy. Dilantin is not a hypnotic and is often used in conjunction with phenobarbital in order to allow better control of seizures with less sedating side effects.

However, Dilantin may cause gastric irritation, dizziness, nausea and vomiting, blurred vision, nervousness, and excessive growth of gum tissue and hair, especially facial hair. Some patients are particularly sensitive to the drug and develop skin rashes, dermatitis, fever; some may have difficulty breathing. Such serious side effects as hallucinations, psychosis, hepatitis, and lupus erythematosus have been reported due to Dilantin therapy.

ANTIPARKINSONS

The three antiparkinson drugs frequently used in treating psychiatric patients are Benadryl, Cogentin, and Artane. These drugs are used to combat the Parkinsonlike side effects often produced when the patient is receiving tranquilizers or other antipsychotic drugs. They reduce muscle rigidity, excessive drooling, and sweating. If the dosage is too high, the patient may have difficulty voiding, blurred vision, and dry mouth. Sucking on hard candies is one way the patient can avoid oral discomfort.

OTHER DRUGS

Some other drugs are used quite often in the treatment of psychiatric patients and, therefore, are included here.

Indoklon. This drug is a central nervous system stimulant administered by inhalation and used instead of electroconvulsive therapy (ECT) to produce convulsions in depressed patients. Its use for this purpose is not widespread.

Lithium carbonate. This drug is used in the treatment of manic-depressive psychoses because it is effective in decreasing the manic patient's excessive motor activity, talking, and unstable behavior by acting on the patient's brain metabolism. Patients should be observed for the following signs of lithium intoxication: nausea, vomiting, diarrhea, sudden loss of appetite, drowsiness, muscle weakness, and poor motor coordination. If these symptoms occur, discontinuation of the drug is required. Knowing that this drug acts on brain metabolism and seeing it drastically improve patient behavior leads many authorities to believe that many of the psychiatric disorders may be due to faulty metabolism and thus may someday be curable through drug therapy.

Brevital. This is a rapid-acting, ultrashort-acting barbiturate administered intravenously and used to induce light surgical anesthesia before ECT treatments.

Succinylcholine chloride (Anectine). This drug is used to produce skeletal-muscle relaxation prior to ECT treatment.

GENERAL CONSIDERATIONS

Drug therapy is not a cure for mental illness; at best it is an adjunct to psychotherapy and other treatment methodologies. It is important, however, because it allows many patients to control symptoms to such a degree that they can function as effective members of society. Just as diabetics may be required to take insulin for the rest of their lives in order to survive, many mentally ill patients must take psychotropic drugs on a long-term basis.

Because most of these drugs are relatively new, it is extremely important that patients taking them be watched for unexpected side effects and complications. The family is usually interested in the patient's progress and should be actively involved in the care plan. Patients should assume the responsibility for taking their own medication when at home and should learn the correct amount and frequency of doses from the staff. The staff should also explain to patients that many of the medications taken are effective because a certain amount of the drug (blood level) is constantly in one's system. If one skips a dose or stops taking the medication, the blood level drops and the medication may become ineffective. Many patients stop taking their medications as soon as they feel better because they believe they are cured. Unfortunately, they fail to realize that the medication has brought about much of their improvement and a relapse will occur if they stop taking their prescribed drug.

Patients and their families should be well informed concerning possible side effects and know to report them to the staff as soon as they appear. Most patients will cooperate in taking medication if they know how it will help and why it is being given.

SPECIFIC NURSING CONSIDERATIONS

Major Tranquilizers

1. Responses are highly individualized, and it is important to find the lowest effective dose for the patient. Also, many signs and symptoms are dose related.
2. Bed rails may be needed for the first few days of therapy because of hypnotensive reactions, drowsiness, and dizziness that may occur in initial attempts to stabilize a dosage.
3. Phenothiazine drugs are not stable when mixed with other medications. Do not mix unless approved by the pharmacy.
4. When giving phenothiazines IM, give them deep to pre-

vent tissue irritation, but avoid injection into the sub-
cutaneous tissue, and inject them slowly.

5. Urinary retention and constipation may occur. Record
intake and output.

6. Upon discharge, make the following clear to patients:
   a. It is important to take medication as ordered to maintain a therapeutic blood level.
   b. Although tolerance can develop, most medications do
   not produce physical dependence.
   c. Patients should refrain from activities requiring mental alertness and coordination until reevaluation by
   the physician.
   d. If in liquid form, medication is sensitive to light and
   must be kept out of direct sunlight.
   e. Medication may turn urine pink to reddish-brown.
   f. Patients should carry identification indicating that they
   are receiving phenothiazine medication.
   g. Patients and their families should understand side
   effects and how to reach the attending physician if
   necessary.

Minor Tranquilizers

1. Unlike major tranquilizers, minor tranquilizers always carry
the possibility of physical and psychologic dependence.

2. Alcohol should be avoided when taking these drugs because
they augment the depressant effects of alcohol.

3. In prolonged Librium therapy, periodic blood cell counts
and liver-function tests are recommended.

4. Prepare IM Librium immediately before administration and
dispose of the unused portion.

5. Intravenous (IV) Valium cannot be mixed with other drugs
or any type of solution. It therefore cannot be added to
intravenous fluids. Administer IV Valium slowly, taking at
least 1 minute for each 5 mg (1 ml).

6. After prolonged administration of Valium or Librium, withdrawal symptoms may occur.

Antidepressants

1. Instruct patients on what foods to avoid when taking MAO
inhibitors.

2. Warn patients against mixing medications with over-the-
counter items such as cough syrup.

3. Monitor effectiveness of the drug as evidenced by patient's

renewed interest in self and surroundings. This is especially important because therapeutic response is so variable, occurring anywhere from 2 days to 2 months from onset of drug therapy.

4. When patients begin showing renewed interest, evaluate and supervise them because the risk of suicide increases when the medication helps patients to feel strong enough to carry out suicidal plans.

5. Patients may require assistance in getting into an upright position during the initial stage of therapy because of orthostatic hypotension.

Sedatives and Hypnotics

1. Barbiturates, especially short-acting ones, may cause dependence; if this occurs, withdrawal may be very serious.

2. Patient should be informed that the use of these drugs with each other or with alcohol may be fatal and should be completely avoided.

3. Barbiturates significantly reduce the effectiveness of the oral anticoagulants; thus these drugs should not be given together.

4. Discourage patients from mixing these drugs with any over-the-counter drugs, especially drugs such as antihistamines that can give additive central nervous system depression.

5. Caution patients against abruptly discontinuing these drugs because withdrawal symptoms may occur.

6. Encourage patients to try some type of relaxation exercises, or other means of decreasing stress, before using these drugs because they are habit forming.

7. Warn patients taking barbiturates not to drive a car or operate machinery.

8. If patients are discharged with a prescription for sleeping pills, encourage them not to keep the pill bottle at the bedside. This may help avoid an accidental overdose.

Anticonvulsants

1. Include patients and their families in health teaching on the use of medication as a part of the therapeutic regimen.

2. Warn that excessive use of alcohol may interfere with drug action.

3. Caution patients to take medication with fluids or food in order to avoid gastrointestinal problems.

4. Stress the necessity of continuing under medical supervision after discharge.
5. Stress that patients should not alter the dosage. If medication is not controlling the seizures, the physician should be notified.
6. Warn patients of things that lower the seizure threshold, such as fever, low blood sugar, and so forth.

Antiparkinsons

1. It sometimes takes 2 or 3 days for these medications to reach therapeutic effectiveness.
2. These drugs have a sedating effect.
3. Monitor intake and output because oliguria can interfere with the excretion of these drugs.
4. Most antiparkinson drugs should be taken after meals.

ANNOTATED BIBLIOGRAPHY

Carey, N., Jones, S.L., and O'Toole, A.W.: *Do you feel powerless when a patient refuses medication?* Journal of Psychosocial Nursing and Mental Health Services, 1990, 28(10):19–25.

> *Explores the issue of the right of patients to refuse medication and the nurse's feelings of powerlessness when this occurs.*

Chapman, T.: *The nurse's role in neuroleptic medications.* Journal of Psychosocial Nursing and Mental Health Services, 1991, 29(6):6–8.

> *Relates the possible side effects of neuroleptic medications and explores the issue of whether the drawbacks to the medication outweigh the benefits.*

Dauner, A, and Blair, D.T.: *Akathisia: When treatment creates a problem.* Journal of Psychosocial Nursing and Mental Health Services, 1990, 28(10):13–18.

> *Explores the symptoms and dangers of akathisia, an extrapyramidal symptom that is a side effect of antipsychotic medications.*

Fritz, J., and Stewart, J.T.: *Lorazepam treatment of resistive aggression in dementia.* American Journal of Psychiatry, 1990, 147(9):1250.

> *Discusses the use of lorazepam for the treatment of aggressive behaviors in dementia patients and gives case examples of its successful use.*

Lund, V.E., and Frank, D.I.: *Helping the medicine go down: Nurses' and patients' perceptions about medication compliance.* Journal of Psychosocial Nursing and Mental Health Services, 1991, 29(7):6–9.

> *Research study on the perceptions of psychiatric patients as compared with the perceptions of nurses on medication compliance.*

Natvig, D.: *The role of the interdisciplinary team in using psychotropic drugs.* Journal of Psychosocial Nursing and Mental Health Services, 1991, 29(10):3–8.

> *Addresses the effectiveness of the team approach in the use of psychotropic drugs as a treatment plan.*

Sachdev, P.S.: *Psychoactive drug use in an institution for intellectually handicapped persons.* The Medical Journal of Australia, 1991, 155:75–79.

> *Research study examining the use of psychoactive drugs for the treatment of long-stay, developmentally disabled individuals in an institution.*

Vernon, A.W.: *Classification of psychotherapeutic drugs.* Journal of Psychosocial Nursing and Mental Health Services, 1981, 19(11):15–17.

> *Discusses classifications and categories of psychotropic drugs, including antipsychotics, antidepressants, antimanics, and antianxiety drugs.*

Wilkerson, L.: *A collaborative model: Ambulatory pharmacotherapy for chronic psychiatric patients.* Journal of Psychosocial Nursing and Mental Health Services, 1991, 29(12):26–29.

> *Discusses the use of the medication clinic and medication group to shift the responsibility for medication management to the patient and family through education and participation.*

Matching I. Match the appropriate item listed in Column B with the descriptive statement listed in Column A.

Column A

_____ 1. Help(s) control severe agitation.
_____ 2. Help(s) elevate the patient's mood.
_____ 3. Combat(s) parkinsonlike side effects.
_____ 4. Used in treatment of manic depressives.
_____ 5. Produce(s) skeletal muscle relaxation prior to ECT.

Column B

a. Antidepressants
b. Lithium
c. Major tranquilizers
d. Indoklon
e. Antiparkinsons
f. Anectine

Matching II. Match the letter of the appropriate item in Column B with the drug in Column A. (Letters in Column B may be used more than once.)

Column A

_____ 1. Valium
_____ 2. Tofranil
_____ 3. Dalmane
_____ 4. Vistaril
_____ 5. Cogentin
_____ 6. Compazine
_____ 7. Dilantin
_____ 8. Aventyl
_____ 9. Mellaril

Column B

a. Major tranquilizer
b. Antiparkinson
c. Anticonvulsant
d. Antidepressant
e. Minor tranquilizer
f. Sedative-hypnotic

True or False. Circle your choice.

T   F   1. Phenothiazines are a cure for mental illness.
T   F   2. The phenothiazine derivatives are the largest group of antipsychotic drugs.
T   F   3. Increased sexual interest is a major problem with patients when receiving phenothiazines.
T   F   4. One of the main difficulties in using minor tranquilizers is that they tend to be habit forming.
T   F   5. MAO inhibitors are usually given with another MAO inhibitor to achieve the desired effect.
T   F   6. Patients no longer need to take their medication when they feel better.

Short Answer. Answer the following questions as briefly and specifically as possible.

1. What effect might one expect the tranquilizers to have on a patient?

   _____.

   _____.

   _____.

2. If a patient is having an autonomic reaction to medication, what is the nursing responsibility?

   _____.

   _____.

3. What are the two categories of antidepressants?

   _____.

4. What are the common side effects to watch for in a patient receiving a tricyclic antidepressant?

   _____.

   _____.

Multiple Choice. Circle the letter or number that you think represents the best answer.

1. Which side effects are characteristic of lithium carbonate?
   a. Diarrhea.
   b. Nausea and vomiting.
   c. Excessive thirst.
   d. Muscle weakness and motor incoordination.
   e. Loss of appetite.
      (1) b and d.
      (2) a, b, and c.
      (3) a, d, and e.
      (4) All of the above.

2. Parkinsonlike symptoms that occur as a side effect of the phenothiazine drugs can best be controlled by:
   a. Mellaril.
   b. Colace.
   c. Artane.
   d. Cogentin.
   e. Compazine.
      (1) a.
      (2) b and e.
      (3) c and e.
      (4) b and d.
      (5) c and d.

3. Jaundice, photosensitivity, and parkinsonian syndrome may occur in patients receiving:
   a. Valium.
   b. Elavil.
   c. Miltown.
   d. Thorazine.
4. Which of the following are true of extrapyramidal symptoms?
   a. They may appear after a single dose of the phenothiazines.
   b. They may appear after prolonged administration of the phenothiazines.
   c. They indicate that the phenothiazines are affecting the deeper brain centers.
   d. They are not controllable.
   e. They are fatal.
      (1) a, d, and e.
      (2) a, b, and c.
      (3) a and d.
      (4) b and c.
      (5) a and c.
5. The time required to reach an effective blood level of antidepressant medication is:
   a. 24 hours.
   b. 2 days.
   c. 2 weeks.
   d. 30 days.
6. Side effects from antipsychotic agents such as Thorazine include:
   a. Extrapyramidal symptoms.
   b. Mental confusion.
   c. Hypotension.
   d. Habituation.
   e. Dryness of the mouth.
      (1) a, b, and c.
      (2) a, c, and d.
      (3) a, b, and d.
      (4) a, c, and e.
      (5) All of the above.
7. In administering medications on a psychiatric service, one should:
   a. Check identification by reading the identification bracelet.
   b. Carry only one drug at a time on a tray.
   c. Mix poorly accepted medications in food or drink.
   d. Inspect the mouth of the patient who is likely or suspected to hoard medications to be sure the medications are swallowed.
      (1) a and b.
      (2) a and d.
      (3) a, c, and d.
      (4) All of the above.

Electroconvulsive Therapy

LEARNING OBJECTIVES

Student will be able to:
1. Describe two theories about why electroconvulsive therapy works.
2. List diagnostic tests necessary before administering electroconvulsive therapy.
3. List general guidelines for caring for the patient before electroconvulsive therapy.
4. List general guidelines for caring for the patient after electroconvulsive therapy.

The purpose of this chapter is to familiarize the reader with the technique of electroconvulsive shock therapy, sometimes called ECT or EST. This technique of treating patients was introduced by Dr. Ugo Cerletti and Dr. Lucio Bini of Rome, Italy, in the late 1930s. Physicians have continued to refine this treatment technique and now administer muscle relaxants and anesthesia prior to the actual treatment, thus reducing the violent aspects of the patient's convulsion. This is done to prevent fractures and contusions, which often occurred before such medications were used. When treatments are given using muscle relaxants and anesthesia, all one observes is a slight tremor in the patient's hands and feet lasting approximately 1 to 2 minutes. Patients do not remember treatment activities, and the only pain they experience is an occasional post-ECT headache.

Although we are not certain why ECT works, two theories are frequently offered. The first of these theories suggests that ECT works by breaking up neural patterns or memory traces in the brain, thus permitting patients to forget, or at least think less about, the painful aspects of their life experiences. The second theory suggests that patients who receive ECT treatments perceive them as a form of punishment and thus improve after treatment because they feel they have been punished for unacceptable thoughts or actions. This latter theory gains much of its support from the idea that ECT seems to work most effectively with depressed patients. As previously discussed, depressed patients frequently have severe guilt feelings. Perhaps ECT reduces guilt by causing the patients to feel that they have "paid" for their sins. We would emphasize the fact that these are only theories about why ECT is effective, and the authors know of no conclusive research demonstrating that either theory is anything more than educated speculation.

Although ECT treatments are performed routinely in many hospitals, it is important to remember that the procedure is a potentially dangerous one and that a great deal of care must be exercised when administering it. All of the following tests should be completed on any patient scheduled for ECT prior to the first treatment:

1. A thorough physical examination.
2. A thorough mental examination.
3. An electrocardiogram (ECG), because ECT places a great deal of strain on a patient's heart.
4. Chest and lumbosacral (spinal) x-rays along with routine blood studies to determine if any abnormalities exist.
5. An electroencephalogram (EEG) to determine whether or not there are any abnormal electrical activities already occurring in the patient's brain. If the possibility of organic brain disease exists, a complete skull x-ray series is also completed, along with a brain scan.

If any significant abnormality is discovered, the physician will likely choose another treatment method. However, in some cases, such as chronically suicidal patients, a physician may decide that the need for the treatment outweighs the potential risks involved.

The 1985 National Institute of Mental Health Consensus Panel on ECT also recommended that ECT be limited primarily to treating depressed patients. Depressed patients, patients with involutional melancholia, and manic-depressive patients seem to be most effectively treated with ECT. These same patients are the ones who are most likely to experience significant guilt feelings and to be anxious and worried. Because they may have heard inaccurate and terrifying stories about ECT, and because of the real dangers that have been explained to them by their physician, these patients are often extremely anxious about having ECT treatments. They require a considerable amount of support and encouragement from the staff. They will likely need to spend a good bit of time just talking about the procedure. This affords them the opportunity to explore their anxieties and feelings openly with a staff member who is familiar with the procedure and who can be friendly, informative, supportive, and attentive. Thus, pre-ECT care and support are vital aspects of the total treatment procedure.

Below are some questions frequently asked by persons who are to receive ECT treatments. We have provided a possible answer to each question, but one should remember that the answer given is by no means the only appropriate answer. Answers may also vary in order to comply with the rules and procedures of a particular institution.

Will I feel any pain?

The only discomfort you might feel would be from the shot that will be given to you immediately prior to the treatment. You will not feel the electricity, and you will not remember anything that happens. You may feel some muscle stiffness for a few hours after the treatment, but usually a warm bath and a little exercise will make you feel much better. Some patients have a post-ECT headache that lasts for a few hours.

Will I die?

No. There is some risk associated with any treatment procedure, but this treatment is safe because we take a great deal of care to be sure that you are able to tolerate the treatment.

Is there a possibility that I could be electrocuted?

It is not possible for you to be electrocuted. The machines used produce only a very small amount of electrical current, and it is not enough to electrocute you.

How many treatments will I have to take?

The number of treatments you will receive will depend on what your doctor thinks is best and on the progress you make after each treatment. Usually between 8 and 12 treatments are used.

Will I lose my memory?

People usually do not remember the treatment itself and may be confused for a few hours or even a few days after ECT treatments; however, there is rarely any permanent memory loss, and you will probably remember everything that you want to remember within a few days to a few weeks after treatment.

Will my mind be ruined?

No. Most people are able to do things as well or better than they could before the treatment. You may be confused immediately following the treatment, but the confusion will go away within a short period of time.

PROCEDURAL GUIDELINES

Presented below are the major tasks that need to be accomplished when a patient is to receive ECT. These are general guidelines, and the particular policies and procedures of each institution must be taken into account.

PRE-TREATMENT

1. At some point prior to the ECT treatment, written informed consent will have to be obtained from the patient. Legally it is the responsibility of the treating physician to explain the procedure to the patient and to be sure that any questions the patient might have are answered. The physician then has the patient sign a written consent form giving permission for the ECT treatment. An ECT treatment should never be administered without the patient's written consent except in the case of an involuntary admission. Even then, the laws for one's particular state should be checked regarding the legality of administering ECT without the patient's written permission.

2. Several hours before the ECT treatment, the patient's chart should be checked to see that all laboratory work, x-rays, and pre-treatment procedures have been completed.

3. The patient will need to be NPO (without food or water) for at least 8 hours before treatment. This should be carefully explained to the patient. If the patient is at all confused or is disoriented or noncompliant, monitoring may be necessary to insure that the patient remains NPO. Sometimes when a patient is ambivalent about receiving ECT, that ambivalence is expressed in efforts to sabotage the NPO rule, thus delaying the onset of treatment. If you suspect this is a problem, it likely means the patient has not been properly emotionally prepared for the treatment.

4. The patient should be given ample opportunity to ask questions and express anxieties. It is important to keep in mind that the patient is likely to be quite anxious and upset prior to treatment and may ask the same questions several times. Members of the treatment team must be supportive during this period and patiently answer any questions a patient might ask, regardless of how many times the question is repeated.

5. Just prior to the treatment, ask the patient to void. This will help to reduce any discomfort and embarrassment the patient might experience from becoming incontinent during the treatment. All watches, rings, hairpins, jewelry, and so forth should be removed from the patient and placed in a valuables envelope. Such items may cause burns or may be lost during or after the treatment procedure. Post-ECT confusion prevents many patients from remembering what

they did with their valuables. Care should be taken to protect their valuables and to reassure them that they are not lost.

6. All objects that are removable should be taken from the mouth (e.g., chewing gum, bridges, or dentures). This is to prevent the patient from aspirating these items during the treatment. Contact lenses should also be removed.

7. Pre-ECT medication is administered by the member of the treatment team responsible for that particular task. It is important that this medication be the accurate amount and that it be given as close to the time specified by the order as possible. The patient may complain of a dry mouth.

TREATMENT

1. All equipment to be used during the treatment should be carefully checked to make sure it is available and functioning properly. This includes the ECT machine, oxygen equipment, the emergency cart, and any emergency trays that might be necessary in case complications occur during the treatment. The patient should be accompanied to the treatment room and asked to lie on the stretcher or operating table where the treatment is to be given. The safety straps should be secured. The straps should be snug enough to keep the patient from falling from the table but loose enough to allow for slight movement when the seizure occurs. Some institutions may require the patient to wear a hospital gown during this procedure.

2. The patient's temporal area, where the surfaces of the electrodes will be placed, should be cleaned prior to treatment. Treatment may be administered by applying electrodes to either one or both temporal areas, depending on the physician's choice of technique. Since cleansing solutions may vary, check your institution's procedure manual for specific instructions. Usually a special paste is applied to the skin of the temporal area in order to keep the electrodes from burning the skin when the electrical activity occurs. After the treatment, this paste will need to be removed with warm water to keep it from caking on the patient's hair and skin.

3. After the operative medication is administered, an airway of some type is generally put into the patient's mouth in order to assure that the patient will continue to have an open airway.

4. A physician should administer the shock. As soon as the electrical current hits the brain, the patient will have a grand mal–type seizure. Thanks to the use of muscle relaxants and anesthesia, the seizures are generally very mild. However, two health workers should be present to help hold the patient on the stretcher or table if the need arises. Care should be taken not to constrict the patient's move-

ments any more than is necessary to insure that the patient does not hurt himself or herself by either a self-inflicted blow or by falling off the table.

5. After the patient has regained consciousness and the physician has determined that the patient is having no difficulty breathing, the patient should be removed to a recovery area. Someone should stay with the patient at all times until he or she is fully conscious.

POST-TREATMENT

1. After the patient has regained consciousness and is able to stand up and move about, a warm bath or mild exercise may help relieve soreness in muscles and joints. The patient should also be given a light breakfast—such as coffee, juice, and toast—because of being NPO for several hours prior to treatment. Many physicians routinely request that 10 grains of aspirin be given as soon as the patient is fully recovered. This is done to relieve post-ECT headaches.

2. The patient may be confused after ECT treatments and thus require a great deal of supervision, assistance, and reassurance. Answer any questions and be as supportive and attentive as possible.

3. Sometimes, even after one or more treatments, the patient may be very uncertain of himself or herself and may develop or retain anxieties about having ECT treatment. In such cases, continual reassurance, support, and attentiveness will be necessary in order to help the patient deal with anxieties about ECT treatments.

ANNOTATED BIBLIOGRAPHY

DeVane, C.L., Lim, C., Carson, S., Tingle, D., Hackett, L., and Ware, M.: *Effect of electroconvulsive therapy on serum concentration of alpha-1-acid glycoprotein.* Journal of Biological Psychiatry, 1991, 30:116–120.

> *Research study examining the effect of ECT on alpha-1-acid glycoprotein and the potential effect this may have on patients receiving both ECT and cyclic antidepressants for treatment of depression.*

Douyon, R., Serby, M., Klutchko, B., and Rotrosen, J.: *ECT and Parkinson's disease revisited: A "naturalistic" study.* American Journal of Psychiatry, 1989, 146(11):1451–1455.

> *Research study examining the possible therapeutic effects of ECT on Parkinson's disease.*

Hertzman, M.: *ECT and neuroleptics as primary treatment for schizophrenia.* Journal of Biological Psychiatry, 1992, 31:217–220.

> *Discusses the advantages of ECT as a treatment for schizophrenia and its use in conjunction with neuroleptics.*

Krystal, A., Weiner, R., Coffey, C., Smith, P., Arias, R., and Moffett, E.: *EEG evidence of more "intense" seizure activity with bilateral ECT*. Journal of Biological Psychiatry, 1992, 31:617–621.

> *Research study testing the ability to separate unilateral and bilateral ECT seizures in order to better characterize seizure generalization, which may be an important factor in the determination of adequacy.*

Scott, A., Gow, S., Garden, W., Shering, P., and Whalley, L.: *Repeated ECT and prolactin release in depressed patients*. Journal of Biological Psychiatry, 1992, 31:613–616.

> *Research study testing prolactin release over a course of ECT in depressed patients who were not receiving neuroleptic drugs in order to evaluate whether prolactin release lessens over the course of ECT treatment.*

True or False. Circle your choice.

T   F   1. ECT is a simple procedure with no risks involved.

T   F   2. Legal consent is not necessary from the patient before ECT is administered.

T   F   3. It is necessary for the patient to go without food or water for 8 hours before an ECT treatment.

T   F   4. When the electric current reaches the brain, the patient will have a petit mal–type seizure.

T   F   5. After an ECT treatment, a patient may be confused and need a great deal of supervision, assistance, and reassurance.

T   F   6. If a patient seems very embarrassed about removing dentures before an ECT treatment, it is all right for the patient to leave the dentures in rather than suffer embarrassment.

Short Answer. Answer the following questions as briefly and specifically as possible.

1. Give two commonly expressed theories as to why ECT is effective.

    _____

    _____

    _____.

2. Why is an ECG completed before the patient receives ECT treatment?

    _____

    _____

    _____.

3. Which psychiatric diagnostic category seems to show the best improvement after receiving ECT?

    _____

    _____.

4. Why is it necessary to remove dentures, bridges, and so forth from the patient's mouth prior to ECT?

    _____

    _____

    _____.

172

Multiple Choice. Circle the letter or number that you think represents the best answer.

1. Mrs. Jones is a patient who is scheduled for shock treatment. Ms. Smith, a student nurse, becomes very anxious and is unable to help with the treatment. What mental mechanism is at work?
   a. Identification.
   b. Denial.
   c. Regression.
   d. Suppression.

2. Which of the following physical complications never occurs as a result of electric shock therapy?
   a. Dislocated jaw.
   b. Compression fractures.
   c. Respiratory arrest.
   d. Electrocution.
   e. Cardiac arrest.

3. ECT is most effective in the treatment of:
   a. Depression.
   b. Neuroses.
   c. Catatonic schizophrenia.
   d. Personality disorders.
      (1) a and b.
      (2) a and c.
      (3) b and c.
      (4) All of the above.

4. An appropriate approach to a patient complaining of amnesia following ECT is to:
   a. Explain that forgetting is the usual reaction and memory will clear up after the treatments are finished.
   b. Help the patient remember those things that have been forgotten.
   c. Tell the patient that the amnesia will subside in a few hours.
   d. Tell the patient that the amnesia is selective and he or she will not forget important things.

5. If Mr. Brown is treated with convulsive therapy, the nurse should:
   a. Take measures to prevent physical injury, especially fractures.
   b. Provide a secure pre-treatment and post-treatment environment.
   c. Monitor vital signs.
   d. Remain with the patient during his confused state.
   e. Assure him that he will not notice any memory loss.
      (1) a and c.
      (2) c, d, and e.
      (3) a, b, c, and d.
      (4) All of the above.

Other Therapies

LEARNING OBJECTIVES

Student will be able to:
1. List and briefly define talk therapies.
2. Define behavior modification.
3. List several advantages and disadvantages of behavior modification.
4. Define auxiliary therapies.

TALK THERAPIES

Psychotherapy, as talking therapy is generally called, can be done either on an individual basis or in groups and may be under the direction of a physician, clinical psychologist, or other therapist. In any case, the aim of the therapy is the same, that is, to help patients gain understanding and/or insight into their problems so that they can learn to deal with them more effectively. Psychotherapy may be used in conjunction with drug therapy, electroconvulsive therapy, art therapy, recreational therapy, and occupational therapy. Frequently a combination of two or more types of therapy will yield best results.

Although there is a great deal of argument about the effectiveness of psychotherapy, and for that matter many other forms of therapy, it is probable that three things are necessary for an improvement in the patient's ability to cope with the stresses of life. First, patients must want to get better. Second, patients must come to a better understanding of what is causing their problems and in turn learn methods or techniques for dealing more effectively with them. Third, an environment in which it is possible for change to take place must be provided.

In many cases, the third task is the most difficult one to accomplish. In the hospital, most treatment teams are successful in creating a therapeutic environment in which desirable changes can occur. How-

175

ever, when the patient goes back home to a nonsupportive environment, it often happens that the best insight and the best treatment available are insufficient to overcome the adverse effects of the patient's environment. In such cases, family therapy is advisable. Otherwise, it is quite probable that the patient will have to return for further treatment, and even then the patient's issues may never be resolved without family treatment.

As a member of a treatment team, one needs to support and reinforce the efforts of the team members who are responsible for individual or group psychotherapy. The skills and techniques presented in Chapter 8 should be helpful in developing support skills for the talking therapies.

BEHAVIOR THERAPY

Behavior therapy is a term used to specify a particular kind of treatment wherein no claim is made to do anything other than change or modify the behavior of the patient. For this reason, it has been called simplistic by many of its critics.

Essentially, behavior therapy consists of deciding which behaviors exhibited by a particular patient are desirable and which are undesirable and then trying to increase the frequency of the desirable behaviors and eliminate or decrease the frequency of the undesirable behaviors. This method of treatment has been particularly effective in the treatment of children and mentally retarded persons.

There are advocates and critics of behavior therapy. The movie *A Clockwork Orange* presented both the capabilities of behavior therapy and some of its drawbacks. In this movie, a young sociopathic person (one who engages in extremely antisocial acts and who demonstrates no remorse for immoral, unethical, or illegal acts) was conditioned, using behavior therapy techniques, against responding to anything in a hostile or sexual way. He had been a very hostile young man who had beaten and mugged several persons and sexually assaulted several others. After he was conditioned not to react to any stimulus in a hostile or sexual manner, he was returned to his community. Of course, because he was unable to respond in a hostile manner, his former enemies and even his friends quickly began to take advantage of him. In the end, he was taken back and deconditioned because of the public uproar over the treatment he had received. Members of his community considered the conditioning technique to be barbaric and inhumane. This points out the fact that just because a particular technique works, it may not be fully used because of social pressures.

Basically, conditioning operates on the idea that people will behave in ways that get them what they want. Each of us responds in this manner every day of our lives. For example, you are reading this book because you wish to gain more knowledge about the subject matter. It may be that you need this knowledge to obtain a degree in some particular area, to get a better job, to be a better mental health worker, or simply because you are curious about the treatment of the mentally ill. You would not be reading this book if it would not help in some way to get you something you want. Factory workers who work 40 hours a week at jobs they find boring usually do so because working at the factory gets them the money they need to obtain other satisfactions in life. Such conditioning factors operate in our lives in other ways. If a 4-year-old realizes that in order to get mother's attention she must lie down on the floor and kick her heels and scream at the top of her voice, she will then engage in that type of behavior whenever she wants her mother's attention. The same is true for the young man who goes to medical school, not because he wants to be a doctor, but because it gains him the approval he so desperately wants and needs from his parents. Sometimes an individual engages in self-destructive behavior in order to gain some apparently superficial end; yet that end has a great deal of meaning to that individual. The idea, again, is that people behave in ways that get them what they want, although they may not always be aware of the long-term consequences of the behavior or even aware that their behavior often appears inappropriate to other people.

In behavior therapy, an effort is made to ascertain which behaviors exhibited by an individual are desirable and which are undesirable, and then to selectively reward the desirable behaviors and ignore the undesirable ones. This is done to increase the desirable behaviors and decrease the undesirable behaviors. Little thought is given to the causes of the behavior or to the dynamics of the behavior in the traditional psychotherapeutic sense. Behaviorists will not ask why a patient is hostile, because hostility is not a concept with which they are willing to deal. Rather, they ask in what behaviors they wish the patient to engage. They want to know what *behaviors* make the patient appear hostile. Behavior therapists argue that the patient only seems hostile because he or she is engaging in certain behaviors and that if the patient were to cease to engage in those behaviors, he or she would not be called hostile.

While some rather astonishing behavioral changes can occur in a relatively short time, this method of treatment has some definite limitations. To begin with, a great deal of control is required over the patient's behavior. It is necessary to be able to control the environment in such a way as to prevent unwanted reinforcement or rewarding of certain behaviors and to be certain that the desired behaviors are rewarded. There is also the problem of maintaining the frequency of the desired behaviors once the patient leaves the controlled environment and the systematic application of reinforcement is no longer possible.

THE AUXILIARY THERAPIES

It has been said that humans are social creatures and therefore that they must respond to a wide range of situations. In order to meet the demands of today's complex and ever-changing society successfully, we must indeed possess a good capacity for flexibility. By and large, mentally ill patients have developed maladaptive ways of responding to their environments and thus, to some extent, lose their social adaptability. Their range of interests and activities becomes quite constricted, and they may or may not lose contact with reality. In general, these patients experience some degree of personality disorganization.

In order to assist mentally ill patients in their attempts to interact effectively with other people again, occupational, art, recreational, adventure, and music therapists provide a wide range of activities. These activities require patients to become involved in something outside themselves, thus affording them less time to dwell on their problems. These activities also require interaction with the therapist and possibly with one or more other patients who are also in the treatment program. If patients are given interesting and challenging projects at a level of difficulty that is appropriate for them, they benefit from their participation. By having to collect their thoughts, organize their actions, and act on their own initiatives, they can be led to become active once again in their own lives as well as the lives of their families and friends. The successful completion of projects can enhance the patients' self-concept and afford the patients a sense of pride or accomplishment that often has been lacking for quite some time. Success also tends to encourage patients to respond to their environment and the people in it in a more healthy fashion.

Not all patients are delighted about the opportunity to participate in such therapeutic activities. Often they prefer to remain in their rooms or to engage in some solitary activity. It is important that they be gently, but firmly, encouraged to participate in therapeutic activities. If patients receive repeated invitations to join the group and are not rejected when they refuse to participate, they may later become more willing to join in such activities. Frequently patients do not wish to participate because they have experienced so many failures; they are certain that they will only fail again. Their anxieties should be taken into account and an effort made to understand them. As is generally the case with mentally ill persons, a great deal of understanding, reassurance, and patience are required in order to help patients feel comfortable enough to engage in any new activity.

It is always important to be certain that once patients agree to participate, they are not expected to engage in some activity that is likely to cause them to be humiliated in front of others or in which they are likely to fail. Activities must be carefully selected and expectations kept in line with their capabilities. If at all possible, conferences among the various members of the treatment team, including those from the various auxiliary therapies, should be held to discuss the patient's progress, treatment goals, capabilities, and needs.

Perhaps the most important thing to keep in mind regarding the various therapeutic activities is that these auxiliary therapies should provide patients with an opportunity to relax, to engage in something that is enjoyable, and to experience a break in the regular therapeutic routine. It should be a time of fun for patients, and patients should be encouraged to participate as freely and as spontaneously as possible.

ANNOTATED BIBLIOGRAPHY

Bond, M.: *Setting up groups: A practical guide.* Nursing Standard, 1991, 5(48):47–51.

> *Describes the concepts and methods used in establishing two distinct types of support groups.*

Bowers, J.J.: *Therapy through art: Facilitating treatment of sexual abuse.* Journal of Psychosocial Nursing and Mental Health Services, 1992, 30(6):15–24.

> *Describes the use of art therapy to help sexually abused patients to access traumatic memories. Includes a case study.*

Buxman, K.: *Humor in therapy for the mentally ill.* Journal of Psychosocial Nursing and Mental Health Services, 1991, 29(12):15–18.

> *Describes the use of humor in a psychiatric setting to promote communication and social interaction and to relieve tension and anxieties in patients.*

Forisha, B., Grothaus, K., and Luscombe, R.: *Dinner conversation: Meal therapy to differentiate eating behavior from family process.* Journal of Psychosocial Nursing and Mental Health Services, 1990, 28(11):12–16.

> *Describes the use of meal therapy with patients with eating disorders to evaluate family dynamics and to work through the meanings that family members have evolved into a system.*

Glaister, J.A.: *The art of therapeutic drawing: Helping chronic trauma survivors.* Journal of Psychosocial Nursing and Mental Health Services, 1992, 30(5):9–17.

> *Describes the use of therapeutic drawing in working with severely traumatized patients. Provides case examples and an explanation of what the patient was trying to express in the drawing.*

Hamer, B.A.: *Music therapy: Harmony for change.* Journal of Psychosocial Nursing and Mental Health Services, 1991, 29(12):5–7.

> *Discusses the successful use of music therapy to strengthen ego, increase socialization, decrease psychotic symptoms, and increase activity in low-functioning patients.*

Hundley, J.: *Pet project: The use of pet facilitated therapy among the chronically mentally ill.* Journal of Psychosocial Nursing and Mental Health Services, 1991, 29(6):23–26.

> *Discusses the benefits of using pets in therapy and offers information on implementing pet-facilitated therapy in an inpatient setting.*

Kreidler, M.C., and Carlson, R.E.: *Breaking the incest cycle: The group as a surrogate family.* Journal of Psychosocial Nursing and Mental Health Services, 1991, 29(4):28–32.

> *Examines the use of the group to help incest survivors work on healing issues and deal with unresolved family issues.*

Zerhusen, J.D., Boyle, K., and Wilson, W.: *Out of darkness: Group cognitive therapy for depressed elderly.* Journal of Psychosocial Nursing and Mental Health Services, 1991, 29(9):16–21.

> *Research study examining the benefits of nurses facilitating cognitive group therapy with nursing home residents suffering from depression.*

True or False. Circle your choice.

T F 1. Basically, behavior modification uses the idea that people behave in ways that get them what they want.

T F 2. Mentally ill patients to a large extent have lost their social adaptability due to their maladaptive ways of responding to their environment.

T F 3. It is the mental health worker's responsibility to see that all patients participate in every activity and not allow excuses from anyone.

T F 4. Occupational therapy is an important measure in the treatment of the psychiatric patient because it offers a means whereby the individual may achieve a feeling of accomplishment.

T F 5. If you were using behavior modification with a patient with poor table manners, you would just accept these manners without comment.

T F 6. Behavior modification is especially helpful in the treatment of children and mentally retarded persons.

Short Answer. Answer the following questions as briefly and specifically as possible.

1. What three things are essential for an improvement in a patient's ability to cope with life's stresses?

   a. _____.

   b. _____.

   c. _____.

2. Which of the above three tasks is the most difficult to accomplish?

   _____.

   _____.

3. What is the primary purpose of psychotherapy?

   _____.

   _____.

   _____.

181

Multiple Choice. Circle the letter or number that you think represents the best answer.

1. Which of the following will probably be most likely to get Mr. Cartwright, a patient on a behavior modification ward, to change his eating habits:
   a. Accept his table manners without comment.
   b. Urge him to eat as the other patients do.
   c. Offer him a reward for each improvement in his table manners.
   d. Point out to him that his eating habits distress the other patients.

2. Limits should be set:
   a. To help patients reduce their anxiety.
   b. To help patients learn to control their behavior.
   c. To establish the authority of the staff over the patients.
   d. To punish inappropriate behavior.
   e. To protect people and property from injury.
   (1) a, b, and e.
   (2) a, b, and c.
   (3) b, d, and e.
   (4) All of the above.

3. Steps and techniques involved in setting limits are:
   a. Identifying the need for the limits.
   b. Helping patients understand the need for the limits.
   c. Allowing patients to verbalize their feelings about the limits.
   d. Consistency.
   e. Evaluating the limits frequently.
   (1) a, c, and e.
   (2) b, c, and d.
   (3) a, b, and d.
   (4) All of the above.

4. Which of the following are advantages of group therapy?
   a. Gives the therapist a chance to supply authoritative answers to problems common to the group.
   b. Provides for the resolution of problems through group discussion and discovery of possible solutions.
   c. Gives the mentally dull an opportunity to reason and form judgments through group interaction.
   d. Allows the therapist to interact with several patients at one time so that they all have access to professional counseling.

5. Occupational therapy is an important measure in the treatment of psychiatric patients because it primarily:
   a. Offers poor patients an opportunity to pay for part of their care by selling items they make.
   b. Provides an opportunity to keep patients active.

    c. Offers a means whereby individuals may achieve a feeling of accomplishment.

    d. Offers an opportunity to observe the patients.

6. A therapeutic health-promoting environment for patients (milieu therapy) provides for:

    a. A testing ground for new patterns of behavior.

    b. Acceptance as individuals.

    c. Unconditional acceptance of behavior.

    d. Protection from self-injury.

    e. A continuous appraisal of patients' needs.

        (1) b.

        (2) b and c.

        (3) a, b, and d.

        (4) All of the above.

7. Which of the following is (are) true about psychotherapy?

    a. The aim of psychotherapy is to help the patient learn new patterns of behavior.

    b. Psychotherapy refers to a certain type relationship between one or more patients and a therapist.

    c. In family psychotherapy, the therapist treats only the neurotic or psychotic family member.

    d. Group therapy, psychoanalysis, and counseling are three common types of psychotherapy.

        (1) b.

        (2) b and c.

        (3) a, b, and d.

        (4) All of the above.

Therapeutic Approaches to Specific Populations

12

Care for Aggressive Patients

There are several groups of behaviors commonly associated with the aggressive patient. These include verbally abusive behavior, agitated or destructive behavior, demanding behavior, lying and stealing, fighting, arguing, irritating behavior, and finally, uncooperative behavior. It is important to keep in mind that although patients behave in an aggressive manner for various reasons, the management of the behavior is generally the same. The specific behaviors usually associated with the aggressive patient are presented individually and discussed in some detail below.

VERBALLY ABUSIVE BEHAVIOR

Patients usually become verbally abusive because of frustrating circumstances that are beyond their control. They then displace the anger and frustration to family, other patients, or staff members. Many verbally abusive patients have developed this pattern of behavior in response to their belief they are going to be rejected. In an attempt to reject before they can be rejected, they become quite hostile to others. Thus others respond to their hostility in a like manner and a vicious, self-defeating cycle begins. This pattern is often referred to as a self-fulfilling prophecy. In order to break this cycle, it is imperative that staff members not respond to a patient's verbal aggression in a punitive, hostile, or rejecting manner.

Therapeutic treatment for verbally aggressive patients often hinges on the ability of staff members to recognize that in most cases these patients do not mean anything personal by their abusive remarks. They are simply displacing their frustration and anger from the object or situation creating those feelings to the staff member. The ability to express negative feelings can be a healthy sign. It may also indicate that patients feel that the staff is capable of accepting the abuse and can deal with it in an effective manner. It also may mean that patients feel comfortable enough to express their frustrations because they know that if they lose control of themselves, the staff will take non-punitive steps to help them regain control. These patients need to be accepted as they are, and staff members must try to understand what the patient is saying from the patient's point of view. When limits must be set, it is important that the limits be on the patient's actions and behaviors, not the patient's feelings. The verbal expression of aggression is an important outlet for the frustrations and tensions that these patients feel.

A key to managing these types of patients is to teach them how to find more socially acceptable ways of expressing their frustrations. Sometimes it is difficult to discourage a particular behavior without appearing to be rejecting, and sometimes the behavior may be so aggressive that it cannot be tolerated. In such cases, it may be necessary to actually tell a patient that although the staff still accepts and cares about him or her as a person, they are not willing to accept the verbally abusive behavior. Judgmental, moralistic, or disparaging remarks about the patient's behavior will typically only make matters worse.

Staff members should be careful not to let patients draw them into arguments. Any time staff members argue with patients, the patients win. Aside from the fact that patients will feel that they have "one up" on the staff member who has lost his or her temper, the staff member has provided an inappropriate role model for the patient. In many instances, patients are not able to use good judgment or act in a rational manner. Staff members, however, are expected to show good judgment, restraint, and socially appropriate behavior. One of the most important therapeutic tools that staff members have is their own behavior. If they provide an acceptable behavioral model, patients are likely to benefit by being able to identify with staff members and pattern their behavior accordingly.

Because verbally abusive patients are quite upsetting to other patients, staff members need to remain calm and controlled when patients have emotional outbursts. If possible, accompany such patients to their rooms or to a more isolated area. There the staff member can reassure and calm the patient while allowing the patient time to regain control. Many patients are later embarrassed by their outbursts and may resent the staff for having permitted them to engage in behaviors that make them look bad in front of their fellow patients. Do not press patients for an explanation of their behavior when they are upset. It is usually more effective to give them time to calm down so that they will be able to discuss their situation in a more rational manner.

When patients become so upset that they have difficulty regaining control, they should be given their prn (*pro re nata*, "as needed") medications. The dosage should not be enough to heavily sedate the patient, just enough to permit resumption of the ability to relate to staff members who are trying to help. When the patient is calm, the staff member can explore the kinds of responses the patient would likely encounter if the same behavior had occurred in everyday life situations. The staff member then has the opportunity to help the patient consider other ways of dealing with the feelings that caused the emotional outburst and the aggressive behavior. By discussing the negative results of previous outbursts, the patient may gain insight about the need for changing his or her behavior.

Finally, staff members should analyze their own response to these patients. If they have any negative or hostile feelings toward a particular patient, they should try to find effective ways of coping with those feelings. It is sometimes helpful to discuss such feelings with a fellow staff member or supervisor. Psychiatric patients are sensitive to the attitudes of others, and a staff member's negative feelings may cause a patient to become even more abusive because of feeling rejected.

VIOLENT, AGITATED, OR PHYSICALLY DESTRUCTIVE BEHAVIOR

There are probably few places that the old adage "an ounce of prevention is better than a pound of cure" applies more than in dealing with patients who are violent, agitated, or physically destructive. Violence usually occurs only when a patient feels threatened and unable to do anything else. Perhaps the most important single factor in dealing with such patients is to learn to recognize danger signals or behaviors that indicate that the patient is about to become agitated or violent. When the conditions are likely to lead to the patient's becoming upset and combative, it is usually wise to use the patient's prn medications and to try to remove the patient to an area where violent behavior could be more easily handled. Frequently, when patients are isolated with only one staff member, they are less prone to be physically assaultive. This is the case because the patient is not stimulated by other patients who are becoming upset and by having a large number of people milling around trying to decide what to do. Patients usually calm down much more quickly when they do not have an audience.

Once such patients are in a quiet area and have been given any needed prn medications, they should be encouraged to talk about their anger and to discuss the reasons they became violent. As with verbally abusive patients, it is also important to explore with patients alternative ways of expressing their anger and hostility and to help them explore similar kinds of behavior or incidents that might have occurred in the past.

Perhaps one of the most detrimental ways to approach patients who become upset and potentially combative is to try to "manhandle" or physically coerce them without giving them an opportunity to accompany a single individual, on their own, to a quieter, more secluded place. Frequently, when patients are very upset, the simple act of a staff member's taking their arm or touching them is sufficient to cause them to lose control completely. Therefore it is probably best never to touch patients who are agitated or out of control until all other approaches have failed. Threatening patients with various forms of punishment—such as shots, locking them in the seclusion room, restraining them to the bed, or other such punitive acts—will further increase their agitation. If a staff member can approach potentially combative patients in a nonthreatening, calm, reassuring manner and if the staff member does not appear to be afraid of such patients, it is likely that the staff member will be able to relate to them in an effective manner. Arguing with agitated patients or otherwise irritating them will practically insure their loss of control. One should try to reduce the patient's perception of threat—not increase it.

With patients who tend to be physically abusive or combative, it is frequently helpful to explain to them very clearly and directly what behaviors are expected of them and then to verbally praise and support them when they make an effort to engage in the expected behaviors. It is especially important that staff members be consistent in their expectations of patients and in reinforcing the expected behaviors. If patients are told that a particular consequence will follow a particular behavior, then it is of utmost importance that the behavior be dealt with in the way the patients were told it would be. Otherwise, patients cannot learn to trust the staff and may be tempted to engage in certain undesirable behaviors just to see if they can get away with them. At the very least, patients may feel that they are unprotected and unsafe and that the staff is not actually in control of the unit.

Another important way of helping patients learn to deal with their physically abusive or combative behavior is to confront them with it and help them understand its inappropriateness. This should never be done at the height of patients' agitation, but rather after the patients have had time to calm down and can be fairly rational in looking at their behavior.

If all efforts to calm violent or destructive patients fail, it will be necessary to physically control their behavior. This is done only to protect the patients themselves, other patients, or staff members, or to prevent the destruction of property. Even in these cases, only the minimum force necessary to control patients should be used. Staff members should use force carefully, but as quickly and efficiently as possible. If a patient has become violent, first remove all other patients and unnecessary staff members from the area. Then collect enough staff members so that there is no doubt about who is going to win the confrontation. Sometimes this will further agitate a patient, but is necessary to assure the proper outcome. At least five people are needed: one for each arm and leg and one to give general assistance. One person should be in charge and receive instant response from the other staff members. Pillows, towels, or blankets may be wrapped around staff members' arms to reduce the force of blows and avoid injury from objects that are thrown. From that point on, the proper procedure is to get the patient off his or her feet and, as gently as possible, placed face down on the floor. Every effort should be made to accomplish this without injuring the patient. Some authorities suggest restraining a patient using the patient's clothing. Others suggest that when the patient's limbs are used to restrain him or her, they should be grasped near the major joints. This should reduce the patient's leverage and thus the likelihood of severe injury to staff involved in restraining the patient.

When the patient is under staff control, the person in charge should decide whether to give a prn medication and whether mechanical restraints are necessary. If mechanical restraints are used, care must be taken to see that they are not unnecessarily uncomfortable for the patient. They should be removed as soon as the patient regains control, and the patient should be told that this is what will happen. Other patients who might have been involved should be reassured and given an opportunity to express their feelings about the incident. The staff should then discuss the incident and try to find ways of preventing future recurrences. In most states it is also necessary to have a physician's or psychologist's order to apply physical restraints. When possible, get the order before initiating the takedown. If the takedown is done in an emergency situation, then call the attending physician immediately after completing the procedure.

DEMANDING BEHAVIOR

One of the most difficult patients to deal with is the passive, whiny patient who constantly seeks a particular staff member's attention and who demands support and reassurance from that person. Such patients frequently become annoying in their demands because nothing the staff member does is enough. First they want their shaving kit, and then they want their toothpaste, and then they want their shoe polish, and then they want their medicine, and then they want to talk, and then they want to make a telephone call, and on and on. Frequently such patients will seek to control all of a particular staff member's time, unconsciously or irrationally believing the amount of time spent with the staff member is an indication of their worth as a person. In other words, such patients' feelings of worth are directly related to how much contact they are able to establish with the staff. Usually, a staff member will find it impossible to attend to all assigned duties if constantly required to deal with a demanding patient. It is more helpful both to the staff member and to the patient if a structured program can be developed wherein the patient is guaranteed access to the staff member at certain times and the staff member makes frequent but brief contacts with the patient at times that are convenient for the staff member. In this way the staff member takes the initiative for the contacts away from the patient, which encourages the patient to be more adaptable in delaying immediate gratification of his or her dependency needs.

Sometimes the most effective thing a staff member can do is ignore the patient who makes constant demands. It is important, however, that the staff member not show annoyance or anger toward the patient. It may be necessary at times to confront such patients with the fact that their behavior is inappropriate and to help them understand that it is necessary to learn other ways of meeting their needs. Frequently patients do not realize that they are unrealistically demanding and are not aware of the effect their behavior has on other people. Verbal reinforcement should be given to patients when they show independent activity and when they are able to meet their need for attention in acceptable ways.

LYING AND STEALING BEHAVIOR

Managing patients who lie and steal is among the most frustrating of all mental health tasks. Frequently, it is difficult to ascertain whether or not a patient is actually guilty of lying or stealing. When confronted with such behaviors, patients are likely to become quite agitated and upset.

One of the reasons that these behaviors are troublesome is that they often involve other patients. For example, one particular patient may steal from other patients, thus irritating and upsetting them, or a patient may lie about a staff member or another patient to a third patient, upsetting and irritating the patient who has been lied about.

If a staff member is certain that Mr. Smith lied or stole something, it is probably best to simply confront him with the behavior rather than asking whether or not the behavior occurred. Asking about the occurrence of the behavior gives Mr. Smith more opportunity to get into trouble because he feels compelled to deny the behavior. The patient later may feel resentful that the staff member caused him to further compound his lies when the staff member was already aware of the truth.

In confronting patients with lying or stealing, it is important to be as nonpunitive and as accepting of them as possible while rejecting the *inappropriate behavior*. If these patients are aware that other patients and staff members know that they have a problem with lying or stealing, they may be encouraged to stop the behavior. It is also important to ask these patients to restore any property that may have been taken and to explore with them the reasons for the lying or stealing. Frequently, it is important to discuss with patients the inappropriateness of such behaviors and the potential consequences of such behaviors in the environment outside the treatment center. Patients should be encouraged to verbalize appropriate behaviors and to explore the effect these behaviors have on their feelings about themselves. It is important to confront patients at a time when other patients will not be able to observe the confrontation. Such confrontations should not be humiliating to patients. Staff behavior that is judgmental or moralistic is inappropriate, and trying to reason with patients on religious grounds is not an effective means of dealing with lying or stealing.

ANTAGONISTIC, INTIMIDATING, OR PHYSICALLY ABUSIVE BEHAVIOR

As in dealing with patients who are likely to become physically abusive, one of the most important things to be done in preventing fights among patients is to recognize potential situations or conditions that are likely to cause patients' tempers to flare. It is also important to recognize personality conflicts among certain patients. Patients who have conflicts might be kept busy doing things that will not bring them into frequent contact with each other. Further, the staff should not permit patients who are likely to have conflicts to engage in activities that might cause their basic personality differences to be exaggerated or that puts them into competition with each other.

If a fight does occur, it is important to separate the participants and to refrain from taking sides unless the staff member observed blatant aggression on the part of one of the patients. The same is true for verbal arguments between patients. If the patients are actually involved in a physical fight, it is important to separate them so that each patient can be dealt with independently. If at all possible, remove the patients to separate areas and away from any audience. If sufficient staff members are not available to physically separate the patients, then a staff member who realizes this might attempt to distract the patients in some way. When appropriate, humor, asking patients to help the staff member with some task requiring some skill the patient possesses, telling the patient he or she needs to go immediately to the lab for tests, or some other distraction may be employed. After the patients have calmed down, it might help to have a therapeutic confrontation, letting the two patients sit down with a staff member to discuss what upsets them about each other. It is sometimes helpful to explore the patients' feelings about themselves as well as their feelings about the other patient. The staff member might then be able to help both patients understand their conflict and to suggest alternative ways of dealing with their feelings about each other. Sometimes patients who have been antagonistic toward each other become good friends once they understand the differences that exist between them and the reasons for their behavior.

One of the most effective things that can be done to help avoid fighting and arguing is to plan a program of activities which will not permit the patients so much free time that they become bored. Group therapy for patients may be used to settle disagreements among patients before they reach the stage of serious arguments and fighting. Again, it is important that staff members provide good role modeling for the patients. Role playing is also sometimes helpful. A staff member may play the part of one or the other of the patients when dealing with patients who have been separated after a serious argument or fight. The staff member would then respond in a manner that would be appropriate if the staff member were actually the other patient. Sometimes it helps to have patients switch roles with each other after they have had time to calm down.

Perhaps one of the most serious staff errors is to ignore or to accept behavior from a particular patient that is known to be annoying or upsetting to other patients. It is also important to remember that a staff member should not intervene in a constructive argument that is being appropriately handled by the patients involved.

UNCOOPERATIVE BEHAVIOR

In the case of uncooperative patients, it is important to be aware of the patient's diagnosis because in some cases a patient is significantly psychologically regressed and is not being intentionally uncooperative. In other cases, patients are uncooperative for what seems to them a legitimate reason. Some of these reasons include being afraid of hospitalization, of medications, or of unusual treatments (such as electroconvulsive shock treatments). One of the least constructive things to do is to approach such patients in a threatening manner and to threaten them with punishment if they do not obey orders or if they do not do what is asked of them. The patient's reasons for being uncooperative should be explored. The staff member should be reassuring and use a kind but firm approach. If a staff member calmly explains the reason patients are being asked to follow directions, they will usually comply. It is almost always detrimental to try to force patients to do anything. Try not to have an audience when asking patients to do things. An audience often makes patients feel they must resist for the benefit of the audience, particularly if the patient has established himself or herself as a "black sheep" among the patients. Because a little humor goes a long way with patients, it can be used to avoid authoritative "orders" that may cause argumentative patient behaviors that sometimes lead to more serious conflicts. A staff member with a smiling face who approaches a patient saying "This little pill is demanding to be swallowed immediately" may get more cooperation than one with a serious face saying "You have to take this medication right now."

It is sometimes necessary to make patient privileges dependent on cooperation with the staff. Within reason, patients must learn to live in accordance with unit policy and regulations. Whenever possible, however, patients should be given a choice of one or more alternatives. Giving patients a choice permits them to maintain a feeling of independence, lets them remain responsible for their behavior, and reduces resentment to complying with requests. When patients do not have a choice in the behavior requested, do not play verbal games with them. For example, if Mr. Smith has to take a certain medication, do not ask him if he would like to take his medicine. In asking that question, one leaves oneself open to a confrontation because Mr. Smith can simply say, "No, I don't want to take my medication." In such situations, it is better to say, "Mr. Smith, it's time to take your medicine. Would you rather have it with water or juice?"

Mentally ill patients will often test the limits set by staff members. Highly manipulative patients especially need to know that the staff is in charge of the unit and that inappropriate behavior will not gain them extra attention or special privileges. They need to know that they are expected to participate in ward activities, work assignments, and therapeutic activities. If patients do refuse to comply or are uncooperative, it is important that they not be rejected by staff members. Such patients should not be made to feel that staff members have a personal dislike for them or that they are annoyed or angry with them. Instead, the staff should stress that the patient is liked and accepted but that the uncooperative behavior is not acceptable.

While it is important to be firm in gaining patients' cooperation with the behaviors expected of them, it is also important to recognize that occasionally a patient has a legitimate reason for not cooperating and understanding is necessary when patients balk for good reason.

SEXUALLY AGGRESSIVE BEHAVIOR

Patients who are sexually aggressive seem to be especially upsetting to many mental health workers. Sometimes this is related to the staff members' moral beliefs. However, personal beliefs must be set aside when treating patients who are mentally ill. While it is not necessary to condone sexual misconduct, it is vitally important that a noncondemning, nonjudgmental approach be used with sexually acting-out patients. Some staff members may be frightened of sexually aggressive patients and may fear for their personal safety. Good unit management requires that such feelings be considered in setting staffing patterns and even in deciding whether a particular patient is appropriate for the unit. Staff members also need to avoid being alone around patients with known sexual acting-out tendencies.

Mentally ill patients have the same basic sexual needs as healthy individuals, but they often find that appropriate outlets (husband or wife, boyfriend or girlfriend) for these needs are far removed, especially when the patient has been hospitalized for a long period of time. In some cases, patients feel too unattractive, too insecure, or too inadequate to find someone with whom they might develop an intimate relationship that might lead to appropriate sexual activity. In other cases, patients have such poor interpersonal relationship skills that they alienate appropriate potential sexual partners. The sexual frustration such patients feel often causes them to engage in inappropriate sexual activities, such as establishing fleeting sexual relationships with other patients or making sexual advances toward staff members. Staff members need to discuss with these patients the inappropriateness of their actions, set limits on their acting out, and try to arrange for appropriate outlets. Very often, the simple arrangement of a weekend pass for a married person will eliminate such inappropriate behavior. Other patients, especially adolescents, have not yet learned how to handle their affectionate and sexual feelings in socially acceptable ways. With adolescents and other patients who have sexual problems, it is important that staff members be firm but supportive when inappropriate behavior occurs. If the behavior cannot be therapeutically ignored, the patient should be confronted and encouraged to discuss the behavior. If it is possible, the behavior might be temporarily ignored until the staff can have an opportunity to discuss the behavior and plan the patient's care accordingly. Motivational considerations other than sexual attraction may need to be evaluated. Sexual behavior may be exhibited by a patient as a way of getting a staff member's attention or as a way of embarrassing a staff member who has caused a patient to feel slighted in some way. It may also be a way of testing limits or of seeking reassurance that inappropriate behavior will be controlled by the staff. Finally, one must consider the possibility that such behavior is motivated by a patient's fear of rejection. Thus the patient tries to provoke anger in an attempt to confirm rejection and reduce the anxiety of unconfirmed rejection.

Staff members must be careful that their warm, friendly, accepting attitudes toward patients do not become seductive. If Mr. Smith does mistake Miss Jones's warmth and acceptance for love or sexual feelings, he may begin to act out sexually toward her. If this occurs, Miss Jones should try to remain calm and say, "Mr. Smith, I like you as a person but it makes me uncomfortable when you say you love me or when you try to touch me." If the behavior persists, Miss Jones should first be sure that her behavior toward the patient is not subtly encouraging him and then firmly tell him, "Mr. Smith, I have tried to be nice about this but you won't let me; your behavior is inappropriate and must stop." If the patient persists further, Miss Jones should ask her supervisor to assign someone else to work with the patient.

Patients do not often act out sexually toward staff members, but when they do, the behavior must be dealt with firmly and with the patient's being able to perceive as little as possible of the staff member's anxiety.

ANNOTATED BIBLIOGRAPHY

Blair, D.T.: *Assaultive behavior: Does provocation begin in the front office?* Journal of Psychosocial Nursing and Mental Health Services, 1991, 29(5):21–26.

Explains how factors such as involuntary admission, dementia or organic brain disorder, staff attitude, denial of the possibility of assault, and the educational level of the staff can all contribute to an assaultive episode.

Blair, D.T.: *Assaultive behavior: Know the risks.* Journal of Psychosocial Nursing and Mental Health Services, 1991, 29(11):25–29.

Discusses the scope and incidence of violence in a psychiatric setting. Also reports on the risk factors, prediction, intervention, and staff members' role in provoking the assaultive behavior.

Blumenreich, P., Lippmann, S., and Bacani-Oropilla, T.: *Violent patients: Are you prepared to deal with them?* Postgraduate Medicine, 1991, 90(2):201–206.

> *Presents information on the signs of impending aggression, how health care workers can prevent or minimize the chance of attack, when to use seclusion or restraint, and intervention methods for dealing with violent patients.*

Cahill, C.D., Stuart, G.W., Laraia, M.T., and Arana, G.W.: *Inpatient management of violent behavior: Nursing prevention and intervention.* Issues in Mental Health Nursing, 1991, 12:239–252.

> *Discusses the critical role of psychiatric nurses in inpatient settings in the management of potentially violent patients.*

Colenda, C.C., and Hamer, R.M.: *Antecedents and interventions for aggressive behavior of patients at a geropsychiatric state hospital.* Hospital and Community Psychiatry, 1991, 42(3):287–292.

> *Explores several aspects of violent behavior, what type of patient is most likely to become volatile, and how staff members may trigger aggression.*

Convit, A., Isay, D., Otis, D., and Volavka, J.: *Characteristics of repeatedly assaultive psychiatric inpatients.* Hospital and Community Psychiatry, 1990, 41(10):1112–1115.

> *Research study examining the relationship between repeatedly violent behavior and gender, age, and diagnosis.*

Monahan, J.: *The prediction of violent behavior: Toward a second generation of theory and policy.* American Journal of Psychiatry, 1984, 141(1):10–15.

> *Discusses the limitations to predicting violent behavior in psychiatric patients and offers possible improvements in predictive technology.*

Murray, M.G., and Snyder, C.: *When staff are assaulted: A nursing consultation support service.* Journal of Psychosocial Nursing and Mental Health Services, 1991,29(7):24–29.

> *Discusses work with violent patients and nursing support services for those who have been assaulted.*

Stevenson, S.: *Heading off violence with verbal de-escalation.* Journal of Psychosocial Nursing and Mental Health Services, 1991, 29(9):6–10.

> *Presents therapeutic communication as a means of altering the course of the aggression cycle before the patient's behavior becomes violent.*

Swanson, J.W., Holzer, C.E., Ganju, V.K., and Jono, R.T.: *Violence and psychiatric disorder in the community: Evidence from the epidemiologic catchment area surveys.* Hospital and Community Psychiatry, 1990, 41(7):761–770.

> *Examines the relationship between violence and psychiatric disorders in nonhospitalized adults.*

True or False. Circle your choice.

T F 1. The key to managing aggressive patients is to teach them to find more socially acceptable ways of expressing their frustrations.

T F 2. It is appropriate and necessary for a staff member to argue with a patient if the staff member is right and the patient is definitely wrong.

T F 3. A staff member's own behavior is often his or her most therapeutic tool.

T F 4. Staff members should not press patients for an explanation of why they behaved in a certain manner.

T F 5. Patients usually become violent only when they feel threatened and unable to react in another manner.

T F 6. Generally, touching agitated patients tends to have a calming effect on them.

T F 7. Sometimes the most effective approach a staff member can have toward patients who make continuous demands is to ignore them.

T F 8. It is often necessary to physically force patients to comply with rules when they are resistant.

T F 9. An effective approach for dealing with hostile patients is to accept their feelings without indicating approval, disapproval, or value judgments.

Multiple Choice. Circle the letter or number that you think represents the best answer.

1. In dealing with a hostile patient, staff members should:
   a. Understand that hostility is the result of a basic character defect.
   b. Be aware of their own reactions to the expressed hostility.
   c. Avoid reacting defensively toward the patient.
   d. Set limits on the patient's behavior.
      (1) a and b.
      (2) b and c.
      (3) b, c, and d.
      (4) All of the above.
2. Effective approaches for dealing with hostility include:
   a. Recognize the patient's feelings of hostility.
   b. Allow the patient to set the pace in the establishment of staff-patient relationships.

199

    c. Accept the patient's feelings without indicating approval, disapproval, or value judgments.

    d. Convey to the patient that it is wrong to feel hostile.

    e. Plan approaches to meet the patient's individual needs.

       (1) a, b, and c.

       (2) b, d, and e.

       (3) a, b, and e.

       (4) a, b, c, and e.

Situation: Mrs. Jones tells you in a loud, angry tone of voice that she is very irritated by the incompetencies of the medical and nursing staff. You say, "You sound angry." Mrs. Jones says, "Wouldn't you be angry if you had to fight for everything you get?" The next two questions apply to this situation.

   3. What would be your most supportive response to Mrs. Jones?

    a. "Yes, I guess I would."

    b. "Tell me about the things that are irritating and make you feel angry."

    c. "The doctor and nurses are trying to help you. Please cooperate."

    d. "You'll have to learn to control your anger."

   4. What would be your most nonsupportive response to Mrs. Jones?

    a. "Yes, I guess I would."

    b. "Tell me about the things that are irritating and make you feel angry."

    c. "The doctor and nurses are trying to help you. Please cooperate."

    d. "You'll have to learn to control your anger."

   5. Mrs. White, a staff member, has been talking to a patient; and as she gets up to leave, he puts his arms around her and tries to kiss her. She should:

    a. Kick him in the groin.

    b. Tell him his behavior is inappropriate.

    c. Tell him that she is going to tell his wife if he does not stop.

    d. Tell him that his behavior makes her uncomfortable and ask him to stop.

Short Answer. Answer the following questions as briefly and specifically as possible.

   1. If a staff member is certain that a patient has stolen an article from another patient, how should the staff member handle the situation?

_____

_____.

2. What is one of the most effective ways to keep patients from fighting and arguing?

_____

_____

_____.

3. When does a patient usually resort to physical violence?

_____

_____

_____.

4. Why is it a good idea to try to isolate patients who appear to be becoming physically destructive?

_____

_____

_____.

13

Care for Anxious Patients

LEARNING OBJECTIVES

Student will be able to:
1. Differentiate between behavioral manifestations of anxiety seen in a healthy person as related to those behaviors seen in a mentally ill patient.
2. List techniques used in working with patients exhibiting compulsive behaviors and patients exhibiting phobic behaviors.

We have already talked about the fear and anxiety felt by many patients. Constant, excessive worry and a high level of physical tension are hallmarks of anxious patients, and many have specific phobias. A large number of patients show restless, somewhat agitated behavior, while others show compulsive, ritualistic behavior. They have a lot of "what if" concerns and a vague feeling that something bad is going to happen. (For a review of symptoms, see Chapter 5.) In practically all cases, the behavior associated with the anxious patient is aimed at reducing the subjective feeling of anxiety that the patient experiences. Anxiety tells the patient and the staff that something needs to be done and often initiates the fight-or-flight stress response in the patient. Another difficulty is that patients are often so anxious that they cannot make a decision. This may occur because the patient sees so many possible solutions that no single solution seems appropriate or "best" and the patient does not want to decide among the alternatives for fear of making the wrong choice. It may also be that the patient cannot find even one solution that is acceptable. Thus nothing is done and the anxiety continues. This chapter discusses many of the behaviors that might be expected from such patients and explores some ways of managing those behaviors. It should be understood that drug therapy is often used in conjunction with the management techniques presented here. Drug therapy is aimed at the physiologic components of anxiety, whereas psychotherapy is aimed at the cognitive and emotional components. One concern with anxiolytic medications is that many are addictive and the patient must be carefully withdrawn when the medications are discontinued after extended use.

It is often the case that anxious patients are upset by new and unfamiliar surroundings. They become more frightened, agitated, and sometimes withdrawn when they do not know what is expected of them and how they should behave. Uncertainty and conflict, often arising out of a fear of loss of control, are the primary causes of anxiety. Therefore, it is important that new patients who are anxious, worried, or upset be introduced to the unit by very carefully explaining what is expected of them, where they will sleep, how they will get meals, when the doctor will come, and what they should do if they need help. These patients frequently need someone to talk to them—to reassure them and simply to provide company. They may have many questions, some of which will be repeated more than once. These questions should always be answered carefully and fully, and patients should be reassured that someone will be available to help if they need anything. On an open unit, anxious patients can frequently be seen moving about searching for someone to talk to about their fears. It is important that staff members take time to talk to such patients and try to help them understand and recognize their fears. Patients can usually be helped to calm down by gradually easing them off the subject of a particular fear or worry and then getting them to talk about things that do not arouse their anxiety or fear and thus are not upsetting to them.

It sometimes happens that highly anxious patients are afraid of other patients on the unit. It may be helpful to introduce such patients to other patients on the unit and to encourage them to talk with some of the other patients. It is sometimes helpful to point out to the anxious patient that all the patients are there for the same reason—to receive help for their difficulties—and that the staff is there to see that everybody receives whatever help they need. Try to avoid situations in which one patient is called upon to express a view or opinion that may conflict with other patients' views.

Frequently, an anxious patient will become upset over something that has a great deal of importance to him or her but that may be of little or no importance either to other patients or to staff members. In such cases, it is helpful to the patient if some specific concession is made that will permit the patient to decrease his or her anxiety or fear by engaging in some particular behavior that would have a calming effect. For example, it is frequently the case that when such patients are about to go on leave or be discharged, they are quite afraid that no one will come to pick them up, and they may want to call their family to be reassured that someone is coming for them. Such patients might be quite relieved, and thus more calm, if allowed to call the family and reassure themselves that someone will come to pick them up.

Cognitive therapists often address anxious patients' tendency to catastrophize, to overvalue certain aspects of a situation, and/or to overestimate the probability of some event. They teach patients to realistically evaluate the probability of some event and to recognize their tendency to make a catastrophe out of something that is highly improbable. This is usually done not by directly challenging a patient's assumptions but rather, for example, by asking questions that point out the overestimation of the likelihood of an event. If the patient says, "I feel like I'm going to die!", the therapist might respond by saying, "I can see you're frightened. What is it you think will cause your death?" The therapist will then proceed through a number of questions that lead the patient to understand that he or she has catastrophized the situation, overestimated the probability of the occurrence, and based these assumptions on beliefs that are irrational. The therapist then will proceed to help the patient supplant the irrational beliefs with rational ones. Relaxation techniques are also often used to treat anxious patients, as is visual-imagery training and systematic desensitization.

RESTLESS, AGITATED BEHAVIOR

Patients who are restless are frequently reassured and calmed by having a mental health team member take them for a brief walk or simply take them to a quiet place and sitting down to talk with them. Usually, if agitated, restless patients are allowed to say what is on their minds, they are able to settle down more quickly and to feel more reassured. Unless patients are allowed to say what is on their minds and to express the things that are troubling them, a great deal of unnecessary angry and frustrated acting out may occur. For example, in one case three attendants were used to restrain one female patient who insisted on being allowed to go into another patient's room. Since nobody thought to ask why the patient wanted to go into another patient's room, she was simply told that she could go into her own room but not into the other patient's room. After a great deal of acting-out behavior and after the patient had been restrained by the three attendants, a nurse asked the girl why she wanted to go into the other patient's room. The patient explained that she had dropped her ring and it had rolled into the other patient's room. When the ring was retrieved, the patient calmed down and was released. The problem could have been prevented by simply asking the patient why she wanted to go into the room in the first place.

If patients are allowed to discuss their anxieties and feelings, much of the emotional pressure they feel seems to be relieved. This is particularly the case at bedtime for patients with anxiety problems. It is usually not a good policy to insist that patients go to bed whether or not they are sleepy. Frequently, patients who are forced to go to bed become quite agitated and restless and are much more likely to act out than if they are taken to a quiet area where they will not disturb other patients who may be trying to sleep. Such patients typically do much better when they are allowed to stay up for a little while and discuss their feelings with a staff member. As soon as the patients calm down, they may then be returned to their room and encouraged to try to go to sleep. Other patients may be able to go to sleep without leaving their rooms if a mental health team member will simply come and sit with them or if they are allowed to leave a light on. Sometimes patients will agree to going to bed if they are given some small favor, such as a glass of juice, a drink of water, a cup of decaffeinated coffee, or simply a chance to walk around for a few minutes before going to bed. Administration of prn medications should also be considered for such patients.

Occasionally, patients seem to become more anxious if staff members or other patients are friendly and supportive of them. In these cases, it is best to maintain a businesslike manner. Such patients need time to accept the idea that others can like them and be interested in them without expecting something in return.

COMPULSIVE BEHAVIOR

One form of anxious behavior that is sometimes difficult to control is compulsive behavior, which may or may not include ritualism. Patients engage in ritualistic behaviors in an effort to "prevent" something bad that they fear will happen. To a lesser degree, many people engage in similar behaviors when they follow superstitions: "Don't walk under a ladder," or "Breaking a mirror means 7 years of bad luck," or "It's bad luck if a black cat crosses the road in front of you." The major problem with compulsive behaviors is that they significantly inhibit a patient's ability to lead a normal life. Some patients carry their ritualistic behaviors to such extremes that they create significant physical problems. One of the most common ritualistic behaviors is that of hand washing. Some patients have been known to wash their hands more than a hundred times a day and continue to wash them despite the fact that their hands are cracked and bleeding from the soap and water and scrubbing. Some cannot leave the house without checking eight times to be certain the door is locked. Such patients should never be approached in a demanding and threatening way because such behavior will only increase the patients' insecurity and anxiety, thus creating more need for the ritualistic behavior.

For many compulsive or ritualistic behaviors it is possible to talk with patients about their behavior and encourage them to try other ways of controlling their anxiety. Sometimes it is possible to help patients begin reducing a ritual by leaving off one of the components of the ritual, and the next day leaving off another component, and the following day leaving off another component until the ritualistic behavior is eliminated. By trying to reduce the compulsive behavior a little at a time, the patient is permitted to adjust to the new conditions slowly rather than having to suddenly deal with all the anxieties that the ritual helped to control. Such treatment techniques should never be used except as part of an overall treatment plan directed, integrated, and controlled by a competent therapist.

It is never helpful to be critical of a patient's ritualistic behavior. It is important to remember that while the behavior may be quite silly to an observer, it has a very real meaning to the patient. The most important thing is to allow patients to know that they and their problems are accepted by the staff members. This usually does more to relieve a patient's anxiety than reassurance that "everything is going to be all right." The patient does not think things are going to be all right and feels rejected if that is all he or she is offered in the way of reassurance. Instead of saying, "Don't worry so much" to a patient, say "I can see that you are upset about this. Why don't we talk about it?" Other reassuring statements include "You seem to feel hurt about Mrs. Jones saying she hates you; let's talk about it" or "Let's talk about why you believe people don't like you" or "I've noticed you always wring your hands and seem upset when your mother calls." Such statements give patients an opportunity to talk if they want to. It is not useful, however, to insist that they talk when they obviously do not want to. More often than not, patients like to talk and a staff member who listens well will be highly valued by patients. The information you gain from listening to the patient may provide valuable cues to the treatment team and should always be reported there.

PHOBIC BEHAVIOR

Phobic patients have specific fears or anxieties and may become quite upset, frightened, or agitated when confronted with the phobic or feared object. Frequently these patients seek reassurance by asking repeatedly whether or not one will be able to help, whether or not they are going crazy, and whether or not they are going to be able to recover from their illness. Perhaps the best reply to such requests for reassurance is to simply tell the patient that you will be happy to talk with the patient about problems any time you are free. The patient may also be told that talking about problems is often the best way to begin solving them.

In managing anxious patients, it is most important that staff members remain calm and restrained. Anxious patients frequently try to provoke anxiety in staff members. If they are successful then, they feel their own anxiety is justified. If they are not successful, then they tend to be reassured. When anxious patients perceive uncertainty or conflict among staff members or other patients, they are likely to respond by becoming even more anxious themselves.

ANNOTATED BIBLIOGRAPHY

Barth, F.D.: *Obsessional thinking as "paradoxical action."* Bulletin of the Menninger Clinic, 1990, 54:499–511.

> *Offers an integration of theoretical approaches to obsessive-compulsive neurosis and attempts to explain the resistance frequently encountered with these patients using Schafer's theory of obsessional thinking as a paradoxical or conflictual action.*

Kercher, E.E.: *Anxiety.* Psychiatric Aspects of Emergency Medicine, 1991, 9(1):161–187.

> *Offers a definition of anxiety, information on prevalence, DSM-III-R classification, theories of anxiety, clinical manifestations of anxiety and management of anxiety in a treatment setting.*

Simoni, P.S.: *Obsessive-compulsive disorder: The effect of research on nursing care.* Journal of Psychosocial Nursing and Mental Health Services, 1991, 29(4):19–23.

> *Discusses the importance of paying close attention to behaviors, feelings, and cognitions when treating patients with obsessive-compulsive disorder.*

Wesner, R.B.: *Alcohol use and abuse secondary to anxiety.* Psychiatric Clinic of North America, 1990, 13(4):699–713.

> *Discusses the prevalence and complications of using alcohol to overcome feelings of anxiety. Offers case examples and treatment plans.*

Whitley, G.G.: *Ritualistic behavior: Breaking the cycle.* Journal of Psychosocial Nursing and Mental Health Services, 1991, 29(10):31–35.

> *Explores biological theories of causation and the use of behavioral and medication therapy as treatments of choice.*

True or False. Circle your choice.

T F 1. Anxious patients are frequently upset by new and unfamiliar surroundings.

T F 2. Phobias are unusual in truly anxious patients.

T F 3. Anxious patients' ritualistic behavior is aimed at reducing their objective feelings of anxiety.

T F 4. Uncertainty and conflict are the primary causes of anxiety.

T F 5. Anxious patients should be encouraged not to talk about their fears because they are unrealistic.

T F 6. Agitated, restless patients should not be allowed to say what is on their mind because they may upset other patients.

T F 7. It is a good policy to insist that patients go to bed whether they are sleepy or not.

T F 8. Sometimes a friendly, supportive staff member can cause a patient to become more upset and anxious.

T F 9. Excessive hand washing is a sign of anxiety.

T F 10. The most effective way to discourage ritualistic behavior is to gently criticize the behavior to the patients. This will allow patients to recognize that their behavior is not helping and that it makes them look bad in front of others.

Multiple Choice. Circle the letter or number that you think represents the best answer.

1. An anxious patient:
   a. Feels threatened by unknown danger.
   b. Is unable to concentrate.
   c. Displays indecision.
   d. May make many demands for attention.
      (1) a and c.
      (2) b and d.
      (3) a, b, and c.
      (4) All of the above

2. The characteristic that distinguishes fear from anxiety is that fear:
   a. Usually has a specific object.
   b. Evokes a milder degree of emotion.
   c. Persists over a longer period of time.
   d. Occurs in the absence of real danger.

209

3. Which of the following are characteristic of anxiety:
   a. Feeling of helplessness.
   b. Reaction to evident danger.
   c. Reaction to future danger.
   d. Many attempts to alleviate by use of defense mechanisms.
   e. Leads to a neurosis if not halted.
      (1) a, b, and d.
      (2) a,.c, and e.
      (3) a, c, d, and e.
      (4) c, d, and e.
      (5) All of the above.

4. The individual suffering from normal anxiety:
   a. Is able to focus on what is happening.
   b. Is able to recognize and face the threat realistically.
   c. Sometimes uses mental mechanisms for relief.
   d. Hears voices.
      (1) a.
      (2) a and c.
      (3) a, b, and c.
      (4) All of the above.

5. Reassurance can be given to anxious patients by:
   a. Remaining calm and confident with them.
   b. Guessing what the patients are worried about and getting them to talk.
   c. Giving correct information when patients need it.
   d. Remaining with them.
      (1) a.
      (2) a, c, and d.
      (3) c and d.
      (4) b, c, and d.

6. A characteristic of anxiety is:
   a. Feeling of helplessness.
   b. Anticipation of pleasure.
   c. Decrease in muscular tension.
   d. Relationship to specific objects.

Situation: Mary, age 18, an honor student at Haven College, is admitted to the hospital during exam week in a state of extreme anxiety. She tells the staff member that if she flunks out, she will not be able to go to medical school as her parents want her to. The next two questions apply to this situation.

7. As Mary and the staff member enter the day room, Mary tries to break away and appears terrified of the group of patients. The staff member should take the following action:

   a. Gently steer Mary to her own room and stay with her.
   b. Call for the orderly to drag Mary away forcibly.
   c. Talk quietly and calmly to Mary as they proceed to her room.
   d. Warn Mary she will he put in restraints if she does not behave.
      (1) a.
      (2) b.
      (3) a and c.
      (4) b and d.

8. The next day Mary is calmer. She tells the staff member how disappointed her parents will be if she flunks. The staff member should:
   a. Tell Mary that her parents will surely love her anyway.
   b. Allow Mary to explore her feelings about this.
   c. Advise Mary to study hard so she can pass.
   d. Ignore the remark.

9. When Mr. Brown has an anxiety attack at night and refuses to remain in his room because he is afraid, you should:
   a. Explain that there is nothing to be afraid of.
   b. Let him sit out in the hall by the nurses' station.
   c. Leave a light burning in his room.
   d. Place him in seclusion room.

10. Which of the following responses is most appropriate in relation to a patient who is pacing the halls, wringing her hands, and crying?
   a. "You seem all upset right now, but I'm sure you won't feel this way much longer."
   b. "Sit here a minute and I'll get your nerve medicine."
   c. "I'll stay with you; perhaps I can help."
   d. "Sit down a while; you'll feel better in a little while."

11. The primary defense mechanism used against anxiety is:
   a. Reaction formation.
   b. Denial.
   c. Suppression.
   d. Compensation.
   e. Repression.

14

Care for Suspicious Patients

In addition to the fearfulness and distrustfulness shown by suspicious or paranoid patients, there is a tendency for such patients to be quarrelsome and aloof. Such behaviors often evoke a great deal of anger in other patients and staff members. This leads to rejection of the suspicious patients, causing them to respond with hostility and confirming their negative expectations about interpersonal relationships. Such patients, therefore, feel ill at ease in interpersonal relationships and tend to interpret minor oversights as significant personal rejections. In fact, they often find slights or injustices where none exist. They are likely to overreact to seemingly insignificant occurrences and are unable to control their feelings and their behaviors in situations where restraint and understanding are appropriate responses. Such patients are frequently overconcerned with fairness and with being certain that they are treated as everyone else is treated.

Projection is the major defense mechanism used by paranoid patients. Many of us without significant mental illness resent in others what we are afraid of in ourselves, and we may or may not have much insight into that tendency. However, without realizing it, paranoid patients project their own hostility and aggressive impulses onto other people. The projection causes the patients to perceive hostility and rejection from others. Thus the patients become fearful, agitated, and overly concerned about their rights. Because they see themselves as the focal point of everybody's behavior, they interpret anything that happens in their environment as having special meaning for them.

Another point to remember in understanding paranoid patients is that they frequently show good ego strength. That is, they appear to be capable people and feel they do not need to rely on anyone other than themselves. They tend to be opinionated, stubborn, and defensive and to react with hostility when their opinions are challenged.

Dealing with suspicious or paranoid patients requires a considerable amount of diplomacy. It is not in the best interest of the patient or the staff member to argue. In an argument, paranoid patients may perceive that they must defend their position and will feel quite self-righteous about venting their hostility, anger, and frustration. They tend to believe that they are defending their position for the benefit of humankind, thus justifying their unreasonable anger.

Paranoid patients sometimes try very hard to get staff members on their side because they see staff members as authority figures. If they succeed, they feel their position is justified. Again, a great deal of tact and preparation is necessary in order to manage this situation effectively. If staff members tell patients that they do not agree with the patients' position, those staff members are inviting an argument that they will almost always lose. They will lose because such patients usually have an extreme commitment to their position and reasoning, by definition, is lost on the irrational patient. On the other hand, making an appropriate interpretive statement may encourage patients to talk and provide an opportunity to move them to an area where their anger and frustration can be vented in privacy. For example, if an angry patient shouts, "You had better not touch me!", it would probably be best to respond by saying, "All right, John, I won't touch you if it bothers you; can you tell me what bothers you about being touched?" rather than saying, "I don't intend to touch you" or "I will touch you if I have to" or "Don't be so afraid of being touched." The first suggested response leaves room for the patient to talk about his reasons for not wanting to be touched and for the staff member to take an opportunity to enter into a discussion with him. This might later lead to the establishment of a relationship in which that patient might learn to trust the staff member.

Because a basic sense of worthlessness and inadequacy underlies much of the paranoid patient's behavior, it is usually not helpful to use flowery language, flattery, or an overabundance of praise in an effort to improve the patient's poor self-concept. It is difficult to "convince" most patients of their worth, but it is particularly difficult to persuade a suspicious patient of increased worth. In grandiose patients, such staff behavior may reinforce the patients' feelings of grandiosity and may at best be inappropriate therapy for them. A staff member also runs the risk of having paranoid patients reject such verbalizations outright, thus breaking off the potential for establishing therapeutic relationships.

Staff members and patients alike are frequently intimidated or made to feel extremely uncomfortable when suspicious patients appear to be visually locked in on them. The "paranoid stare" occurs when patients stare intently, trying to observe everything that is occurring in their environment. The fact is that such patients miss very little. For example, when staff members or others look away from staring patients, the patients sometimes feel that others are afraid of them or that they cannot stand the scrutiny of such a righteous person. If a staff member is in a visual confrontation with a paranoid patient, it is best not to avoid the stare but to observe the patient closely for a brief period. The patient may then decide that the staff member is not afraid and is willing to pay close attention to what he or she has to say. A long staring duel may be avoided by staff members if they move quickly to distract the patient by suggesting some diversional activity or direct the patient's attention to a picture in a magazine or on the wall.

Paranoid patients seem to have a great many religious delusions. A staff member should listen quietly as the patients talk about their delusions and take the first opportunity to ask them to help with some particular task or to engage them in a more reality-oriented conversation. As little reference as possible should be made to the delusional concerns. Argument is inappropriate and useless because patients will feel compelled to defend their delusions.

Suspicious or paranoid patients have a strong fear of developing a close relationship with another person. This is related to their fear of being rejected, because patients can only feel rejection if close relationships are established. These patients are most likely to establish a relationship with a staff member who is honest and forthright. If Mr. Jones believes that you are going to hurt him, simply reassuring him that you are not going to hurt him will not allay his suspicions. However, if a staff member recognizes Mr. Jones's suspiciousness by saying, "I know you don't trust me and that's all right; I just want to talk," the patient may be helped to understand that he is not going to be rejected because he is distrustful.

Another way of managing a patient who presents outlandish demands or who demands acceptance of obviously delusional ideas is to say to the patient, "I know you believe you have a light bulb turned on inside your head, but I can't see it." To say anything more might lead to an argument the staff member could not win and might escalate the patient's anger. If pushed, one might say, "I know you believe it's true, but you wouldn't ask me to believe something I know nothing about, would you?" That last statement runs the risk of asking for a rational response from an irrational person, but all rationality is not always lost, even in people with irrational thoughts and beliefs. If you do not believe that, just look at some of our politicians!

A reason for not agreeing with patients' delusions is that patients frequently retain some contact with reality and will be quite mistrustful if they are able to convince the staff member that a delusion is true. If Mr. Jones has convinced the staff member of the truthfulness of his delusion, he may have enough rationality to know that the staff member may not be as mentally healthy as he is. In many cases patients' stories are close enough to rationality that it is difficult to know whether they are being truthful. For example, one of the authors once treated a patient who was convinced a family member was trying to steal money and property left to her by her father. She was so convincing the author had to advise that an attorney be brought in to evaluate the situation. In fact, she was right. Just because patients are irrational about one thing does not mean they cannot be rational about other things. Always try to verify things that are not obviously absurd. For example, it might be difficult to verify a delusion such as "I'm on a special mission to prepare the way for aliens from Mars; I'm a Martian princess and I own half of the land on the planet."

To sum up these last few comments, a rule of thumb may be appropriate: *Do not participate in a patient's mental games because you do not know the rules and therefore cannot hope to win.* Finally, it is important to realize that patients' suspiciousness and attentiveness to the things going on around them frequently make them a source of anxiety and provocation for staff members. A paranoid patient may make offensive, yet accurate, criticisms of staff members, unit policies, and unit procedures. It is of absolute importance that staff members not respond to these criticisms by becoming anxious or by rejecting these patients. This is a difficult lesson to learn. Paranoid patients are likely to be kind at some times and vicious at others. This inconsistency in behavior makes them difficult to manage successfully. It is the staff's responsibility to provide such patients with firm, consistent, supportive care.

ANNOTATED BIBLIOGRAPHY

Epstein, L.J.: *Paranoid illness in the elderly.* Consultant, 1980, 20(9):95–102.

> *Relates range of etiologic factors contributing to paranoid behavior in the elderly. Author states opinions on the goals of treatment.*

Hawes, M.J., and Bible, H.H.: *The paranoid patient: Surgeon beware!* Ophthalmic Plastic and Reconstructive Surgery, 1990, 6(3):225–227.

Provides a case example of a plastic surgeon's work with a patient with a paranoid disorder. Incudes suggestions for detecting and managing these patients.

Koontz, E.: *Schizophrenia: Current diagnostic concepts and implications for nursing care.* Journal of Psychosocial Nursing and Mental Health Services, 1982, 20(9):44–48.

Explores schizophrenia from the DSM-III multiaxial approach. Describes the various types of schizophrenia: disorganized, paranoid, catatonic, undifferentiated, and residual.

The Quality Assurance Project: *Treatment outlines for paranoid, schizotypal and schizoid personality disorders.* Australian and New Zealand Journal of Psychiatry, 1990, 24:339–350.

Presents treatment outlines for paranoid, schizotypal, and schizoid personality disorders using advice from expert committees, review of the literature, and the opinions of practicing psychiatrists.

True or False. Circle your choice.

T F 1. Usually a patient's delusions have some basis in reality.

T F 2. It is therapeutic for patients to discuss their delusions at length.

T F 3. The paranoid patient is likely to be warm and kind one moment and then become very anxious the next moment.

T F 4. The major defense mechanism used by the paranoid patient is projection.

T F 5. Suspicious patients often interpret minor oversights as personal rejection.

T F 6. Since a basic sense of worthlessness and inadequacy underlies much of the paranoid patient's behavior, it is helpful to use flattery and a great deal of praise to improve the patient's self-image.

T F 7. Paranoid patients may have a great many religious delusions.

Multiple Choice. Circle the letter that you think represents the best answer.

Situation: Mr. White is a 49-year-old man who has spent much of his life drifting from place to place. He was admitted to the hospital because of extreme suspiciousness of others and visual hallucinations. The next four questions apply to Mr. White's situation.

1. Which approach by the staff would be the most threatening to Mr. White?
   a. Forthright and honest.
   b. Friendly and emotionally detached.
   c. Warm and nurturing.
   d. Permissive and reserved.

2. Mr. White is sitting quietly next to a staff member in the day room. He seems to be mumbling to himself. Which comment would best serve to get the patient's attention?
   a. "Tell me what you are thinking, Mr. White."
   b. "Why are you mumbling, Mr. White?"
   c. "I understand you are angry, Mr. White."
   d. "Let's look at this magazine, Mr. White."

3. You are talking with Mr. White and suddenly he says: "What are you asking me all this for? I've already told this to my doctor. I suppose you're trying to find out if my answers will be the same." Which of the following responses would be best?

218

a. "Why do you think I would do that?"
b. "I'm only trying to help you."
c. "It seems to you I've been prying."
d. "I'm sorry you feel that way. Let's talk about something else."
4. The chief mental mechanism Mr. White is using is:
a. Rationalization.
b. Reaction formation.
c. Projection.
d. Introjection.
e. Conversion reaction.

Situation: Mr. Green has voluntarily admitted himself to the state hospital on the urging of his physician. Mr. Green has lived alone most of his life and has no known friends. Recently, he had been phoning his neighbors, accusing them of "bugging" his house and plotting to kill him. The next two questions apply to this situation.

5. During the admission procedure, Mr. Green refuses to take off his clothes and get into bed. Which approach by the staff member would be most helpful at this point?
a. Get another staff member to assist in removing the patient's clothes.
b. Leave the room and send an orderly to undress the patient.
c. Find out why the patient does not want to undress.
d. Let the patient keep on his street clothes.
6. Mr. Green in angrily telling you about what people have been doing to him. Your best response is:
a. To say nothing.
b. "I don't blame you for being angry. That's a terrible thing for them to do."
c. "Why are you angry at me? I haven't done anything to you."
d. "It doesn't really make any sense, does it, that your neighbors would be doing this?"
e. "It must be difficult to feel all alone and threatened like that."

15

Care for Depressed Patients

LEARNING OBJECTIVES

Student will be able to:
1. Identify symptoms of depression.
2. List techniques for dealing with the depressed patient.
3. Identify different modes of treatment for depression.

Depressed patients are the patients who usually get the most sympathy from a therapeutic staff. However, if these patients' depression does not lift as treatment progresses, they may experience a great deal of rejection and hostility from staff members.

Depressed patients have such a multiplicity of symptoms and problems that effective management is difficult. These patients frequently have a decreased appetite, a significant weight gain or loss, a loss of interest in activities of daily living, difficulty sleeping, and many other physical problems. Usually, their self-esteem is poor and, when depression is severe, personal hygiene is neglected. Depressed patients are likely to be tearful, upset, and apathetic. Since their activity level is low, there is a predisposition to certain physical problems. Bedsores, skin rashes, boils, scalp infections, constipation, and nutritional deficiencies may occur. These problems may be reduced or prevented by attentive staff, although extra effort is required.

The treatment of depressed patients requires a great deal of careful observation and supportive therapy. Frequently the patients' lives are at stake because of suicidal feelings. These patients often have exaggerated feelings of guilt and believe that their life is not worth living. Sometimes their feelings of uselessness and worthlessness are such that they feel they do not deserve to live and would rather die. During this time, it is important to prevent these patients from destroying themselves while trying to help them understand that times and circumstances change, as does the availability of love objects, and that they may hope for a better situation at sometime in the future. Most depressed patients, however, are strongly oriented to the present and have very little wish to consider a future for themselves. They lose sight of the fact that things do change and seem to believe that things will always be as painful and hurtful as their current circumstances.

Inexperienced staff members sometimes allow themselves to become trapped by agreeing not to disclose a patient's suicidal thoughts. One should never agree to keep anything concerning a patient's welfare from other staff members or from the patient's physician. If, in reality, patients do not want the information known, it is unlikely they would share it with anyone.

It is important to recognize that depressed patients frequently deny their need for human company and for the support of persons in their environment. Although depressed patients may indicate that they do not want to talk and do not want company, they are usually comforted by someone's paying attention to them and by knowing that someone is willing to talk to them. This subtly bolsters their self-esteem and helps them to feel that they are worthwhile individuals. Even if patients do not appear to notice that a staff member is present, it is quite likely that they take comfort in the knowledge that someone cares enough to sit with them in their misery. If at all possible, patients should be encouraged to talk about their feelings and problems. Patients' verbalizations should be responded to in an understanding and nonjudgmental way. Patients should be supported in their efforts to talk about their problems and should be permitted to express their discomfort and hurt by crying if they feel the need to cry. Patients should almost never be told not to cry.

Sometimes a crying or weeping patient causes discomfort among staff members. A crying patient, however, will usually respond to a calm, soothing voice and an arm around the shoulders. Comments such as "Everything will be all right" and "The sun will shine tomorrow" are not comforting to these patients because they are not consistent with their feelings. Instead, depressed patients should be encouraged to talk about what makes them feel like crying. Comments such as "Would you like to talk about what is making you cry?" or "Something must be hurting you very much" may encourage the patients to talk. The idea is to focus more on the feelings than the content of what the patient is saying.

Depressed patients also suffer from sleep disturbances. They may require medication for sleep and may need to talk or sit with someone before they can calm their fears and become sleepy. In other cases, depressed patients may sleep 12 to 14 hours a day as a means of escaping from feelings of guilt and depression.

Because depressed patients have low activity levels, it is often necessary to encourage them to participate in a wide range of activities so that they may begin to reestablish social relations that have been ~~social~~ neglected. Involvement in as many activities as possible should be encouraged. This is particularly true of activities that will permit the establishment of social relationships, which increase patients' confidence and improve their self-esteem. Depressed patients usually need to begin to establish relationships on a one-to-one basis. As their condition improves, they should be encouraged to become involved in group interactions. Sometimes when depressed patients do not believe they can help themselves, they will willingly do things to help others. Such interactions may prove to be quite therapeutic.

Depressed patients should be encouraged to get out of bed, to go to breakfast, to go to all their meals, to make up their beds, and to attend to matters of personal hygiene.

Staff members can help depressed patients regain pride in their personal appearance by making sure that they are provided with clean, attractive clothing and that they are neatly dressed and well groomed. Family members should be encouraged to bring favorite articles of clothing or perhaps a new shirt or a new dress. Barbers and beauticians may be needed to help with improving patients' physical appearance. Staff members, however, should be careful not to overwhelm depressed patients with too many extravagances because the patients may respond by withdrawing further, believing they are not worthy of all the attention.

Small meals, selected from favorite foods and presented attractively, help to restore lost appetites and to improve nutrition. It may be helpful to sit with such patients at meals and to offer verbal encouragement. Sometimes it is necessary for staff members to feed severely withdrawn patients.

It is important not to be critical of the level of involvement that a patient might show in some particular activity. Proficiency will improve with regular exposure and a developing interest in the activity. In the beginning, praise and reinforcement for simply showing up at a particular activity is important, and any efforts made toward becoming involved in activities should also be praised. Frequently, efforts to get a particular patient involved in activities will require a number of attempts. Staff members should not become discouraged or irritated if patients will not respond immediately to their efforts. Persistence and kind, gentle persuasion will often result in the desired involvement. Force is not helpful. It will instead produce resentment or guilt feelings and more withdrawal. New patients especially need time to adjust to the clinic or ward routine and to learn what is expected of them.

On occasion, a crying, whining patient will become attached to a particular staff member and will make that staff member's life miserable. In such cases, it is helpful if other staff members approach that patient with suggestions for activities and with requests for assistance on some minor task. This encourages interaction with other staff members. Encouragement to become involved in activities that require spending some time doing something independently or with another patient is desirable.

It is likely that there will be a few patients who will remain withdrawn despite the intensive efforts of the staff to draw them out and to get them involved in activities. In such cases, visits at regular intervals by particular staff members enable these patients to look forward to having company. This should be done even if it results in no conversation or interaction with the staff members. During such visits, staff members might perform small tasks for the patient that let the patient know of their care and concern. If the patient is in bed, a staff member might smooth the bedcovers, quickly brush the patient's hair, or suggest some makeup, a change of bedclothes, or some other aspect of personal care. Without appearing overly cheerful, staff members can encourage a positive outlook on life and a discussion of activities that might interest the patient. Patients should be encouraged to attend activities that are of interest and even to attend some activities that may not be of interest but could simply help pass the time.

In talking with the depressed patient, a staff member might try a broad range of topics of possible interest. Usually even severely depressed patients are interested in something. The trick is to discover what that something is and then to use it to further the patient's interest in other activities.

It is critically important to remember that, although depressed patients may not show it, they want and are much in need of a relationship with another person. They are often afraid that they will not be able to fulfill their part of a relationship and thus are reluctant to become involved. Once they are involved, however, much therapeutic good can be accomplished.

Because depressed patients almost always have poor self-esteem, they may respond well to assisting staff members with minor tasks. This allows patients to feel somewhat special and important, thus improving their self-esteem. A patient may have a particular talent or characteristic that can be pointed to with respect and admiration by staff members and other patients. Ancillary therapy activities, such as art, occupational, recreational, adventure, and music therapy, frequently offer an opportunity for patients to do something that can be recognized and appreciated by both staff members and other patients.

Two other modes of treatment for depressed patients are medication and electroconvulsive therapy (ECT). Since both of these treatment modes have been discussed in detail previously (see Chapters 9 and 10), details are not repeated here. It is sufficient to say that they require special attention and must be taken into consideration in treatment planning for a given patient. It might be helpful to review these procedures when beginning to care for depressed patients.

ANNOTATED BIBLIOGRAPHY

American Psychological Association: *Prevalence of Depression and the Effectiveness of Psychotherapy in Ameliorating Depressive Symptoms*. APA, Washington, DC, 1991.

> *Research study examining the prevalence, cost to employers, and effectiveness of treatment of persons suffering from depression.*

Bieliauskas, L.A., and Lamberty, G.J.: *Simple Reaction Time and Depression in the Elderly*. Veterans Administration Medical Center and University of Michigan, Ann Arbor, 1991.

> *Research study examining the role of depression in psychomotor slowing and deficits in recall in the elderly.*

Hewitt, P.L., and Flett, G.L.: *Dimensions of perfectionism in unipolar depression*. Journal of Abnormal Psychology, 1991, 100(1):98–101.

> *Research study testing the hypothesis that self-oriented perfectionism, other-oriented perfectionism, and socially prescribed perfectionism are related differentially to unipolar depression.*

Joseph, S.G.: *Facing the darkness*. Insight, 1991, 12(2):25–31.

> *Discusses the combination of biologic, psychologic, and social factors contributing to depression in women.*

Swanson, B., Cronin-Stubbs, D., and Colletti, M.: *Dementia and depression in persons with AIDS: Causes and care*. Journal of Psychosocial Nursing and Mental Health Services, 1990, 28(10):33–39.

> *Discusses the importance of distinguishing depression from AIDS dementia complex and presents treatment plans for both disorders in order to promote the quality of life.*

Ugarriza, D.N.: *Postpartum affective disorders: Incidence and treatment*. Journal of Psychosocial Nursing, 1992, 30(5):29–36.

> *Divides postpartum depression into three distinct syndromes: postpartum "blues," postpartum psychosis, and postpartum depression. Discusses treatment issues surrounding each postpartum affective disorder.*

Zerhusen, J.D., Boyle, K., and Wilson, W.: *Out of the darkness: Group cognitive therapy for depressed elderly.* Journal of Psychosocial Nursing and Mental Health Services, 1991, 29(9):16–21.

Research study examining the benefits of nurses' facilitating cognitive group therapy with nursing home residents suffering from depression.

True or False. Circle your choice.

T F 1. Depressed patients usually have poor self-esteem.

T F 2. Often depressed persons feel so worthless that they feel they do not deserve to live.

T F 3. Depressed patients often convey a strong need for companionship.

T F 4. Upon approaching tearful, depressed patients, it is helpful to remind them that things will be better tomorrow.

T F 5. Depressed patients frequently suffer from sleep disturbances.

T F 6. A high activity level is often seen in depressed persons.

T F 7. A staff member caring for depressed patients should have a friendly, cheerful outlook in order to encourage the patients to feel the same.

T F 8. Two important modes of treatment of depressed patients are medication and electroconvulsive therapy (ECT).

T F 9. Depressed patients should be encouraged to talk about their feelings and problems.

T F 10. Depressed patients should not be encouraged to participate in activities but should be left alone to participate at their own pace.

Multiple Choice. Circle the letter or number that you think represents the best answer.

1. While planning activities for depressed patients, the staff member should understand that the patients need:
   a. Variety and challenge to lift them out of their depression.
   b. Competitive activities with the group.
   c. Activities that require exertion of energy.
   d. Simple and structured activities at first.

2. Which of the following are characteristic of depression:
   a. Early morning wakening.
   b. Good appetite.
   c. Lack of guilt feelings.
   d. Worse mood in the late afternoon.
   e. Enjoys life.
      (1) a and d.
      (2) a, b, and e.
      (3) c and e.
      (4) c, d, and e.
      (5) None of the above.

227

Situation: Thirty-five-year-old Mrs. Brown, a mother of three, part-time bookkeeper, and part-time cosmetics salesperson, was brought to the hospital by her husband. She had become progressively unable to sleep, eat, talk, or perform housework. She sat for long periods of time, smoking one cigarette after another, seemingly unaware of people or things around her. The next two questions apply to this situation.

3. Mrs. Brown's depression is probably the result of:
   a. Paralyzing fear.
   b. Conflicting responsibilities.
   c. Physical exhaustion.
   d. Internalized aggression.
4. The feeling Mrs. Brown is most likely to demonstrate during her depression is:
   a. Suspicion.
   b. Fear.
   c. Loneliness.
   d. Worthlessness.
5. An attempt to commit suicide is most likely to occur during which of the following phases of hospitalization?
   a. Immediately following hospital admission.
   b. At the point of deepest depression.
   c. When depression begins to lift.
   d. Shortly before hospital discharge.
6. Mrs. Adams expresses to a staff member that she is feeling depressed about the recent death of her father. Which of the following responses by the staff member would communicate understanding and acceptance?
   a. "I know just how you feel."
   b. "Everyone gets depressed when they lose a loved one."
   c. "This must be very difficult for you."
   d. "Try to think positive. He was ill only a short time and didn't have to suffer long."

16

Care for Suicidal Patients

LEARNING OBJECTIVES

Student will be able to:
1. Describe different treatment modes for dealing with the suicidal patient.
2. List steps to create a safe environment for the suicidal patient.
3. Define SIRS.
4. List therapeutic approaches to the suicidal patient in each of the SIRS categories.

In the United States, suicide is currently the tenth leading cause of adult deaths and the third leading cause of death among college students. Suicidal deaths persist despite the advent of psychotropic drugs, open-door hospitals, community mental health centers, suicide prevention centers and hot lines, and a significant increase in the number of professionals available to treat patients.

It has been estimated that more than 27,000 Americans die each year by their own hand. Alec Roy (1989), a suicide expert and researcher, reports that the Golden Gate Bridge in San Francisco is the number-one suicide site in the world. He further reports that about 75 people kill themselves every day, and many experts believe this figure is actually far below the number of suicides that occur. They reason that many suicides are made to look like accidents or that they are recorded as such in order to protect the feelings of surviving family members. It is also difficult, and sometimes impossible, to collect life insurance if the insured committed suicide.

For each completed suicide, estimates suggests there are 10 to 20 unsuccessful attempts. Statistics further show that men are more likely than women to succeed in committing suicide. The difference seems to be due to the fact that men and women choose different types of suicidal weapons. By using firearms, knives, poisons, rope (hanging), or automobiles, men end their lives in painful, violent ways that tend to be extremely lethal. Women seem to prefer drugs, often those that have been prescribed by their physicians. Since it takes quite a while for drugs to be absorbed from the stomach into the circulatory system, overdoses are often discovered and medical treatment provided before death can occur. This method also provides the opportunity for a change of mind by telling someone what has happened.

The possibility of suicide is higher for certain groups of people than it is for the general population, and there is some evidence that genetic factors may predispose people to suicide. In addition to the genetically vulnerable, these groups include persons who have previously attempted suicide, the terminally ill, the elderly, the alcoholic, the severely emotionally ill, persons in families who have successful suicides among members, and people who associate socially with persons who have made suicide attempts. Highly stressful situations and the availability of lethal weapons also increase the likelihood of a suicide attempt.

TREATMENT

ALL SUICIDE ATTEMPTS SHOULD BE TAKEN SERIOUSLY. Members of health teams sometimes find this very hard to do, especially if a person has made what seem to be several superficial suicide attempts. One may hear someone say, "Oh, they're just trying to get attention." This statement may be true to some extent, but it is therapeutically significant that someone is so starved for human attention as to resort to such drastic measures.

The human desire to be loved and to feel worthwhile is universal. Suicidal patients desperately wish to communicate and relieve their feelings of worthlessness, abandonment, rejection, helplessness, and hopelessness. Their inability to do so may result in a sense of rage or anger that they direct toward themselves. Something as temporary as losing one's job may create such momentary feelings of worthlessness that a person commits suicide. The anger is actually toward a world that is perceived as so unsupportive and uncaring that the solution may be to remove oneself from it. Shneidman (1986) reports that the most common reason for suicide is to seek a solution, the most common goal is a cessation of consciousness, the most common stimulus is intolerable psychologic pain, the most common stressor is frustrated psychologic needs, and the most common emotions are hopelessness and helplessness. Other motivational factors in suicide include identification with someone who has killed themselves, revenge, sacrifice, religious fantasies about joining a lost loved one, punishment of a jilting lover or for any number of acts against the suiciding person, and cult ideologies such as those of the followers of Jim Jones at Jonestown. In adolescents, family turmoil, loss of love objects, and physical and psychologic illness are leading causes of suicides. Data indicate that in the United States an adolescent commits suicide every 90 minutes.

Unfortunately, many suicidal patients do not realize that they are unhappy, depressed, or anxious. They may not be aware of the cause of their suicidal impulses or the fact that they need help. Frequently one finds in the pre-attempt history of the suicidal patient an overinvolvement in work, career, or love objects. For example, a young wife who merges her identity with that of her husband, thus losing her own sense of being a capable person, may attempt suicide if something happens to break up that relationship. Such overidentification frequently masks underlying feelings of worthlessness, insecurity, and inadequacy. To feel worthless is to feel unloved, unlovable, and unwanted. Self-esteem is reduced significantly.

Suicide attempts should be viewed as an effort on the part of the individual to communicate emotional pain and a need for help. They should also be taken as a signal that something is drastically wrong in the individual's life and that change and improvement are necessary if the person is to survive.

Available research indicates that the vast majority of patients who commit suicide have openly expressed their intention to kill themselves well in advance of the act. Many of these people have discussed their plight with friends and relatives. They may have been told that they should not have such thoughts or have been completely ignored and thus rejected. In fact, Shneidman (1986) says the most common interpersonal act in suicide is communication of the intention to commit suicide. Any time anyone reacts to suicidal patients in a rejecting manner, their desire to commit suicide may be increased since their feelings of worthlessness have once again been reinforced. Suicidal persons need someone with whom they can talk, someone willing to listen, and someone sincerely interested in their problems. Anyone with emotional or physical problems may be suicidal. This is especially true if the individual has suffered a recent loss, such as the death of a loved one, divorce, loss of a body part, or the loss of positive feelings of self-worth due to divorce, business losses, or the loss of a job. As mentioned earlier, terminally ill patients are likely to attempt suicide. This is especially true if they believe that their impending death is likely to be painful.

RECOGNIZING BEHAVIORAL CLUES

Depressed patients are a large group of potential suicides. Since they tend to stress physical complaints rather than suicidal ideas, the staff may overlook their suicidal potential. Thus, in order to help prevent suicides among such patients, one must pay particular attention to their emotional state. For example, if patients who have been agitated and upset suddenly become calm, outgoing, and happy for no apparent reason, they may be "telling" you that they have decided to commit suicide. Patients seem actually to feel relieved and happier after deciding that the solution to their problems is to end their lives.

The following are other behavioral clues that may indicate the possibility of a suicide attempt. These patients deserve your close attention:

1. Patients who have extreme difficulty sleeping and especially those who also experience early-morning (3 to 6 A.M.) awakenings.
2. Patients who continually talk about committing suicide, particularly those who have made a previous attempt.
3. Patients who express feelings of hopelessness and helplessness.
4. Patients who are very tearful and dwell on sad thoughts.
5. Patients who show the vegetative signs of depression (loss of sleep, appetite, and interest in their appearance and usual activities).
6. Patients who show unusual interest in getting their affairs in order and who may even try to give away their belongings.
7. Patients who are hallucinating (hearing voices, seeing things, and so forth) and/or who feel persecuted. Patients who are hallucinating may commit suicide because the voices they hear tell them to do so, or in an attempt to get away from those voices, or to escape from the frightening creatures that they see.

CREATING A SAFE ENVIRONMENT

The creativity shown by patients in finding weapons with which to harm themselves is truly amazing. If one considers the fact that many suicide attempts seem to occur as a result of a momentary impulse over which the patient seems to have no control (common in alcoholics and individuals with personality disorders), the necessity for making sure that weapons are not available becomes obvious. Patients have broken mirrors, light bulbs, and lamps and then used the glass to cut themselves. They have been known to wet themselves all over and then try to electrocute themselves by sticking something metal in an electrical outlet. They may try to stab themselves with pens, pencils, nail files, or dull dinner knives; to hang themselves with belts, simple household string, or knotted bed sheets; to poison themselves by eating abrasive cleansers or drinking shaving lotion, mouthwash, or lighter fluid; or to drown by submerging themselves in the bathtub. They may also try to drown themselves by holding their head under water in the sink, pouring gargling solution down their nose, or sticking their heads in mop buckets full of water. Others may jump out of windows, step in front of cars, or set themselves on fire. Depressed patients may simply refuse to eat in an attempt to starve. There are many other suicidal methods not listed above, and it is a real challenge to stay one step ahead of patients in keeping their environment as safe as possible.

Suicidal patients often need to remain under constant supervision, and alertness is the staff's best defense. If the staff members maintain a warm, friendly, supportive attitude while carrying out assigned responsibilities, patients may reap a special benefit. Not only will they be prevented from ending their lives before treatment has had a chance to work, but they may feel that all the attention they are receiving means that they are truly important and that people care about what happens to them. Perhaps they may even begin to feel that life really is worth living.

TECHNIQUES FOR EFFECTIVE INTERACTION

To relate effectively to suicidal patients, one should realize that these patients may feel particularly discouraged and hopeless if they do not perceive a steady improvement in their condition. Such feelings are increased if these patients are led to believe that their lack of improvement is due to poor motivation or lack of willpower.

Some suicidologists believe that instead of placing the responsibility for improvement on the skills of the staff or on the patient's willpower, the responsibility should be assigned to the medication the patient is receiving. This tends to neutralize the patient's sense of guilt and thus reduces symptoms. Realizing that it takes days or weeks for some of the antidepressants to reach an optimal therapeutic level in the bloodstream can allow the staff to approach the patient in an optimistic and hopeful way. Such knowledge may also make it easier for the patient to understand and tolerate a slower-than-expected rate of recovery. Because suicide is permanent, the necessity of communicating a sense of hope to these patients is of utmost importance. Life circumstances and personal aspirations vary and change. If a patient, therefore, is prevented from committing suicide and is able to internalize a sense of hope, there is a good possibility for a good recovery. The authors are constantly impressed with the fact that intensely suicidal patients shake their heads in wonderment after their suicidal crisis has passed and seem not to understand their own behavior. Many realize they would have killed themselves but for the work of the staff—and most are truly grateful.

In working with suicidal patients, one may expect that a great deal of time will be spent with a few patients who generate crisis after crisis by making repeated suicide attempts. Dealing with such patients is often exasperating and anxiety provoking. Perhaps one of the reasons for this anxiety is that staff members perceive the anger the patient is experiencing but are unsure of how to deal with it. Unfortunately, the most common way of reacting to anger is to respond with anger. If the staff reacts in this manner, patients only feel more rejected and their anger is increased. Staff members must realize that the ability to react appropriately is essential. They must be interested in and understanding toward the patient but must not assume the patient's emotional burdens and attitudes. When they do so, they become ineffective in helping the patient deal with suicidal feelings.

It is important to remember that patients expect staff members to be calm and controlled even in the face of their own hostility and anger. They depend on the staff to recognize the destructive elements in their behavior that they cannot see and to provide a safe, structured environment in which they can regain a sense of hope. Suicidal crises can best be handled with genuine human concern and understanding. An honest attempt on the part of a staff member to reach out and help will eventually be accepted by most suicidal patients.

SUICIDAL INTENTION RATING SCALE

Since treatment plans will vary with the intensity of a patient's suicidal impulses, a Suicidal Intention Rating Scale (SIRS), which has been developed and found useful by the authors, is presented below. It provides a systematic procedural guide that can be used in the day-to-day management of hospitalized suicidal patients. It is the responsibility of the patient's physician or the R.N. in charge of the unit to rate the patient and then notify the rest of the staff of the preventive measures to be instituted. Even though all hospitals do not use such a tool, it is included to suggest some practical approaches to the care of the suicidal patient. A recent survey of public and private psychiatric hospitals indicates that most hospitals follow a procedure similar to the one presented here when caring for suicidal patients.

The SIRS values and suggested therapeutic approaches are as follows:

0. A SIRS value of zero (0) is assigned to a patient when there is no evidence that the patient has (or has had in the past)

suicidal ideas that have been brought to the attention of another person.

Nursing Approach: A patient with a SIRS value of 0 follows usual admission procedures and hospital routines.

1+. A SIRS value of one plus (1+) is assigned to a patient when there is some evidence of suicidal ideas but no actual attempts. This patient does not have a history of repeatedly threatening to commit suicide.

Nursing Approach: A patient with a SIRS value of 1+ follows usual admission procedures and hospital routines. However, the patient should be quietly and unobtrusively observed and evaluated for evidence of recurrence of suicidal thoughts.

2+. A SIRS value of two plus (2+) is assigned to a patient when (a) there is evidence that the patient has attempted suicide in the past but is not now actively thinking about suicide or (b) when the patient is having suicidal ideas but is not threatening suicide. For example, the patient may say, "I have thought about suicide but I don't believe it is the way out."

Nursing Approach: A patient with a SIRS value of 2+ follows usual admission procedures and hospital routines. The patient is allowed to use the following items but must return them to be locked up after use:

   a. Shaving kit (including razor, blade, aftershave, cologne, shaving cream).
   b. Mouthwash in glass bottles.
   c. Belts.
   d. Fingernail files and fingernail clippers.
   e. Knives of any description, including penknives. These may be used under supervision only.
   f. Hair picks and hair lifts.
   g. Any cosmetics in glass containers.
   h. Plastic clothes coverings.
   i. Hairspray.

3+. A SIRS value of three plus (3+) is assigned to a patient who has been making serious suicidal threats. For example, the patient may have said, "If they don't stop bothering me, I'm going to kill myself."

Nursing Approach: Upon admission, a patient with a SIRS value of 3+ must be searched to determine if there are instruments on his or her person, in his or her clothes, or in his or her room which may possibly be used for self-destruction. This procedure should be performed in a professional manner, with the staff being extremely careful to protect the patient's dignity. The patient will then be allowed to use the following items only under direct supervision:

a. Shaving kit (including razor, blade, after shave, cologne, shaving cream).

b. Mouthwash in glass bottles.

c. Belts.

d. Fingernail files and fingernail clippers.

e. Knives of any description, including penknives.

f. Hair lifts or hair picks.

g. Any cosmetics in glass containers.

h. Hairspray.

i. Plastic clothes coverings.

j. Medications brought in on admission.

k. Coat hangers.

l. Lamps or any other breakable item from his or her room.

m. Eyeglasses. (*Note:* These should be removed only when a patient is extremely suicidal and may use the glasses as a weapon. It must be kept in mind, however, that the removal of eyeglasses may add to confusion and depression.)

This patient should be observed at least every 30 minutes and more often if at all possible. Eating meals in the dining room is permissible, but a staff member should be present at the table during the meal. Unless otherwise ordered by the physician, the patient is not permitted to leave the unit for recreational or occupational therapy activities, and visitors are restricted to immediate family.

Note. It is wise to encourage patients with a SIRS rating of 3+ or below to stay out of their rooms and in the company of other patients and staff. They can thus be watched more closely. Usually other patients on the unit know when a patient is suicidal. They often take it upon themselves to help watch the patient and will notify staff members of behavioral changes.

4+. A SIRS value of four plus (4+) is assigned to a patient who has been brought to the hospital because of an active suicide attempt or as a precaution against such an attempt.

Nursing Approach:

a. The patient will be admitted to a seclusion room. This is for protection, not punishment. Staff members should take care to explain why this procedure is necessary. It is much easier to observe and limit behavior in a smaller area, but the staff should spend as much time as possible with the patient interacting on a one-to-one basis. With the permission of the attending physician, a family member(s) acceptable to the patient should stay around the clock while the patient is in seclusion.

b. The nurse in charge will search the patient's clothing and body, taking care to conduct such a search in a professional manner with concern for the patient's dignity. A very thorough search should be carried out. Sometimes it is necessary to carefully check the patient's hair, ears, between toes and fingers, and other parts of the body where harmful objects might be concealed. In females, the admitting physician may consider it necessary to examine the vaginal area to be sure that nothing has been concealed there. This may seem to be an extreme precaution: however, a loaded .22-caliber pistol has been found in a vagina. There are numerous cases of drugs being concealed in this manner.

c. The patient will be clothed in a hospital gown.

d. Any clothing, supplies, or other items that are brought to the hospital and that may be needed when suicidal precautions are removed will then be placed in the patient's locker outside the seclusion room. All unnecessary items brought to the hospital will be sent home.

e. All items brought to the hospital by the family will be thoroughly inspected by the nurse on duty, and anything that might be used in a suicide attempt will not be given to the patient.

f. The door to the seclusion room should be locked at all times when the patient is alone.

g. Meals will be served in the seclusion room, and only paper dishes will be used if a staff member is unavailable to supervise the meal. If at all possible, a staff member should spend time with the patient during meals.

h. It may be necessary to remove all linen from the bed and a staff member must stay with any patient trying to commit suicide by banging his or her head on the walls or door of the seclusion room.

i. Anytime the patient is allowed out of the security room, a member of the hospital staff must be in attendance.

j. Under no circumstances will the patient be allowed to leave the psychiatric unit without a direct order from the attending physician. In cases where the patient has the permission of the attending physician, the patient should be accompanied by an attendant at all times (for example, to x-ray, lab, and so forth).

k. Visitors will be restricted altogether. The only persons allowed to visit will be those who have specific permission from the attending physician.

Ideally, all patients assigned a 2+, 3+, or 4+ suicidal rating would be closely or continually observed on a one-to-one basis (one staff member to one suicidal patient). In most hospitals, however, such a staffing ratio is impossible, and many hospitals now use closed circuit TV monitoring to provide constant supervision for one or more patients simultaneously. One should note that drastic intervention procedures such as placing the suicidal patient in a seclusion room or searching the patient for potential weapons may become necessary. These protective measures are used as a means of preventing suicide until treatment measures such as medication and psychotherapy begin to take effect. The items taken from the patient or the fact that a patient is placed in seclusion is not as important as the manner in which these procedures are performed.

All suicidal patients should be watched closely at shift change and in the early morning hours. Patients who have been unable to sleep all night often decide that they are not going to face another such night and make a suicide attempt. Others who are waiting for their unobserved chance to commit suicide often find it during the confusion of increased activity that occurs at shift change.

After visiting hours or activity periods, it may be necessary to closely check the environment, and possibly the patient, for objects (potential weapons) that may have been given or unintentionally left by a visitor. When hospital workers must make repairs on the unit, be sure that patients do not take their tools and that the workers do not leave any of their supplies on the unit when they leave.

If one finds a patient who has attempted suicide or who is about to do so, do not leave the patient. If alone, call out for help. Then, while waiting, speak to the patient in a calm, reassuring manner. If the patient wants to talk about feelings, allow him or her to do so. If not, try to distract the patient from the suicidal intention by whatever means available.

If one finds a patient who is already unconscious, call for help and then start appropriate first-aid measures.

ANNOTATED BIBLIOGRAPHY

Allgulander, A.P.: *Suicide among young men: Psychiatric illness, deviant behaviour and substance abuse.* Acta Psychiatrica Scandinavica, 1990, 81:565–570.

A longitudinal study analyzing the role of psychiatric illness as opposed to social and behavioral risk factors for suicide.

Anderson, D.B.: *Never too late: Resolving the grief of suicide.* Journal of Psychosocial Nursing and Mental Health Services, 1991, 29(3):29–31.

A nurse comes to grips with the suicide of her mother when she was a young child by discussing the incident with her father several decades later.

Blumenthal, S.L.: *Youth suicide: Risk factors, assessment, and treatment of adolescent and young adult suicidal patients.* Psychiatric Clinics of North America, 1990, 13(3):511–557.

> *Provides epidemiological information on suicide, sociocultural and psychologic explanations of suicide risk factors, and assessment and treatment for suicide attempts.*

Conrad, N.: *Where do they turn? Social support systems of suicidal high school adolescents.* Journal of Psychosocial Nursing and Mental Health Services, 1991, 29(3):14–20.

> *Discusses the prevalence of suicidal behaviors in adolescents and the social supports that can be utilized to decrease these behaviors.*

Daniels, S.M., Fenley, J.D., Powers, P.S., and Cruse, C.W.: *Self-inflicted burns: A ten-year retrospective study.* Journal of Burn Care Rehabilitation, 1991, 12:144–147.

> *Research study reviewing the characteristics of self-inflicted burn patients, including psychiatric history, in order to better understand these patients and design methods to identify patients at risk.*

Davis, A.T., and Schrueder, C.: *The prediction of suicide.* The Medical Journal of Australia, 1990, 153:552–554.

> *A review of the literature addressing suicide prediction, role of the clinician in evaluating the risk of suicide, and directions for future research.*

Hendin, H.: *Psychodynamics of suicide, with particular reference to the young.* American Journal of Psychiatry, 1991, 148(9):1150–1158.

> *A review of the literature on the psychodynamics of suicide, focusing on the evaluation and treatment of the young suicidal patient.*

Milch, W.E.: *Suicidal patients' psychological attacks on the therapist.* Bulletin of the Menninger Clinic, 1990, 54:384–390.

> *Discusses the tendency for suicidal patients to psychologically attack the therapist and the feelings this generates in the therapist. A case report is provided to further demonstrate this concept.*

Peterson, L.G., and Bongarm, B.: *Repetitive suicidal crises: Characteristics of repeating versus nonrepeating suicidal visitors to a psychiatric emergency service.* Psychopathology, 1990, 23:136–145.

> *Discusses the characteristics of suicidal patients seen in the hospital setting multiple times in a 1-year period for suicide attempts.*

Rygnestad, T., and Hauge, L.: *Epidemiological, social and psychiatric aspects in self-poisoned patients.* Social Psychiatry and Psychiatric Epidemiology, 1991, 26:53–62.

> *A 10-year study examining the epidemiological, social condition, and psychiatric diagnosis of deliberate self-poisoning patients seen at a medical department.*

Schotte, D.E., Cools, J., and Payvar, S.: *Problem-solving deficits in suicidal patients: Trait vulnerability or state phenomenon?* Journal of Consulting and Clinical Psychology, 1990, 58(5):562–564.

> *Research study examining the stability of interpersonal problem-solving skills in suicidal patients.*

Valente, S.M.: *Deliberate self-injury: Management in a psychiatric setting.* Journal of Psychosocial Nursing, 1991, 29(12):19–25.

> *Discusses self-injury, the potential dangers, and how to manage these behaviors in a psychiatric setting.*

REFERENCES

Roy, A.: Suicide. In Kaplan, H.I., and Sadock, B. (eds.): *Comprehensive Textbook of Psychiatry*, Vol. 2, ed. 5. Williams & Wilkins, Baltimore, 1989, p. 1414.

Shneidman, E.: *Definition of Suicide.* Wiley, New York, 1985.

Schneidman, E.: Some essentials of suicide and some implications for response. In Roy, A. (ed.): *Suicide.* Williams & Wilkins, Baltimore, 1986.

Judgment Exercises. Although a doctor or an R.N. will usually rate the patient's suicidal potential, try rating the following patients according to the SIRS scale given in this chapter. Knowledge of this scale and the signs and symptoms that patients exhibit in each category will make one a better observer of the behavior of suicidal patients. You often will be the one who reports to the other team members behavior that indicates the need for a change in suicidal precautions. Rate the following patients according to the type of SIRS rating they should be given.

_____ 1. Mrs. Brown, a 30-year-old divorced mother of three, has been hospitalized on the psychiatric unit for 2 weeks due to severe depression. She has spent most of this time alone in her room crying and pacing the floor. She has been your patient during her entire hospitalization, and on several occasions she has verbalized to you her belief that the only solution to her problems is to end her life. She has also expressed such feelings to other staff members. You come on duty one morning and, much to your surprise, Mrs. Brown is in the day room and cheerfully says "Good morning" as you approach her. She then immediately states the following: "You can stop worrying about me now. I know everything's going to be all right."

_____ 2. Mrs. Green is admitted to the hospital due to severe depression that began 3 weeks after the death of her husband. She says that she guesses that she has thought about suicide but that she has never seriously considered taking her life.

_____ 3. Mrs. Farmer, a 23-year-old female, is admitted to the unit. She immediately begins to order people around and to be generally uncooperative. She says that she wants to kill herself because nobody likes her.

_____ 4. A private detective, Mr. Jones, is admitted to the unit following a self-inflicted gunshot wound to the head. He says that he is tired of the world and that he no longer wishes to live. He says that as soon as he gets out of the hospital he will kill himself.

According to your hospital's routine, what approach would be used with each of the patients described above? (Be specific.)

241

1. Mrs. Brown: _____

_____

_____

_____

_____

2. Mrs. Green: _____

_____

_____

_____

_____

3. Mrs. Farmer: _____

_____

_____

_____

_____

4. Mr. Jones: _____

_____

_____

_____

_____

Short Answer. Answer the following questions as briefly and specifically as possible.

1. For each successful suicidal attempt, records indicate that there are approximately how many unsuccessful attempts?

_____.

2. What specific groups in the general population are more likely to attempt suicide?

_____

_____

_____.

3. What is an individual who has made a suicide attempt trying to communicate?

_____

_____

_____.

4. As a mental health worker in a hospital setting, what is one of the best defenses available in the prevention of suicide?

_____.

5. List three behavioral clues that would be indicative of a possibility of a suicide attempt.

a. _____.

b. _____.

c. _____.

True or False. Circle your choice.

T F 1. In the United States, suicide is at present the tenth leading cause of adult deaths.

T F 2. Women are more likely to be successful in their suicide attempts than men.

T F 3. When individuals have made several superficial suicide attempts, it is not necessary to take them seriously because they are only trying to get attention.

T F 4. Research indicates that the majority of individuals have made successful suicide attempts have expressed their intention in some form before doing so.

T F 5. Patients often appear quite happy or relieved once they have decided that suicide is the answer to their problems.

T F 6. All suicidal attempts should be taken seriously.

T F 7. Patients who are hallucinating (for example, hearing voices, seeing things) may commit suicide because the voices they hear tell them to do so.

T F 8. A SIRS value of one plus (1+) is assigned to a patient when there is evidence that the patient has attempted suicide in the past but is not now actively thinking about suicide.

T F 9. A patient admitted with a SIRS of four plus (4+) is admitted to a seclusion room for punishment.

T   F   10. A suicide note is a bid for attention and should not be taken seriously.

T   F   11. It is usually harmful for patients to talk about their suicidal thoughts and their attention should be diverted from such topics.

T   F   12. Suicidal patients whose spirits seem to suddenly improve should be observed closely, for it is likely they have decided on a suicidal plan and intend to carry it through.

T   F   13. Professionals in the field of medicine usually respond in a very positive manner toward patients who have attempted suicide.

T   F   14. The more violent or painful suicide method chosen, the more serious the intent of suicide.

T   F   15. Persons who abuse alcohol or drugs are prone to suicidal behavior.

Matching. Match the SIRS value(s) listed in Column B with the appropriate statement in Column A (more than one answer may be used).

Column A	*Column B*
_____ 1. Allowed shaving kit with razor and blade.	**a.** SIRS 0
	b. SIRS 1+
_____ 2. No evidence that the patient is actively thinking about suicide, but evidence shows has attempted suicide in the past.	**c.** SIRS 2+
	d. SIRS 3+
	e. SIRS 4+
_____ 3. "If I don't get some relief, I'm going to kill myself."	
_____ 4. Admitted and remains in seclusion room for his or her own protection.	
_____ 5. No history or evidence of suicidal ideas.	
_____ 6. Admitted to hospital because of an active suicide attempt.	

Multiple Choice. Circle the letter or number that you think represents the best answer.

1. Among adults, suicide is the _____ leading cause of death in the U.S.
    a. First.
    b. Fifth.
    c. Tenth.
    c. Fifteenth.

2. Which of the following losses might be significant enough to motivate a person to attempt suicide?
   a. Death of a loved one.
   b. Loss of health due to a chronic illness.
   c. Loss of a job.
   d. Loss of a loved one via divorce.
   e. Loss of beauty.
      (1) a.
      (2) a, b, and e.
      (3) b, c, and d.
      (4) All of the above.

3. A person attempting suicide is likely to have recently experienced which of the following feelings?
   a. Guilt and a wish for punishment.
   b. Hopelessness.
   c. Anxiety.
   d. Worthlessness.
   e. Exuberance.
      (1) b.
      (2) a and d.
      (3) a, b, c, and d.
      (4) All of the above.

4. Establishing a therapeutic relationship with the suicidal patient contributes to which of the following:
   a. The patient's feelings of self-worth.
   b. The patient's desire to live.
   c. The patient's feeling of being overprotected and dependent.
   d. The patient's belief that others want him or her to live.
      (1) a.
      (2) b and c.
      (3) a, b, and d.
      (4) All of the above.

5. Which of the following behaviors might be clues preceding a suicidal act?
   a. Sudden changes in behavior from depression to cheerfulness.
   b. Talking directly or indirectly about suicide.
   c. A history of a previous suicidal attempt.
   d. Giving away items of great sentimental or monetary value.
      (1) a and c.
      (2) a, b, and c.
      (3) a, c, and d.
      (4) All of the above.

Care for Patients Who Have Lost Contact with Reality

LEARNING OBJECTIVES

Student will be able to:
1. Identify behaviors associated with a patient who has lost contact with reality.
2. Define and give an example of a delusion, an illusion, and a hallucination.
3. Describe techniques for dealing with the patient who has lost contact with reality.

Patients who hallucinate or exhibit other bizarre behavior are usually suffering from one of the psychotic disorders (schizophrenia, senile dementia, affective psychosis, and so forth). Such behaviors, however, may also occur if there is organic brain disease, traumatic injury to the brain, a high fever, or if the individual has taken certain drugs such as LSD or other hallucinogens. Regardless of the cause, these patients pose unique problems for staff members and can be quite upsetting to other patients.

If the symptoms are recognized soon enough, quiet attention and support from staff members can often keep hallucinating or delusional patients from losing control. Therefore staff members must constantly be alert and attuned to behavioral cues that indicate impending problems. For example, a manic patient may first exhibit loud talk, rapid pacing, and grandiose ideas before becoming agitated and destroying the day room.

On the other hand, staff members must be careful not to reinforce bizarre behavior. This happens if the behaviors exhibited by patients get them what they want. For example, if a patient begins dancing up and down the hall with her dress tucked in her panties in order to

247

get attention, the staff should kindly, but firmly, inform the patient to go to her room. When the patient has no audience, the behavior will cease. If the staff and other patients stop to watch, to clap and giggle, the patient's inappropriate behavior will be rewarded and will most likely increase.

Patients who show bizarre behavior often need help in understanding why their behavior is inappropriate and what effect it has on others. They may benefit from appropriate confrontation with the fact that their behavior is not socially acceptable. Such confrontations should only be done by a staff member who is well trained and experienced in psychotherapeutic techniques.

Patients who are hallucinating or showing other bizarre behaviors do not respond well to demands or orders. They do, however, usually respond to kind but firm structuring (instructions on appropriate behavior).

Patients who are totally out of contact with reality also exhibit behavior that is bizarre but that is far more disturbing. Staff and patients are often at least tolerant of vulgar language, unusual makeup, or other inappropriate behavior but may be frightened by people who hear voices, see visions, and act in unusual ways because of their hallucinations. There are three types of reality distortions which indicate that a patient may have lost contact with reality. They are delusions, illusions, and hallucinations.

A delusion is a false belief that cannot be corrected by reasoning. For example, a delusional patient may believe that someone is trying to poison him by putting something in his food and, therefore, may refuse to eat.

An illusion is a false interpretation of a real sensory impression or image. An example of an illusion would be when Mrs. Jones thinks she sees a man in her room when it is only the shadow of her bathrobe hanging on the door, or Mr. Brown who thinks he hears a gunshot when he actually heard a car backfire as it passed his window.

A hallucination is an idea or perception that does not exist in reality. Patients who hear voices telling them to do things when no one is talking to them, or patients who see things that no one else sees, are said to be hallucinating. The most common hallucinations are visual and auditory, but patients occasionally smell things (olfactory), taste things (gustatory), or feel things (tactile) that are not real.

These patients should be shown a great deal of kindness and concern, for their hallucinations, delusions, or illusions are often quite frightening. Voices may say scary things to them or tell them to do dangerous or evil things or to kill themselves or someone else (command hallucinations). They may see snakes crawling on their beds or feel that there are lice all over their bodies. Although none of this is really happening, it is very real to the patients and they are often panic stricken. It is helpful to stay with these patients until their prn medication can begin to calm them. Sometimes they will become quieter and more in contact with reality if they are simply removed from the environment (often busy, rushed, and overstimulating) in which they started to lose touch. Talking to the patient in a quiet, soothing manner is also helpful, especially if the nurse tries to steer the conversation back to reality. For example, Mrs. Jones states that she just heard God telling her how to save the world. Instead of asking the patient to explain further (which would be focusing on the hallucination), the staff member should try to draw the patient's attention back to reality, for example, by commenting on the needlework the patient has been doing and asking to be shown how to do a particular stitch.

Patients who tend to lose contact with reality should not be allowed to spend a great deal of time alone because this encourages their bizarre behavior. Some authorities believe that hallucinations begin because a person is lonely and anxious and has no "real" person with whom to talk. Patients then "create" someone in their mind with whom they can have an interpersonal relationship. In the beginning, the imagined people or voices tell the patient what they want to hear and allow them relief from their anxiety. Thus patients begin to allow more time for their imagined relationship and less time for real people. They need to be around other people and, if possible, to sit and talk quietly with someone. A staff member who cares can help a great deal if the caring attitude and feeling are communicated to the patient. Staff members must begin to replace the imaginary people.

When patients experience a hallucination or delusion, they should be told that the staff member knows they are upset and knows they hear the voices or see the snakes, but that the staff member cannot hear or see them. Staff members must serve as a healthy role model and someone with whom the patient can test what is real and what is unreal. For this reason, it is extremely important for staff members never to tell a patient that they too can hear the voices or see the snakes.

Some authorities suggest that after staff members have established a working relationship with patients, they should tell the patients to dismiss the voices any time they are hallucinating. For example, the staff member might say, "Mrs. Jones, tell those 'voices' to go away—I'm real; they aren't." Once again, focus the patient's attention on something else—something real.

Finally, it is important that staff members not argue with patients who are hallucinating. Arguing forces patients to defend their false perceptions and may cause them to become violent. Avoid making statements that might be misinterpreted by patients and always try to be supportive of patients' feelings about their perception without supporting the misperceptions themselves. For example, the patient who says he is being chased by FBI agents would not benefit from a staff member's saying: "Mr. Jones, it's ridiculous for you to believe FBI agents are after you. That's nonsense. Just stop believing that and you'll be all right." Neither would it be helpful to respond by saying, "Gee, that really sounds interesting, Mr. Jones; please tell me more about it." It would be better to respond by saying, "Mr. Jones, I know you believe the FBI is after you, but it doesn't seem that way to me. It's a very pretty day. Why don't we take a walk." Then try to interest Mr. Jones in things that are reality oriented.

ANNOTATED BIBLIOGRAPHY

Blair, D.T., and Hildreth, N.A.: *PTSD and the Vietnam veteran: The battle for treatment.* Journal of Psychosocial Nursing and Mental Health Services, 1991, 29(10):15–20.

> *Focuses on the professional bias, personal issues, countertransference, and pathologic staff dynamics encountered by many patients treated for post-traumatic stress disorder (PTSD). Also presents characteristics of PTSD and the complications of diagnostic confusion in treatment.*

Chapman, T.: *The nurse's role in neuroleptic medications.* Journal of Psychosocial Nursing and Mental Health Services, 1991, 29(6):6–8.

> *Neuroleptic medications for the treatment of schizophrenia often have adverse side effects. Patients were allowed to express their attitudes concerning the need for these medications.*

Curl, A.: *Agitation and the older adult.* Journal of Psychosocial Nursing and Mental Health Services, 1989, 27(12):12–14.

> *Focuses on agitation in elderly patients caused by delirium, dementia, parkinsonism, and depression and the appropriate management of these behaviors by nursing staff.*

Dauner, A., and Blair, D.: *Akathisia: When treatment creates a problem.* Journal of Psychosocial Nursing and Mental Health Services, 1990, 23(10):13–17.

> *Explains the symptoms and dangers of akathisia (a side effect of antipsychotic medications) and gives several case examples of patients suffering from these symptoms.*

Deutsch, L.H., and Rovner, B.W.: *Agitation and other noncognitive abnormalities in Alzheimer's disease.* Psychiatric Clinics of North America, 1991, 14(2):341–349.

> *Presents the behavioral symptoms of Alzheimer's disease, such as agitation, wandering, passivity, psychosis, and sleep disturbances and discusses*

the importance of understanding the nature and treatment of these symptoms.

Dzurec, L.C.: *How do they see themselves? Self-perceptions and functioning for people with chronic schizophrenia.* Journal of Psychosocial Nursing and Mental Health Services, 1990, 28(8):10–14.

Research study describing the relationship between the self-perceptions of schizophrenic patients and their level of daily functioning.

Malone, J.A.: *Schizophrenia research update: Implications for nursing.* Journal of Psychosocial Nursing and Mental Health Services, 1990, 28(8):4–8.

Discusses the scientific advances made in the understanding and treatment of schizophrenia, what areas need to be further explored, and the implications for nursing practice.

Swanson, B., Cronin-Stubbs, D., and Colletti, M.: *Dementia and depression in persons with AIDS: Causes and care.* Journal of Psychosocial Nursing and Mental Health Services, 1990, 28(10):33–39.

Discusses the importance of distinguishing depression from AIDS dementia complex and presents treatment plans for both disorders in order to promote the quality of life.

True or False. Circle your choice.

T F 1. Patients who are hallucinating or exhibiting other bizarre behaviors respond best to direct demands.

T F 2. Patients who hear voices telling them to do things when no one is talking to them are said to be experiencing illusions.

T F 3. The most common hallucinations are visual and auditory.

T F 4. Patients who tend to lose contact with reality should be left alone a great deal of the time because this tends to decrease their bizarre behavior.

T F 5. Some authorities believe that hallucinations begin because a person is lonely and anxious with no "real" person with whom to talk.

T F 6. A delusion is a false belief that cannot be corrected by reasoning.

Multiple Choice. Circle the letter or number that you think represents the best answer.

1. Which of the following is not appropriate when responding to disoriented, confused, or incoherent patients?
   a. Giving the patients necessary information and assistance as needed.
   b. Helping the patients to hurry through activities so they get exposure to all areas of the ward routine.
   c. Being kind and firm yet help the patients when appropriate.
   d. Providing reality-oriented conversation topics.

2. When working with persons who have a distorted perception of reality, the mental health worker will generally be most effective if he or she:
   a. Encourages the patients to discuss the voices they hear.
   b. Continually tries to draw the patients' attention to the here and now.
   c. Avoids all unnecessary physical contact.

3. In working with patients who are hallucinating, appropriate approaches include:
   a. Carefully watching what you communicate nonverbally.
   b. Providing a structured environment.
   c. Conveying to patients that you believe the "voices" are real.

    d. Asking concrete, reality-oriented questions.
    e. Increasing social interaction rapidly.
        (1) a, b, and c.
        (2) a, b, and d.
        (3) b, d, and e.
        (4) c, d, and e.
        (5) All of the above.

Short Answer. Answer the following questions as briefly and specifically as possible.
  1. List two psychiatric disorders mentioned in this chapter that are likely to have hallucinations as one of their major symptoms.

    a. _____.

    b. _____.
  2. What behavioral clues would be indicative of a patient who is about to lose control?

    _____

    _____

    _____.

  3. List the three types of reality distortions which indicate that a patient has lost contact with reality.

    a. _____.

    b. _____.

    c. _____.
  4. Define *illusion:*

    _____

    _____

    _____.

  5. Define *hallucination:*

    _____

    _____

    _____.

18

Care For Patients with Neurologic Deficits

Mental health professionals have coined the term *JOCAM* to describe the group of symptoms often shown by patients who suffer from neurologic deficits. Of course, patients with other psychiatric illnesses may exhibit these same behaviors, and one's approach to them may be the same. When used in reference to a patient, the term *JOCAM* means that the patient has difficulty in the following areas:

J = judgment

O = orientation

C = confabulation

A = affect

M = memory

When working with patients who exhibit behaviors indicating problems in the above areas, staff members need to maintain a warm, accepting attitude. Because these patients often show poor judgment, they must be supervised closely to prevent them from bringing physical harm to themselves (such as wandering off or getting lost, falling, drinking or eating inappropriate things, not paying adequate attention to environmental hazards). Often these patients know they are confused and become quite frustrated and agitated because they cannot correct the problem. Measures such as supportive understanding from the staff, a supervised warm bath, a well-lighted room that eliminates shadows that might be misinterpreted, playing soft music, or mild tranquilizers may be used to help these patients relax.

Some patients with neurologic deficits have excellent memories for past events but forget new information and experiences rather quickly. It may be necessary for the staff to repeat information several times. The staff should use a kind, quiet tone of voice and give simple, short explanations and answers. This is especially important because the patient's attention span may be short. Loud voices and long explanations tend to bewilder these patients and may not be remembered at all.

Because it is embarrassing not to be able to remember, patients who are forgetful often make up information (confabulation) to fill in information gaps and cover up the things they have forgotten. It is important, therefore, to listen carefully to what the patient is saying. If the information is made up or incorrect, the patient should be corrected in a gentle, nonpunitive manner. A staff member might say, "I know you're having trouble remembering where you lived last year, but your family says it was with your son, not in a home for the aging" or "I know you miss your mother but she died a long, long time ago." If such explanations bother patients or worsen their depression, you might try distracting them from the thoughts and say something like: "I know you miss your mother. Would you like to help me with this game? I think it goes like this"—then proceed to engage the patient in the game.

Calendars with large print and clocks with large numbers and hands help keep patients with neurologic deficits oriented to the date and the time. These should be placed around the unit in the areas where these patients spend most of their time. Ideally, there should be a clock and a calendar in every patient's room.

It may also be helpful to label certain areas such as the nurses' station and bathrooms, and to even put the patient's names in large letters on their bedroom doors. Staff members should wear easy-to-read, large-print, name tags at all times, and it is helpful if the tag also states the person's position (such as R.N., Aide, Dietitian, or Social Worker).

When patients with neurologic deficits are admitted to the hospital unit or come to a community mental health center for treatment, they should be carefully oriented to their new environment. These patients are extremely sensitive to change and may become confused in new surroundings. They like to follow a stable routine, and changes make them feel anxious and insecure. These patients should not be hurried and should be assisted whenever they need help. Because they may not always ask for assistance when they really need it, the staff must observe them carefully and give assistance when the situation warrants it. Mr. Green may be able to dress himself but may put his shoes on the wrong feet or may have forgotten how to tie his shoestrings. Mr. Jones may remember the general location of the bathroom but forget which is for the men and which is for women; he may therefore use the wrong one. Patients with these problems should never be scolded or embarrassed in front of other patients or staff members. Instead, staff members should help them correct the inappropriate behavior or learn the necessary task. These problems occur because older patients who have brain damage often have trouble generalizing their learning experiences. For example, an older gentleman who learns to walk with the aid of a walker in physical therapy may be unable to remember how to use the walker when he returns home or to his room on the unit. Therefore elderly patients have to be taught in a setting similar to the one in which they will use whatever skill is being learned or they should have supervised practice in that area.

When neurologically deficient patients talk in a nonsense manner, they should be told that the staff member does not understand what they are saying and the subject should be changed back to a reality-oriented topic.

Confusion can be kept to a minimum by allowing patients to bring familiar objects from home, such as a favorite chair, a nightstand, or pictures of their families. Also, it is helpful to place their personal items (clothing, toilet articles, and so forth) in an area to which they have easy access. If Mrs. Jones is found wandering around nude, she should be taken back to her room and helped to dress. The reason Mrs. Jones was wandering around nude may be that she was tired of wearing the same dirty dress and could not find her clean ones, which were hidden away in her suitcase on the top shelf of the closet, out of reach and out of mind.

Another way to help decrease patient confusion and forgetfulness is to teach them to use lists and/or appointment books. If Mrs. Green has trouble remembering her daily schedule, help her write it down in a small notebook so that she can review it as needed. If she forgets and asks a staff member about a scheduled event, she can be referred to her notebook. A list taped next to the mirror in his bathroom may help Mr. Green remember to shave, comb his hair, and brush his teeth each day. Lists and appointment books are a socially acceptable means of keeping one from forgetting important matters and may even improve the patient's self-esteem.

Sometimes normal unit activities, such as a simple birthday party for another patient, can confuse patients with a neurological deficit. If this happens, patients should be removed to a quieter area. A staff member should stay with the patients while they eat their cake in peace and quiet so that they do not feel that they are being rejected or punished.

Affect refers to the feelings experienced with an emotion. Patients with problems of JOCAM are often described as having flat affects. They seem to be neither happy nor sad and show little, if any, emotion about anything; they simply exist. Sometimes, however, their affect may be quite inappropriate. Patients may cry uncontrollably because they cannot get a letter open or may laugh when they hear that a friend has died. When such patients have reason to be upset, they need to express their feelings even if the wrong emotion is used. The appropriate emotion can sometimes be obtained by simply telling the patient, "I know you are upset; you might feel better if you cried" (or whatever the appropriate emotion might be). This technique structures the situation for the patient and gives information about the type of behavior expected. Another technique the staff can use in handling excessive emotional outbursts is distraction. Mrs. Brown, a patient who is crying uncontrollably, may be stopped by calling her attention to an interesting activity occurring across the room or by involving her in that activity.

The language of patients with neurologic deficits may also be inappropriate. If Mr. Jones swears and screams obscenities at a staff member who has moved his eyeglasses from their usual resting place, the staff member might respond in the following manner: "Mr. Jones, you're right. I should have put your glasses back where you keep them. I'm sorry, but screaming and saying what you did will only make people angry. Next time, try not to get so upset. Just ask for what you want and we will help you." If this is too long an interaction for the patient's neurologic condition, shorten it by saying: "You're right. Just ask if you need anything else." This acknowledges the patient's frustration and provides structure without involving a long interaction.

When a patient is being corrected, the correction should occur immediately after the inappropriate behavior takes place and it should be done privately. Otherwise, the patient may not remember what he or she said or did that needs changing and may become embarrassed or angry. When a patient acts in an appropriate way or learns a new task, be sure to give immediate feedback in the form of praise and approval.

It is the responsibility of staff members to recognize that brain-damaged patients depend on routine and structure to help them stay oriented. Anything that disturbs their "world" is likely to upset them. In the situation of the misplaced eyeglasses discussed above, it was, in fact, the staff member who caused the situation leading to Mr. Jones' inappropriate behavior.

Patients who have neurologic deficits are not hopeless. There are now drugs available that help clear their thinking by increasing the brain's metabolism and use of oxygen. Further, great strides in helping such patients cope with their environment and illness can be made by a kind, understanding staff that rewards appropriate behavior and rechannels inappropriate behavior.

Staff members should remember that other physical problems such as infections, kidney problems, high fever, or adverse drug reactions, may cause or exacerbate the behaviors described in this chapter. Staff members must be constantly alert to the possibility of such factors when JOCAM problems are discovered.

ANNOTATED BIBLIOGRAPHY

Beck, C., Heacock, P., Mercer, S., and Walton, C.G.: *Dressing for success: Promoting independence among cognitively impaired elderly.* Journal of Psychosocial Nursing and Mental Health Services, 1991, 29(7):30–35.

> *Cognitive impairment often encourages excess disability. Ideas on fostering independence in this population are presented.*

Bemporad, J.R.: *Dementia praecox as a failure of neoteny.* Theoretical Medicine, 1991, 12:45–51

> *Discusses the possible causes of chronic mental illness and the significance of the loss of neoteny (juvenile traits that encourage learning) in these patients.*

Curl, A.: *Agitation and the older adult.* Journal of Psychosocial Nursing and Mental Health Services, 1989, 27(12):12–14.

> *Focuses on agitation caused by delirium, dementia, parkinsonism, and depression and the appropriate management of these behaviors by nursing staff.*

Deutsch, L.H., and Rovner, B.W.: *Agitation and other noncognitive abnormalities in Alzheimer's disease.* Psychiatric Clinics of North America, 1991, 14(2):341–349.

> *Presents the behavioral symptoms of Alzheimer's disease, such as agitation, wandering, passivity, psychosis, and sleep disturbances, and discusses the importance of understanding the nature and treatment of these symptoms.*

Hom, J.: *Effect of Duration of Alzheimer's Disease on Higher Cognitive Function.* Department of Psychiatry and Neurology, University of Texas Southwestern Medical Center, 1991.

> *Research study examining the effect of duration on the general and specific neuropsychologic functioning of patients with Alzheimer's disease.*

Lohr, J.B.: *Oxygen radicals and neuropsychiatric illness: Some speculations.* Archives of General Psychiatry, 1991, 48:1097–1106.

Explores the relationship between free radicals and neuropsychiatric conditions that are marked by the gradual development of psychopathologic symptoms and movement disorder. Radical-induced damage may be important in Parkinson's disease, tardive dyskinesia, metal intoxication syndromes, Down's syndrome, schizophrenia, Huntington's chorea, and Alzheimer's disease.

Masters, J.C., and O'Grady, M.: *Normal pressure hydrocephalus: A potentially reversible form of dementia.* Journal of Psychosocial Nursing and Mental Health Services, 1992, 30(6):25–28.

Discusses the symptoms, diagnosis, etiology, treatment, and nursing care for normal pressure hydrocephalus (NPH), a form of dementia that has proven to be reversible.

Samuel, W.A., Henderson V.W., and Miller, C.A.: *Severity of dementia in Alzheimer disease and neurofibrillary tangles in multiple brain regions.* Alzheimer Disease and Associated Disorders, 1991, 5(1):1–11.

Research study examining the relationship of numbers of neurofibrillary tangles (NFTs) in selected cortical and subcortical sites to the duration of clinical disease and the severity of dementia.

Multiple Choice. Circle the letter or number that you think represents the best answer:

1. Organic brain disorders are caused by:
    a. Interpersonal traumas.
    b. Anatomic damage.
    c. Physiologic damage.
    d. Trauma to the psyche.
    e. A too-strong superego.
        (1) a, d, and e.
        (2) b, c, and d.
        (3) d and e.
        (4) a, b, and c.
        (5) b and c.
2. Choose the items that can be features of organic brain disorders.
    a. Impairment of memory for past events.
    b. Impairment of judgment.
    c. Good control of emotions.
    d. Personality changes.
    e. Hallucinations.
        (1) All of the above.
        (2) b, d, and e.
        (3) a, b, and c.
        (4) a, c, and e.
        (5) None of the above.
3. Confabulation is:
    a. A type of hallucination.
    b. An effective medication.
    c. Fragmented thinking.
    d. Echolalia.
    e. Filling in memory gaps.
4. In treating a patient with organic brain disorder caused by cerebral arteriosclerosis, the mental health worker should:
    a. Understand the patient's personality before illness.
    b. Give individualized care.
    c. Know that memory for recent events is better than memory for past events.
    d. Provide a disordered environment
    e. Be optimistic, emphatic, and clear.
        (1) All of the above.
        (2) None of the above.

(3) a, b, c, and d.

(4) a, c, and d.

(5) a, b, and e.

5. The relatively permanent impairment of cerebral function that occurs in chronic organic brain damage produces defects in:

a. Memory.

b. Orientation.

c. Judgment.

d. Comprehension.

e. Affect.

(1) a, b, c, and e.

(2) a, b, and c.

(3) a, b, c, and d.

(4) All of the above.

6. The premorbid personality of a patient with organic brain disorders:

a. Usually has little to do with the type of illness he or she develops.

b. Usually determines the behavior he or she shows.

c. Is usually impossible to determine.

d. Usually is the opposite of that shown.

7. A senile patient is withdrawn and negativistic. The best approach to the patient might be:

a. "Would you like to go to your room where you can be alone?"

b. "I need a partner to play checkers with me."

c. "Your family will be terribly disappointed if you don't go to O.T. [occupational therapy]."

d. "Your doctor wants you to participate in activities."

8. Which of the following is not appropriate when responding to disoriented, confused, or incoherent patients?

a. Giving the patients the necessary information and assistance as needed.

b. Helping the patients to hurry through activities so they get exposure to all areas of the ward routine.

c. Being kind and firm yet helping patients where appropriate.

d. Providing reality-oriented conversation topics.

True or False. Circle your choice.

T F 1. Organic brain disorders (chronic type) can be reversible.

T F 2. Good psychologic adjustment to life prior to the onset of cerebral arteriosclerosis is a determining factor in the prognosis of the disease.

T F 3. Patients with organic brain damage often have short memory spans.

T   F   4. It is frequently helpful to "make an example" for other patients by choosing a particular brain-damaged patient to keep correcting until he or she does almost everything in the desired manner.

T   F   5. Patients should not be allowed to bring personal items from home because it only makes them cry and want to go home.

Short Answer. Answer the following questions as briefly and specifically as possible.

1. Fill in the term which corresponds to the letter given:

   J = _____

   O = _____

   C = _____

   A = _____

   M = _____

2. The best way to explain something to an organically impaired person is:

   _____.

3. Brain-damaged patients often have difficulty with maintaining a good orientation to a new environment. List five things a mental health worker can do to reduce disorientation.

   a. _____.

   b. _____.

   c. _____.

   d. _____.

   e. _____.

4. When it is necessary to correct a patient, why should it be done immediately following the inappropriate behavior?

   _____

   _____

   _____.

5. The two most important factors in helping brain-damaged patients to stay oriented are:

   1. _____.

   2. _____.

THE JOURNEY

What is this affliction that causes the pain,
*   that produces feelings of inferiority and shame?*
What is this force that drives me to be,
*   something I hide and fear others might see?*
How do I handle the turmoil within,
*   and how long do I wait for my soul to mend?*
How do I handle the despair that I feel,
*   when I don't know fantasy—and I don't know real?*

I must lay down my guilt and give up my lies,
*   and I'll view the world through different eyes.*
Say goodbye to the past, anticipate the new,
*   reach out to others, giving them a chance too.*
I must know that I'm worthy and know that I'm strong,
*   with my new inner peace, I will not go wrong.*
What was this affliction that caused the pain?
*   and what will I do with the insight I've gained?*
I will live out my life one day at a time
*   knowing whatever the outcome, the decision is mine.*
Feelings still surface every now and then,
*   But none that would take me to where I have been.*

Diane Quinn

19

Care for Patients with Eating Disorders

DIANE QUINN, R.N., M.S.N.

LEARNING OBJECTIVES

Student will be able to:
1. Define *anorexia nervosa, bulimia nervosa,* and *compulsive overeating.*
2. Identify behaviors associated with anorexia nervosa, bulimia nervosa, and compulsive overeating.
3. Plan appropriate nursing interventions for patients with eating disorders.

While there are no absolute standards of beauty, we learn at an early age what is attractive and acceptable and what is not. Because the society in which we live equates beauty with thinness, many adolescents and young adults are obsessed with their physical appearance. In their quest for the ideal, they practice extreme and bizarre eating behaviors. While some risk their lives by denying their need for food, others with unmet needs turn to food for consolation.

Eating is one of the earliest forms of nurturance; it is the process by which attachment between infant and mother begins. For many people, eating represents parental love, but for others, eating is symbolic of quite a different parental relationship. Throughout life, attitudes toward food continue to impact human interaction. When the bond between certain individuals and food becomes more than a life-sustaining activity, then quality of life is compromised. In addition, current emphasis on personal control and increased cultural pressures for thinness have created a preoccupation with physical appearance and produced a major health care concern in the United States.

Anorexia nervosa, bulimia nervosa, and compulsive overeating are the three major eating disorders discussed in this chapter. Unfortunately, as we will see, their etiology is unclear, the physiologic and psychologic complications are debilitating, and the cure is uncertain. Effective treatment is complex and involves skilled interventions based on knowledge and understanding of the disorder. Patients with eating disorders offer a challenge to every health professional involved in their care, and the role of the nurse is often critical.

ANOREXIA NERVOSA

Anorexia nervosa is a severe form of self-starvation that may lead to death. Essential characteristics of the disorder include extreme weight loss, usually of more than 25 percent of beginning body weight, intense fear of fatness, disturbed body image, bizarre attitude toward food, and amenorrhea in females. Anorexia nervosa is found predominantly in adolescent females with above-average intelligence and increases with socioeconomic status. The onset of anorexia nervosa tends to be associated with stressful life situations with which the individual is unable to cope. It is not unusual, however, for one single event to mark the beginning of a rigid program of food avoidance. Case histories are often complex, but certain patterns emerge. Consider the following:

> Carla is a shy, soft-spoken girl who was considered a loner by her friends and a "model" daughter by her parents. Carla described herself as very active and ambitious but admitted that no accomplishment had ever reaped her self-satisfaction.
>
> At 16, Carla applied for a part-time modeling job at a local department store. When she did not get the job, the 5-foot 6-inch, 130-pound Carla was convinced it was because she was too fat. She decided to diet. Carla ate only nibbles in her family's presence, and when they questioned her eating behavior, she always managed to minimize their questions regarding her well-being.
>
> Carla spent many hours vigorously exercising. She weighed herself several times a day. If she did not like what the scales showed, she exercised more.
>
> Carla masked her thinness with loose-fitting clothes. One evening Carla's mother walked into Carla's room and was frightened by the emaciated body of her daughter. The next day Carla visited the family physician, who encouraged her to eat more and prescribed vitamins. To Carla's mother, the physician's advice was, "Don't worry, it's just a phase she's going through."
>
> On Carla's 17th birthday, her parents threw her a surprise party, complete with cake and ice cream. Carla reacted by screaming accusations at her parents: "You are trying to make

me fat! I don't want to gain any weight! Take it away—take it all away!"

Carla was admitted to the psychiatric unit of the local hospital. Her admission weight was a mere 92 pounds. Carla's parents were unaware of their daughter's condition.

History

Obtaining accurate data from the patient with anorexia nervosa may be difficult. The anorectic may be unable or unwilling to provide the necessary information. The family, however, is usually able to describe the characteristics of the patient's behavior in great detail. Typically, the anorectic has been well adjusted, highly conforming to aggressive parental expectations, perfectionistic, and achievement oriented. These young men and women are described as being impeccably groomed and orderly. As the condition worsens, this compulsive neatness is sometimes replaced with a lackadaisical attitude toward hygiene and appearance. Other characteristics of anorectics include empathy and sensitivity toward the feelings of others and an intense fear of criticism.

The history of an anorectic often reveals that dieting began with a casual remark from a significant other about a girl's figure or weight. At a time when body image plays such a critical part in one's self-esteem, misperceptions of self-worth are enough to initiate a pattern of self-destructive behaviors.

The anorectic may begin by skipping desserts and sweets and progress to skipping meals. As food restriction increases, exercise increases. Many anorectics loose considerable weight and avoid gaining weight by restricting intake and by exercising. Unsure of the degree of control they have, some resort to vomiting and to abusing laxatives, enemas, and diuretics.

Signs and Symptoms

Anorectics may appear to be healthy, considering the degree of emaciation. As a result, novice nurses may have difficulty assessing the severity of the condition.

Patients with anorexia nervosa perceive themselves as over-weight, no matter how thin they may be. Despite severe wasting, patients may deny that anything is wrong and can always find some body part they believe is fat (Chitty, 1992). The anorectic may insist that everyone is unduly concerned.

Anorectics think endlessly about food and at the same time are obsessed with controlling their own intake. Even though they deliberately refuse to eat, anorectics' appetites are not suppressed. They usually have a broad knowledge of the nutritional and caloric value of food. Despite the fact that they rarely eat the food themselves, anorectics collect cookbooks and recipes, prepare elaborate meals, and take great pleasure in watching others eat. This food refusal is exhilarating to the patient, therefore they withdraw from anyone who encourages them to eat.

Anorectics have an insatiable compulsion for vigorous exercise. They may engage in lengthy sessions of aerobics or jog for miles every day. Terrified of gaining even a pound and losing control, anorectics push themselves to greater levels of endurance until they experience a sense of triumph. Excellence in academics may be maintained but requires increasing hours of study. Many continue to be active in sports and other extracurricular activities. Some may have several part-time jobs. Sometimes as little as 2 to 3 hours a night is spent sleeping.

Anorectics frequently deny that they have a weight problem and insist they feel fine. They plead with their parents to cease the nagging about eating behaviors and body weight. They are proud of their self-denial and their low weight and just want to be left alone. Anorectics admit feelings of loneliness and isolation, but they have difficulty forming healthy relationships.

The advanced anorectic patient is emaciated and skeletal in appearance. The cheek bones are prominent, and the eyes are sunken. The upper torso appears particularly thin, with the ribs and clavicles highly visible. When the disorder is in the advanced stages, fine downy hair (lanugo) may be present on the face, trunk, and extremities. The hands and feet may be cold and mottled. Other physical symptoms include bradycardia, hypotension, and anemia. High serum calcium indicates osteoporosis.

NURSING INTERVENTIONS

Once the patient's life is out of danger, treatment is aimed at restoring normal nutrition and eating habits and at dealing with psychological issues associated with the eating problem (Lucas, 1991).

Ineffective coping, misperceptions of body image, and poor self-esteem are subjective emotional experiences of the anorectic. Nursing interventions, directed toward promoting improvement in these areas, are included in the following discussion.

Trust is the foundation of the therapeutic relationship. In therapeutic relationships, there are certain expectations of both the nurse and the patient. The nurse has the responsibility to maintain the therapeutic relationship and guide it toward the achievement of goals. The attitudes and skills of the nurse are of crucial importance to successful treatment. Chitty (1992) emphasizes that anorectics are extremely resistant to change. Progress may be slow and recovery, at best, may be defined as a lessening of symptoms.

PROMOTING IMPROVED NUTRITION

If the patient is medically unstable, intravenous (IV) therapy or tube feedings may be necessary. Nurses must evaluate their own strengths and have an honest awareness of their feelings toward the patient if treatments are to be carried out in a nonjudgmental manner. Daily weights and accurate records of input and output (I&Os) are effective interventions for monitoring progress.

The nurse must avoid discussing food and eating behaviors with the patient. Such self-centered issues reinforce maladaptive behaviors by allowing the patient to avoid dealing with the hidden causes of the disorder. Refer the patient for dietary consultation and assist with the development of realistic dietary goals.

Provide for a stress-free mealtime environment. Large meals overwhelm anorectic patients. Small frequent ones are more manageable and will be better accepted by them. Because anorectics are masterminds of manipulation and procrastination, it is helpful to set time limits for meals. Acknowledge efforts of patients who meet the established goals, but remember that due to their mistrust of others, anorectics will not accept excessive praise.

Behavioral interventions such as rewards for new adaptive behavior may be incorporated into the management plan for the anorectic. Privileges need to be linked to caloric intake, however, and not to weight gain. Consistency in the treatment approach must be maintained throughout hospitalization to prevent manipulation of the staff by the patient.

PROMOTING EFFECTIVE COPING

The nurse must be sincere in his or her approach to anorectic patients. Using empathy and active listening shows concern for patients. At first, patients may be in a dependent patient role, but as the condition improves, the nurse should encourage patients to assume more responsibility for their behavior and feelings. Having patients participate in their treatment planning fosters independence and maturity and facilitates the development of healthy coping mechanisms.

The nurse must demonstrate a belief in patients' abilities to improve their maladaptive behaviors and provide encouragement for accomplishments. Patients should be allowed some flexibility in daily routines, but the treatment team must set and maintain limits. Limit setting not only provides the structure necessary to assure the safety of the patient but also reflects a sense of caring.

Patients need to be encouraged to explore their fears and feelings about gaining weight. Help them understand and accept these fears. Gaining insight into their relationships with others can help patients deal with their disorder. As patients risk self-disclosure, their anxiety may intensify. The nurse must have advanced preparation and the skills necessary to prevent a new crisis. For the inexperienced nurse, spending time with the patient, observing the behavior, and documenting accordingly are valuable contributions to the success of the treatment.

PROMOTING IMPROVED PERCEPTION OF BODY IMAGE

Body image reflects a person's attitude and reveals something about his or her self-concept. Body image constantly changes in response to life's experiences and perceptions. During adolescence, when the fear of rejection is great, perceptions of body size and weight play a major role in self-concept.

Anorectics have extreme misperceptions of their body size. No matter how thin they are, what they see in the mirror is someone who needs to lose weight. Encourage anorectic patients to express these feelings. Be accepting of the patients' mental mistakes. Help patients accept both their strengths and weaknesses.

PROMOTING FEELINGS OF SELF-WORTH

Anorectics refuse to accept reinforcement for anything less than perfection. Help patients identify and focus on their positive attributes. Encourage patients to ventilate their true feelings in whatever ways they find comfortable.

The nurse must offer an unconditional acceptance of both the negative and positive feelings expressed by patients. Discounting patients' feelings will only increase their humility. Acceptance helps patients to realize that negative feelings are normal, that mistakes are tolerated, and that perfection and acceptance are not synonymous. For anorectics, the ability to compromise indicates progress and a greater level of personal awareness.

PROGNOSIS AND OUTCOME

The effect of interventions in the treatment of anorexia nervosa is not well understood, and the outcome is uncertain. Some anorectics recover, while others become permanently incapacitated or die. Both resolution of the underlying psychological problem and nutritional counseling are crucial to recovery. Comerci, Kilbourne, and Harrison

(1989) point out that early motivation for change is believed to be a good prognostic sign.

BULIMIA NERVOSA

Bulimia nervosa, more commonly known as binge eating, is the frequent compulsion to ingest large amounts of food in a short period of time (usually less than 2 hours). Bulimia nervosa is a disorder closely related to anorexia nervosa in that feelings of lack of control and distorted body image are present, but bulimia is a distinct eating disorder in itself. Bulimia is characterized by episodes of overeating and purging through self-induced vomiting, laxative and/or diuretic use, fasting, or vigorous exercise. These episodes are followed by post-binge guilt, self-deprecating thoughts, and depression. Bulimia occurs in anoretic, normal weight, and obese individuals. Most bulimics are young white females of high school or college age, middle to upper-middle class, well educated, and intelligent.

Nicole, a 21-year-old part-time secretary and full-time nursing student, came to the Mental Health Department because of binge eating. She complained that while she was concerned about her body image and weight, she regularly went on eating binges that lasted 2 to 5 days. These episodes left her nauseated and weak. Nicole expressed feelings of guilt and shame over her lack of will power. She admitted to abusing alcohol and drugs.

The initial interview with Nicole revealed a significant family/psychosocial history. Nicole lived with her mother, her alcoholic stepfather, and a sister who was viewed by the family as the "pretty one." Nicole related a history of sexual abuse by her grandfather between the ages of 10 and 13. She confided in her mother on several occasions regarding her grandfather's incestuous behavior but was told by her mother "you will get over it." Nicole had never mentioned it again.

Psychotherapy with Nicole involved helping her to identify inner conflict and self-defeating behaviors. As she began to discuss her feelings openly and honestly, the need for indirect expression of her anger lessened, and the binge eating subsided.

HISTORY

The nurse may be astonished by the bulimic's obsession to control eating and the inability to do so. The consumption of food is described more as an addiction, an escape from life's pressures, than a means of satisfying hunger. There is usually a failure at many "quick" weight-loss endeavors, causing the patient to lose control and binge. Weight fluctuations are common with bulimics, as are night binges.

Family characteristics as perceived by the bulimic include a high level of conflict, low emphasis on independence, and little appreciation for the open expression of feelings (Laraia & Stuart, 1990).

Many bulimics were formerly anorectics, while others may become anorectic. The nurse must keep in mind that these two conditions, although different, often coexist. Bulimics, like anorectics, are usually very secretive about their eating habits. Feeling ashamed, the bulimic will often withhold information about symptoms.

SIGNS AND SYMPTOMS

Patients with bulimia nervosa have feelings of low self-esteem, lack of control, worthlessness, and guilt. They are embarrassed and ashamed of their binges (eating three or four bags of chips, two or three pizzas and several dozen cookies is not unusual). Bulimics live daily in a state of mental chaos. They want to give up on life, and they want to keep their habit. Binging is their means of escaping life's pressures, but it results in feelings of worthlessness.

Anxiety, limited impulse control, unsatisfactory interpersonal relationships, and chronic depression are characteristics of this disorder. Bulimics are preoccupied with food and cannot delay gratification; therefore gorging becomes a compulsive ritual. Unlike anorectics, bulimics recognize their bizarre eating behaviors and may self-refer to an eating-disorders program.

Bulimic patients are usually of average or slightly above average weight. Their appearance may not offer any significant clues to the disorder. Bulimic patients are usually older than anorectics and more outgoing. They may engage in impulsive behaviors, such as gambling, shoplifting, and alcohol or drug abuse. On the unit, bulimics may steal others' food.

Physical signs of bulimia nervosa include hoarseness and esophagitis, enlarged parotid glands, dental enamel erosion, muscle weakness, and lacerations of palate and calluses on knuckles (sometimes called Cooper's sign) due to self-induced vomiting. In the advanced stages, amenorrhea may be present. Bulimic patients may complain of weakness and fatigue. Laboratory tests may reveal electrolyte abnormalities; potentially fatal cardiac arrhythmias could occur.

NURSING INTERVENTIONS

For bulimics, the goal of nursing interventions is to promote effective coping skills, help them recognize anxiety-producing events, and help them avoid binging and purging in response to anxiety (Chitty,

1992). In order to establish a therapeutic relationship with the bulimic, the nurse must be genuine and reassuring. Scheduled contact with the patient should be provided. The nurse should define in simple terms the role and responsibilities for both patient and nurse. Once trust is established, help the patient identify the situations that produce anxiety. What were the coping behaviors prior to binging and purging? What are healthier ways of handling anxiety?

USING PATIENT CONTRACTS

Patient contracts may be useful with bulimics. Contracts define the expectations of the patient as well as the reinforcement from the staff. The contract should be a mutual endeavor between the patient and the nurse and must be renegotiated at intervals. Such a contract might look like the one shown below (adapted from Steckel, 1982, p. 44):

PATIENT CONTRACT

I, _____ , will _____
            (patient)   (behavior)

in return for _____ .
                     (reinforcement)

Patient _____

Nurse _____

Date _____

(Room at the bottom of the contract page should be used to record information about items in the contract that may need further explanation or that need to be spelled out in greater detail. The space may also be used to record other information needed by either the patient or the therapist.)

PROMOTING EFFECTIVE COPING

Help the patient to identify the triggers that cause binging. What emotions precipitate the binging? Fear? Boredom? Anger? Loneliness? Once these high-risk situations are identified, the nurse can help the patient identify alternate behaviors, such as exercise, a hobby, or a warm bath. Encourage the patient to express feelings that have been suppressed because they were considered unacceptable. Help the patient to identify healthier ways to express those feelings.

The exaggerated sense of guilt and inferiority that bulimics feel is overwhelming. Role playing with the nurse is an effective way for patients to deal with these feelings and experiment with new behaviors.

Involve the patients in their discharge planning. Compliance is improved when they have an active part in goal setting. The discharge plan for the bulimic should include the productive use of time, appropriate expression of feelings, and nutritional counseling. Goals should be realistic. One small win can reinforce another and build confidence.

Intrafamilial conflicts reinforce maladaptive eating behaviors; therefore families must be included in the plan of care for the patient. Listen to the family's concerns and fears about the patient's bulimia. Encourage the family to identify their own strengths and weaknesses and to explore together their own coping mechanisms. Encourage the family to share their feelings with one another. Help the family understand the needs of the patient. Social support is an important determinant in one's ability to make stressful decisions. Make appropriate referrals to community resources.

PROGNOSIS AND OUTCOME

Generally, the prognosis for bulimia is less favorable than for uncomplicated anorexia nervosa. Polivy and Thomsen (1988) point out that the abnormal cycle of binging and purging is difficult to break because, to the bulimic, it means control over the body as well as control in other areas of personal functioning. Serious complications, including death, may occur as a result of electrolyte imbalances. Comerci, Kilbourne, and Harrison (1989) note that because depression is so prevalent in bulimics, the risk of suicide is also greater.

COMPULSIVE OVEREATING

Compulsive overeating has not long been recognized as an addiction. Obesity, a symptom of compulsive overeating, historically has been the focus of treatment rather than the addiction itself.

Obesity is generally defined as body weight exceeding the recommended weight by 20 percent. Obesity is found among the affluent as well as in lower socioeconomic groups and is common among both women and men. Obesity is most prevalent between the ages of 20 and 50.

Emotional factors have always been linked with obesity. In times past, emotional disturbances were viewed as causes of obesity, but it is now believed that these disturbances are the result of obesity.

The nurse cannot assume that all obese individuals are emotionally disturbed because many appear to be well adjusted. The focus of the following discussion will be on the obese patient who is psychologically impaired.

Phillip is 44 years old, 6'1", and weighs 300 pounds. He has been on many diets over the past several years. The last attempt at weight loss consisted of eating only grapefruit and eggs, lasted 2 weeks, and netted a total weight loss of three pounds.

Phillip went to a private psychiatrist with complaints of depression. He reported that his problems began 8 years ago when his wife left him. Unable to find a satisfying relationship with another woman, Phillip turned to food for comfort. His weight had escalated from a previous 200 pounds to his current weight.

Phillip was so discouraged every time he looked into the mirror that he would consume huge quantities of food just to feel better. His sense of satisfaction was short lived, however, and soon after binging, he would feel guilty. He stated he felt under constant scrutiny by others and perceived himself as a total failure.

Psychotherapy with Phillip involved helping him to explore his feelings about the meaning of obesity and body image. With encouragement and support from his therapist, Phillip began to explore feelings about his relationships with others. Soon he began assuming responsibility for himself. With the help of his therapist, Phillip was able to set realistic weight-loss goals, initiate an exercise program, and identify healthier coping strategies.

HISTORY

Most obese patients report a lifetime of noncompliance with various weight-loss methods. Between-meal snacking and late night eating are common to the obese. Because genetics and family traditions and beliefs contribute to obesity, obtaining a family history is useful. People with eating disorders are likely to have a history of chemical dependence. Any preexisting medical condition, as well as any medication, should be ruled out as a cause of the weight gain. Many obese people live a sedentary lifestyle and engage in few recreational activities.

SIGNS AND SYMPTOMS

Not only do obese individuals suffer from the sigma of obesity, but they are blamed for being fat. Fatness is not valued in our society as thinness is; thus overweight people are stereotyped. Such societal labels as "lazy," "weak," and "self-indulgent" add to the patient's poor self-esteem. These individuals are not weak. They are, in fact, usually very determined overachievers, searching for acceptance from others, and grateful for any crumb of human kindness. Patients who compulsively overeat may feel hopeless over their failure to lose weight. It is important to recognize that obesity is a complex problem and that the relationship one has with food is influenced by many biopsychosocial factors.

Many obese patients live out their fantasies through food. Roth (1985) believes that "many compulsive overeaters eat because they don't know that they are allowed to express the anger they carry inside" (p. 64). Emotions were meant to be expressed; if they are not, they can all be displaced onto food. Because food asks nothing in return, it is perceived as safer and more predictable than interpersonal relationships for those who fear rejection.

Obese people tend to be less active than normal-weight individuals, but the total energy expenditure is no different from that in the nonobese. The reason for this is that it requires increased energy to move the excess body fat.

The pain experienced by compulsive overeaters comes neither from the weight gain nor from the negative comments about their bodies. The pain comes from within as these messages are translated into a measure of self-worth. To some, in a culture where the social pressures for body thinness are so powerful, being fat is the ultimate failure!

Obesity may result in feelings of depression, anxiety, low self-esteem, and social isolation. These negative mood states may produce the need to turn to something that never fails us—food.

NURSING INTERVENTIONS

The nurse must approach obese patients in a supportive, nonjudgmental manner and accept them as people. The ultimate goal of treatment is to help patients achieve a balance between caloric intake and energy expenditure. Nursing interventions should focus on ways to teach patients good nutrition, to improve their current nutritional status, and to promote social interaction and a sense of well-being.

TEACHING GOOD NUTRITION

Some obese patients demonstrate a basic knowledge of good nutrition, while many others have a nutritional knowledge deficit. The nurse must recognize that patients' negative self-concepts potentiate the need for emotional nurturing, that is, food. Because of their impulsiveness and inability to delay gratification, many compulsive over-eaters cannot distinguish emotional hunger from biological hunger.

The nurse can discuss the basic food groups with patients and encourage them to select favorites from each group. Emphasize to patients the importance of examining food labels. Written nutritional materials are also helpful.

IMPROVING NUTRITIONAL STATUS

Help patients establish realistic goals for improving their nutritional status. Help them explore ways to change eating habits. Establishing a program of exercise helps to achieve a more acceptable energy balance.

Keeping a food journal helps patients identify not only patterns of eating but also the relationship between emotions and eating. Review the journal with patients weekly and help them identify techniques for dealing with the urge to eat. Stress that relapse may be prevented by using delay and distraction strategies in high-risk situations.

Give positive feedback when patients achieve any small weight loss. "Slips" in progress can provoke a variety of responses, generally negative ones. Help patients to avoid overreacting to these experiences and use them constructively. Teach patients how to make healthy selections when dining out.

PROMOTING SOCIAL INTERACTION

For the socially isolated patient, the nurse can offer companionship while making no demands. Frequent, brief visits indicate interest and acceptance of the patient. Engage the patient initially in a non-competitive, one-to-one activity, then gradually progress to group activities. Allow the patient the freedom to leave the group if anxiety becomes a problem. Recognize any time spent socializing as positive, and reinforce that behavior in the patient.

PROMOTING A SENSE OF WELL-BEING

Many compulsive overeaters experience feelings of hopelessness and social isolation but feel powerless to change. The nurse can promote hopefulness in obese patients by spending time with them. Encourage obese patients to express both negative and positive feelings. Listen with an empathetic ear and an accepting attitude.

Parent and Whall (1984) found that there was a positive relationship between physical activity and self-esteem. Encourage daily exercise for obese patients. Promote good grooming and hygiene because this heightens self-esteem.

Encourage patients to make eating the primary focus at mealtime. Teach them to eat slowly and put utensils down between bites.

This can slow the eating process and demonstrate that change is possible.

Teach patients about obesity and its physiologic and psychologic implications. Involve them in the decision making regarding their care. Reaching an understanding of one's condition promotes hope. Encourage patients to share experiences with other eating-disordered patients. Self-esteem increases with the ability to help others. Reinforce any expression of hopefulness.

PROGNOSIS AND OUTCOME

The key to successful weight loss is motivation. Compulsive overeaters must admit a personal need for help and commit to change. Without this, no amount of intervention from others will be effective. They must realize that losing the weight is only part of permanent weight control. Maintenance of a normal weight is the ultimate goal. Patients must gain insight into their relationships with others as well as their relationship with food. In giving up the security of food and smothering relationships, self-doubt vanishes and a new freedom is found.

SUMMARY

Whatever the cause of eating disorders, all affected individuals demonstrate pathologic coping skills. These maladaptive behaviors are manifested in eating-disordered patients through physiologic and psychologic alterations, self-esteem disturbances, and body-image distortions.

Recovery from eating disorders is a long journey filled with uncertainty. Eating-disordered patients must recognize the importance of small wins and set their goals accordingly. They must come to realize and appreciate that balance is the way to physical and mental health. They must let down their psychologic defenses, face their denial, and give up the struggle to be someone else. Colvin and Olson (1985) believe that these individuals must stop blaming others and go from self-delusion to self-honesty.

Patients may sometimes fail to respond to the best of efforts, and the nurse may feel defeated. The satisfaction that comes, however, with knowing that you have made a difference in these individuals' lives more than compensates for the frustrations experienced along the way.

ANNOTATED BIBLIOGRAPHY

American Psychiatric Association: *Diagnostic and Statistical Manual of Mental Disorders*, ed. 3, rev. APA, Washington, DC, 1987.

Chitty, K. K.: Eating disorders. In Wilson, H. S., and Kneisl, C. R. (eds.): *Psychiatric Nursing*. Addison-Wesley, Redwood City, CA, 1992, pp. 469–486.

> *Chapter defines eating disorders and describes both historical and theoretical foundations of each. Major focus: nursing care plans and appropriate nursing interventions for both client and family.*

Christie, C.: *Compulsive Eating, Anorexia, and Bulimia.* Institute for Natural Resources, Berkeley, CA, 1990.

> *Defines compulsive eating, bulimia, and anorexia. Profiles of each to include etiology, symptoms, and treatment.*

Colvin, R. H., and Olson, S. C.: *In search of thinness: Secrets of people who have lost weight permanently.* New Woman, November 1985, pp. 77–83.

> *Authors identify four common phases that successful dieters experience during weight loss. Identifies strategies of once-obese now permanently slim individuals.*

Comerci, G. D., Kilbourne, K. A., and Harrison, G. G.: Eating disorders: Obesity, anorexia nervosa, and bulimia. In Hofmann, A., and Greydanus, D. (eds.): *Adolescent Medicine*, ed. 2. Appleton & Lange, Norwalk, CT, 1989, pp. 441–461.

> *Chapter reviews each eating disorder in detail, including radiologic and laboratory findings. Major focus on medical evaluation, assessment, and treatment.*

Deters, G. E.: Problems of nutrition. In Lewis, S. M., and Collier, I. C. (eds.): *Medical-Surgical Nursing: Assessment and Management of Clinical Problems*, ed. 2. McGraw-Hill, New York, 1987.

> *Chapter describes essential components of sound nutrition and medical/nursing management of bulimia and anorexia nervosa.*

Laraia, M. T., and Stuart, G. W.: *Bulimia: A review of nutritional and health behaviors.* Journal of Child and Adolescent Psychiatric Mental Health Nursing, 1990, 3(3): 91–97.

> *Epidemiology, physiology, and precipitating factors are reviewed. Treatment from a holistic approach is explored.*

Lucas, A. R.: Eating disorders. In Lewis, M. (ed.): *Child and Adolescent Psychiatry*. Williams & Wilkins, Baltimore, 1991, pp. 573–583.

> *Chapter looks at adolescents and eating disorders from a developmental prospective. Biologic as well as psychologic theories are discussed. Family and interpersonal dynamics as well as environmental and social influences are explored as causes of eating disorders.*

Parent, C., and Whall, A.: *Are physical activity, self-esteem, and depression related?* Journal of Gerontological Nursing, 1984, 10(9): 8.

> *This study identifies the positive relationship between self-esteem and physical activity in the elderly.*

Polivy, J., and Thomsen, L.: Dieting and other eating disorders. In Blechman, E. A., and Brownell, K. (eds.): *Handbook of Behavioral Medicine for Women.* Pergamon, New York, 1988, pp. 345–352.

> *Chapter focuses on eating disorders from compulsive eating to anorexia and bulimia and attempts to answer why the disorders are an issue in women's health.*

Roth, G.: *Feeling fat doesn't have to mean feeling you're a failure.* New Woman, September 1985, pp. 62–64.

> *Article examines perceptions of obese women in regard to self-worth; emphasizes positive self-talk.*

Steckel, S.B.: *Patient Contracting.* Appleton-Century-Crofts, Norwalk, CT, 1982.

Sundermeyer, C. A.: *Emotional Weight.* New Outlook, Ann Arbor, MI, 1989.

> *Looks at the causes of obesity—both psychologic and nutritional. Forces reader to identify true emotions and relationship with food.*

Multiple Choice. Circle the letter that you think represents the best answer.

1. One predominate characteristic of anorectics is:
   a. Anxiety.
   b. Anemia.
   c. Depression.
   d. Preoccupation with food.

2. The percentage of total body weight lost in anorexia nervosa is often:
   a. 5 percent
   b. 20 percent
   c. 25 percent or more.
   d. 40 percent or more.

3. One of the diagnostic criteria for bulimia is:
   a. Weight loss of 15 percent.
   b. Refusal to maintain minimal body weight.
   c. Under 20 years of age.
   d. Awareness of abnormal eating patterns.

4. One of the many physical complications of binging/purging is:
   a. Hypotension.
   b. Pathologic fractures.
   c. Decayed teeth.
   d. Throat cancer.

5. Characteristics of the compulsive overeater might include all of the following except:
   a. Knowledge deficit in regard to nutrition.
   b. Hopelessness.
   c. Social isolation.
   d. Laziness.

6. Treatment for the compulsive overeater should include all of the following except:
   a. Calorie restriction of 600 calories per day.
   b. Nutrition education.
   c. Keeping food records.
   d. Daily exercise.

Short Answer. Answer the following questions as briefly and specifically as possible.

281

1. Describe the primary nursing interventions in the treatment of anorexia nervosa.

_____

_____

_____.

2. Describe the primary nursing interventions in the treatment of bulimia nervosa.

_____

_____

_____.

3. Describe the primary nursing interventions in the treatment of compulsive overeating.

_____

_____

_____.

True or False. Circle your choice.

T   F   1. The client with anorexia nervosa may have secret rituals about food.

T   F   2. Anorectics usually are not able to exercise because of their weakened condition.

T   F   3. The bulimic is usually very withdrawn.

T   F   4. The bulimic is very open and honest in regard to binging/purging.

T   F   5. The compulsive overeater should eat three well-balanced meals a day.

20

Care for Chemically Dependent Patients

LEARNING OBJECTIVES

Student will be able to:
1. Identify factors that influence the use and abuse of alcohol.
2. Identify Jellinek's four stages of alcoholism.
3. Define the term *cross tolerance*.
4. Identify methods of treatment for alcoholism and other drug abuse.

The abuse of alcohol and other drugs represents a significant problem for health authorities in the United States. In fact, alcohol abuse alone has been said to be the third-largest health problem in America. When abusers of other drugs are added to the ranks of those who abuse alcohol, the problem becomes even more devastating. Although many people believe that only members of the lower socioeconomic groups abuse alcohol and other drugs, statistics indicate that abusers are found in all socioeconomic groups.

Although the deaths of athletes who die from cardiac arrhythmias associated with cocaine use frequently make the headlines, and although large heroin and cocaine busts make sensational news stories, alcohol remains the most commonly abused drug in the United States. Alcohol is more readily available than other drugs, it is legal, and its use is socially accepted by our society. In fact, the drunk seems to occupy a special place in our society. If our friend John Smith gets drunk at a party, he is laughed at when he stumbles over a table, curses loudly, or makes a pass at a friend's wife. All of his behavior is forgiven because he is not considered to be responsible because of his drunkenness. If Mr. Smith engaged in these behaviors under other circumstances, he would quickly become a social outcast or would be jailed for assault.

We are a nation of drug takers. The television daily presents the virtues of every conceivable form of pain relief, sleep inducer, muscle relaxer, and vitamin supplement. If creatures from outer space were to observe our television commercials and report back to their leaders, they probably would say that we are a nation of people who never sleep and who suffer constant low back pain, nasal congestion, bronchial spasms, gastric indigestion, tension headaches, aching feet, bloodshot eyes, and premenstrual pain and tension. They might also say that the life-sustaining substances on earth are so poor that they must be supplemented daily with many different kinds and colors of special vitamin tablets and that, indeed, things are so bad that humans even have to have special foods for their animals that include the same kinds of supplements. Television commercials market all these various pills, along with alcoholic beverages, as a sure means of making life more tolerable and thus more pleasurable. Most drug abusers (remember that alcohol is a drug) drink or take pills in an attempt to withdraw or sedate themselves to escape from the realities, or as many say, the boredom, of the world in which they live.

Unfortunately, the most significant impact created by media advertising of alcohol and pills lies in the promotion of an attitude rather than promotion of the products themselves. For the most part, the products are not harmful. On the other hand, the attitudes created by the media indicate that it is okay for people to seek happiness, escape, excitement, or pleasure from a pill or a bottle with seemingly little regard for the possible psychologic or physical addiction that may occur as a consequence of their drug-taking behavior.

The following sections present information related specifically to abusers of alcohol and abusers of other drugs. Although there are similarities and differences between the two groups (Table 20–1), they are presented separately in order to emphasize differences in treatment and management approaches.

ABUSE OF ALCOHOL

The *DSM-III-R* (p. 173) divides the category of alcohol abuse into three main subtypes: (1) regular daily intake of large amounts of alcohol, (2) regular heavy drinking limited to weekends and (3) long periods of sobriety interspersed with binges of daily heavy drinking lasting weeks or months.

People who abuse alcohol are known by a variety of names ranging from *problem drinker* to *alcoholic, wino, lappster, derelict,* and *bum.* The term *problem drinker* is usually applied to a person who does not have the obvious symptoms associated with clinically diagnosed alcohol dependence. *Alcohol-dependent* is the term used in the

Table 20–1.

COMPARISON OF ALCOHOLICS AND OTHER DRUG ABUSERS

Similarities	Differences
1. Addicts in both groups come from all sociologic and economic levels.	1. Men outnumber women 3:1 in drug abuse. The ratio of men to women for alcohol abuse is 1:1.
2. Basic personality structures for both include dependency, low self-esteem, inability to tolerate tension, immaturity, and difficulty in accepting responsibility for their own actions. They often blame their problems on someone else or on some event in their lives.	2. The average age for alcoholics is substantially higher, being 30 to 55 years for alcoholics and 16 to 25 years for other drug abusers.
3. Both cause psychologic and physical dependence, with psychologic dependence occurring first.	3. Alcohol is much more socially acceptable than other drugs.
4. Abusers often start the habit for the same reason—to feel accepted or to gain a feeling of social well-being.	4. It usually takes longer to become addicted to alcohol than to other drugs. Persons may become psychologically dependent on other drugs after the first dose; this is not so with alcohol.
5. Both begin behavior leading to addiction because of psychologic maladjustment and access to drugs or alcohol.	5. Alcohol withdrawal symptoms may appear from 1 to 8 days after the last drink; drug withdrawal symptoms begin to occur 12 to 16 hours after the last dose.
6. In advanced stages, both present a basically poor general appearance and look extremely malnourished because they spend more on their habit than on food.	6. Persons withdrawing from alcohol suffer tremors, increasing jitters, spasmodic gait, nausea and vomiting, loss of consciousness, convulsions, hallucinations, and death. Persons withdrawing from drugs other than alcohol often have teary eyes, persistent yawning, a runny nose, increasing restlessness, hostility, and severe abdominal cramps.
7. Both cause severe economic problems for the themselves and their families due to the cost of addiction.	7. Alcoholic withdrawal is frequently a more acute medical problem.
8. Both have impaired judgment.	

Table 20–1.

COMPARISON OF ALCOHOLICS AND OTHER DRUG ABUSERS *(Cont'd)*

Similarities	Differences
9. Both initiate treatment because of an acute medical problem or the concern of someone else for them—rarely of their own initiative; both use massive denial. In treatment, both need patience, understanding, consistency, a structured environment, and empathy—not sympathy.	8. Alcohol is taken by mouth; other drugs can be taken by mouth but are frequently taken intravenously or subcutaneously (skin popping) to increase and speed up the desired effect. Other drugs may also be sniffed or snorted.
11. Both need increasingly larger doses of their drug to produce the desired effect, with the end result being an increased intake not to feel good but to keep from feeling bad and to prevent withdrawal symptoms.	9. Unpredictable bad trips are often experienced with drugs other than alcohol.
12. Both types of addiction cause severe medical complications.	10. Blood pressure, pulse, and respiration are depressed with an overdose of drugs other than alcohol; in an alcohol overdose, pulse is often rapid (over 100), respiration is increased (often exceeding 30), and blood pressure is frequently normal.
13. It is often necessary in planning treatment to include family members.	
14. It is difficult for people in the medical field to accept drug abuse as an illness; therefore they are reluctant to treat abusers and sometimes feel that they are wasting their time.	11. Possession of drugs other than alcohol without a prescription is illegal, while alcohol is legally sold to anyone over 21 years of age.
15. Both addictions are curable but not arrestable.	
16. After initial addiction, each may become more of a physical problem than a mental one.	

DSM-III-R to describe those persons with drinking characteristics generally called "alcoholism," which along with the term "alcoholic" was coined in 1849 by Magnus Huss. In this chapter, we will use the term alcoholic as synonymous with the *DSM-III-R* term alcohol-dependent. Individuals are diagnosed as alcoholics when they have lost control of their drinking to the extent that interpersonal, family, and community relationships have become seriously threatened, dis-turbed, or significantly impaired. Although superficially alcoholics can be witty, charming, and friendly, a great number of them are destruc-tive and aggressive when they have been drinking.

Long-term alcoholics tend to be pale, thin, and poorly nourished because they spend their money on alcohol rather than food and because they forget to eat when they are drinking. Long-term male alcoholics may have dilated blood vessels in their faces and a bulblike, fleshy nose, which is frequently referred to as a "whiskey nose." The alcoholic individual often has bloodshot eyes and a generally disheveled appear-ance. Poor personal and dental hygiene are likely, as are a hoarse voice, hand tremors, and "the jitters." Alcoholics also tend to have a spasmodic work record or show decreased work proficiency. Of the approximately 5 to 10 million alcoholics in the United States today, only 5 percent are of the stereotyped skid row bum–type. *Most do not fit the description just presented.* Instead, they are our neighbors, relatives, and friends. They go to work every day wearing neatly pressed clothes and they have families, go to church on Sunday, live in suburbia, and generally keep up a good front. With seemingly so much going for them, one might wonder why such people become alcoholics.

FACTORS INFLUENCING ALCOHOLISM

Some authorities report that alcoholics have ambivalent feelings about living and dying and that chronic alcoholism represents a slow form of suicide. Alcoholics often have a long-established pattern of self-medication using alcohol. They "medicate" themselves for pro-motions, weddings, new babies, job changes, and so forth, until finally they find themselves "medicating" in order to just make it through the day at the office. Many authorities see alcoholism as a lifestyle, a means of adjusting to a particular combination of circumstances and personality types. One frequently finds in the history of alcoholics a very poor mother-child relationship and significantly poor self-esteem. Many alcoholics have passive and dependent personality traits and thus have difficulty facing up to life's daily problems. They often lack the confidence to make choices and feel inadequate to face the basic tasks of life.

Alcoholics may be very angry about being so dependent and thus become frustrated and hostile. Because hostility often creates more hostility in relationships, alcoholics are likely to be rejected by others and may indeed begin to experience difficulty in meeting their basic needs because of such rejection. Alcoholics typically have difficulty tolerating tension and appear to always be wrapped up in their own problems. Personality tests given to alcoholics frequently reflect a cyclic pattern in their personalities. Alcoholics feel tense and depressed and try to relieve these feelings by drinking. When they are rejected for becoming drunk, they become even more depressed and guilt ridden. They then drink more to reduce their new feelings of guilt and depression and a vicious cycle has begun.

Besides these psychological factors, a constitutional or genetic factor has also been suggested as a possible reason that some people who drink become alcoholic while others do not. Within the last few years much effort has gone into demonstrating the presence of an alcohol "gene" that is passed on to the children of alcoholics. This gene is thought to make persons more susceptible to becoming addicted than the general population. Although there is still not a great deal of research data to substantiate this belief, and still a lot of controversy about the gene theory, many people believe strongly that there is an inborn metabolic vulnerability that causes people to become alcoholics. We do know that some individuals cannot tolerate alcohol and may become drunk after only one drink or may become pathologically intoxicated after using only a small amount of alcohol.

Social factors may also contribute to alcoholism. The ads for alcoholic beverages stress the "good life," and society in general is very accepting of the use of alcohol. An individual drinks with others and feels accepted. Cocktail parties abound, and alcohol is served at practically every social function. Alcohol is generally considered to be a social facilitator, and three out of four American adults drink to some extent.

While many authorities believe that all drinkers begin to drink for the same reason, most do not believe that an individual chooses to become an alcoholic. That is, it is not an act of will. Rather, alcoholics begin to drink in order to sedate themselves so that they do not have to face the pain or boredom they perceive as inherent in living out their daily lives. The drinking temporarily makes it easier for them to face their problems or insecurities or shyness or disappointment or hurt or perceived failure. As these individuals begin to drink more and more, their self-esteem problems are severely compounded. When they do go for treatment, they often speak of having a "drinking problem" but somehow divorce themselves as people from the "drinking problem." If one did not know better, one might think that alcoholics were talking about someone other than themselves. Alcoholics use massive denial as a defense mechanism and have much difficulty accepting personal responsibilities for their drinking problem. The process of being able to accept the fact that one is an alcoholic seems to be a major key in the treatment of alcoholism. Most treatment programs stress that once a person becomes addicted to alcohol, that person will always be addicted and can never regain the ability to tolerate alcohol. Alcoholics Anonymous (AA) and other such groups stress the fact that a "recovered alcoholic" must never drink; if that person does drink again, he or she is considered to have relapsed.

Although there are many theories about what causes alcoholism, there is very little disagreement over the fact that there is both a psychologic and a physical addiction to the drug. In fact, momentarily setting aside the gene theory, psychologic dependence usually occurs before physical dependence. An individual drinks, feels relief, drinks more, feels more relief, and so on, eventually becoming physically addicted. At that point, the alcoholism often becomes as much a physical problem as a mental problem.

PHYSIOLOGIC EFFECTS

It is important to remember that alcohol is a poison and, therefore, is highly toxic to the body. It may sedate one to the extent that the problems of daily life become more tolerable, but it irritates practically every organ system in the body. It inflames the gastrointestinal tract (including the pancreas and the liver). It depresses the production of bone marrow and thus the production of red blood cells, increasing the individual's susceptibility to infection and bruises. Alcohol causes both brain tissue changes and scar tissue formations in the liver (cirrhosis). It may also cause significant damage to the heart. It decreases metabolic efficiency and reduces the individual's ability to absorb vitamins. The liver may become increasingly enlarged, less functional, and, therefore, less able to rid the body of toxic substances. Because alcohol sedates the cerebral cortex, an individual who is drinking is less able to think discriminately, which results in impaired judgment and motor function. Therefore, when individuals are intoxicated, they are much more likely to fall and hurt themselves. Alcoholics who are seen in the emergency room should be carefully checked for subdural hematomas and other signs of trauma, such as bruises, contusions, and fractures. Sexual impotence may also be a complication of alcoholism, further increasing the marital discord that is prominent when one or both marriage partners are alcoholic.

RECOGNIZING ALCOHOLIC TENDENCIES

Because alcoholics tend to use denial as a defense against having to face their alcoholism, they are likely to go for a long time without treatment. Because alcoholics are not likely to identify themselves as such, it is helpful to treating professionals to be able to recognize a person who may be alcoholic. The following questions are provided as a means of assessing whether or not an individual may be an alcoholic. Of course, when asking these questions, it is important to keep in mind that the denial mechanism may cause the person being questioned to lie or to otherwise distort the truth.

1. Have you ever lost work or been late for work because you were drinking?
2. Do you and your spouse ever argue about whether you drink too much?
3. Do your friends consider you to be a heavy drinker?
4. Are you quiet and withdrawn but become the "life of the party" after a few drinks?
5. Have you ever felt sorry about your drinking behavior?
6. Do you need a drink at certain times during the day, or do you usually drink throughout the day?
7. Do you often want a drink soon after waking in the morning?
8. Does drinking make it easier for you to get through the day?
9. Do you drink by yourself a good deal of the time?
10. Do you ever have difficulty recalling activities that occurred while you were drinking?
11. Do you feel better about yourself as a person when you are drinking?

A "yes" answer to any one of the preceding questions suggests the strong likelihood that an individual is alcoholic, and a "yes" answer to two or more questions increases the probability significantly.

THE ALCOHOLIC PROCESS

The process of becoming an alcoholic has been broken down into four stages by Jellinek (1960).

1. *Prealcoholic symptomatic phase.* In this phase, alcohol is first used to avoid problems or to bolster confidence during moments of stress or crisis. The drinking behavior takes the place of the development of adequate coping mechanisms, and, as stress occurs more often, the individual's drinking becomes more frequent. There is also an increase in the individual's ability to tolerate alcohol.

2. *Prodromal phase.* In this phase, the individual drinks heavily and the heavy drinking frequently leads to unconsciousness and memory blackouts. The individual cannot wait to get a few drinks but then feels guilty about drinking. There is usually no one to talk to about the problem.

3. *Crucial phase.* During this phase, there is a loss of control

and the individual is unable to abstain from drinking. The individual is likely to drink continuously until nausea or unconsciousness results. The individual may exhibit grandiose or aggressive behavior while drinking, along with remorse, self-pity, and resentment toward anyone who tries to prevent his or her drinking. Withdrawal symptoms will occur if the individual stops drinking.

4. *Chronic phase.* The behavior in this stage is marked by frequent "benders" and prolonged periods of intoxication. There is usually daily intake of alcohol in response to the physical craving that occurs as a result of metabolic changes. Nutritional deficiencies occur, as well as organ-system difficulties and behavior problems. Individuals in this stage frequently lose their jobs because they are unable to work effectively. They are also likely to experience severe marital disruption and lose the family through divorce. If individuals in this stage are not treated, death may occur within a relatively short period as a result of malnutrition, infection, or acute problems that occur when the person is unable to obtain alcohol. At this point, alcoholic hallucinosis (hallucinations after stopping drinking) and acute delirium tremens ("the DTs") are likely.

Jellinek stresses that not all of the phases and symptoms are experienced by every alcoholic and that they do not always occur in the same sequence.

TREATMENT

Although we have already said that society tends to tolerate and even accept the individual who is drunk, patients who are diagnosed as alcoholic are often rejected not only by family and friends but also by the medical personnel who are assigned to care for them. Although medical personnel tend to view alcoholism as a disease and are usually able to view it more objectively than the alcoholic's family and friends, many are still ambivalent toward the alcoholic. The professional person may feel frustrated by alcoholics and unconsciously reject them. Some authorities believe that the longer one works with alcoholics, the more negative one becomes toward them. Alcoholics tend to relapse frequently and resume drinking; thus it is often difficult for staff members to determine if they are making progress.

Medical personnel like to see their patients "get well" and do not like to see patients return. When alcoholic patients return time after time for detoxification, the treatment team has a tendency to become discouraged. The frequent return rate has been suggested as one of the main reasons alcoholics have difficulty finding acceptance among treatment team members. This is particularly true if patients do not appear to be trying to help themselves or if their will power is so poor that the very afternoon they are discharged, they are returned to the unit unconscious from an alcohol overdose. One must remember, however, that alcoholism is a chronic illness and, as in all chronic illnesses, the patient is subject to relapses.

Because alcoholics are not well received by treatment teams, family members, and friends, it is no wonder that a great many people have difficulty admitting their alcoholism. Perhaps for this reason, among others, the denial mechanism mentioned earlier is brought into play by the individuals as a defense against admitting their alcoholism. The alcoholic's massive use of denial is a major obstacle throughout the treatment process. Because of the denial, alcoholics often feel obligated to refuse treatment and detoxification because to allow treatment would be to admit their alcoholic condition. Alcoholics' use of denial, abusive language, belligerence, and manipulative behavior is severely detrimental to good patient-staff relationships. At first it may be difficult to understand why alcoholics behave as they do, but if one examines the way alcoholics enter treatment, it is somewhat easier to see the reasons behind their behavior.

WAYS OF ENTERING TREATMENT

Alcoholics usually enter treatment in one of four ways. The most frequent way an alcoholic begins to receive treatment is through recognition of the alcoholic status by someone in the general hospital when the alcoholic has been admitted for some other reason. The patient may have sought medical attention for stomach ulcers, "nerves," urinary problems, liver disease, gastrointestinal problems, or other physical complaints; or the patient may complain of depression or anxiety. Most often the physical illness is secondary to the primary problem of alcoholism. A second way alcoholics may enter treatment is that they are brought by the police after being picked up for public drunkenness. In the past, public drunks were thrown into jail to "dry out," and research indicates that many people died from delirium tremens. Today, however, most states have legislation requiring that persons who are picked up for public drunkenness be taken to a hospital or to a treatment center for alcoholics. The third way an alcoholic may begin treatment is when a family member, concerned friend, employer, or health care worker becomes aware of an individual's drinking problem and is able to convince the person to seek treatment. The fourth, and perhaps the least likely, way for an alcoholic to begin treatment is through self-referral.

There is, however, one diagnostic category of alcoholics who usually do seek treatment on their own initiative because they realize something is really wrong and want help. This category is pathologic intoxication, or *alcohol idiosyncratic intoxication*, as specified in the third revised edition of the *Diagnostic and Statistical Manual of Mental Disorders (DSM-III-R)*. In pathologic intoxication, the individual becomes extremely intoxicated after only one or two drinks. Such individuals may be hostile, belligerent, and suicidal or may become severely depressed. For either type of reaction, symptoms usually last from a few hours to several hours, and there is often amnesia about the events. The cause of these idiosyncratic reactions is not known, but there is known to be greater susceptibility among persons with a history of neurologic trauma or neurologic disease processes as well as people who are fatigued or are in a weakened state from some other disease process.

RECOGNIZING SIGNS AND SYMPTOMS

Because alcoholic patients are not likely to tell treatment team members that they are alcoholics, it is important for all team members to be aware of the signs and symptoms that indicate the possibility of a patient's being alcoholic. Of course, if the patient smells of alcohol when admitted, many people are immediately alerted to the problem. However, if there is no reason to suspect that a patient is drinking, one must become attuned to other symptoms. Alcoholics may not go into active delirium tremens for a period of 1 to 8 days after their last drink. However, many other symptoms do appear 12 to 48 hours after the patient's last drink. Anxiety and irritability are often the first symptoms to appear as the alcohol begins to be processed out of the patient's system. Patients may then develop shakiness or tremors, begin to make unreasonable demands, or have temper tantrums. They may become so nauseated that they vomit or show evidence of dehydration. They may be extremely restless, agitated, aggressive, and confused. Alcoholics can become disoriented and may sometimes begin to hallucinate. To keep environmental factors from increasing the hallucinating behavior of alcoholic patients, staff members need to maintain an attitude of caring concern and frequently reorient patients to reality and to their environment. Explain to them who you are and restrict all visitors unless otherwise ordered. Place patients in a quiet room with no shadows so that they will not be subjected to unnecessary stimulation from television, radio, other patients, or shadows on the wall (which are often misinterpreted as demons or people intending harm).

At any point during withdrawal, alcoholic patients may begin to convulse and will die if not carefully managed. As a matter of fact, a significant number of patients in active delirium tremens die if treatment is inadequate. Some patients continue to deny their alcoholism despite the presence of such significant and dangerous symptoms. One point of considerable interest to people working in general hospitals and outpatient clinics is the way in which one can tell the difference between a drug overdose and an alcoholic withdrawal reaction. Although there may be some individual differences, a general rule is that although both drug and alcohol withdrawal cause slowed motor responses, drowsiness, and confusion, in the toxic alcohol state, the patient's vital signs are usually elevated. The patient has rapid respirations, a rapid pulse (over 100), and a normal blood pressure. In drug overdose, all vital signs are usually depressed. It is important to keep in mind, however, that alcoholics can become so acutely ill and have such poor circulation that they show a drastically lowered blood pressure. If this occurs, they must receive immediate emergency medical treatment in order to survive.

METHODS OF TREATMENT

Medical treatment of alcoholics in the prealcoholic and prodromal stages usually consists of some type of group therapy or, in some cases, individual psychotherapy. Treatment of alcoholics who are in the crucial or chronic phase not only requires group psychotherapy (there is no evidence that individual psychotherapy is beneficial) but often requires hospitalization or at least treatment in a special outpatient detoxification unit. Treatment of acute withdrawal from alcohol is accomplished primarily through the use of medication. These patients are given intravenous fluids to combat dehydration and minor tranquilizers to help calm them and help protect them from seizures. They are also thought to help reduce anxiety and guilt.

Librium is the tranquilizer most commonly used in the treatment of alcoholics, but other minor tranquilizers are also used. By the time alcoholics are in the crucial or chronic phase of alcoholism, they usually have decreased liver function due to cirrhosis or scarring of the liver, and Librium is not as difficult for the liver to metabolize as many of the other tranquilizers. Another reason physicians treat alcoholics with Librium is that while this drug is chemically similar to alcohol, it does not depress the brain centers. Anticonvulsants may be needed to further reduce convulsive activity in these patients, and multivitamin therapy is essential to replace the vitamins lost due to poor nutrition. In particular, thiamine deficiency and a deficiency in the B vitamins have been shown to be associated with Wernicke-Korsakoff syndrome and peripheral neuropathy, respectively. Alcoholics must always be considered to have a malabsorption syndrome until proven otherwise. Antacids are given for gastric distress, and anti-emetics are given for severe nausea and vomiting. Again, it is important to realize that these patients are severely ill and may die without adequate care.

A great deal more than the appropriate use of medications is involved in the successful treatment of alcoholics. Most treatment programs make sure that alcoholics learn about the effects of alcohol on the body. Treatment teams try to provide alcoholics with psychologic support while at the same time teaching them how to become more independent as they gradually learn to cope with the stress and problems involved in daily living. It is necessary to accept these patients without moralizing or blaming them for their behavior. On the other hand, it is necessary to help them begin to realize that they are responsible for their own behavior. Staff members need to be consistent and should not let alcoholic patients manipulate one staff member against another, as they often try to do. It is important to evaluate physical complaints carefully. If there are valid problems, they should be treated, but staff members should not let patients manipulate them into giving extra medications for nonexistent ills. At times, alcoholics going through detoxification become so desperate for alcohol that they will drink anything they think might have some alcohol content, including mouthwash and hair tonic.

It is important to point out realities to alcoholic patients and to try to keep them functioning in the here and now. If they are expressing remorse about what has happened in their lives or are expressing unrealistic plans for their future, they may be doing so in order to avoid coping with current problems. Activities that increase alcoholics' interaction with staff members and others help to build their self-esteem. It is important to reward or reinforce appropriate behaviors exhibited by alcoholics and to be sure that they receive recognition for all accomplishments.

Insofar as outpatient or follow-up care is concerned, inpatient hospital staffs and outpatient clinic staffs are rather limited in their effectiveness. Maintenance of sobriety depends primarily on the alcoholic. Most treatment centers try to work with the family while the patient is in treatment. Their acceptance of the patient and willingness to help are vital links in the recovery process.

After discharge, many alcoholics take a drug called Antabuse (disulfiram) to discourage them from drinking. If they take even one drink while on Antabuse, they experience severe nausea and vomiting, redness of the face and trunk, headaches, heart palpitations, a drastic lowering of blood pressure, and sometimes even death. Patients who have tried to drink while taking Antabuse indicate that the reaction is so severe that they will never drink alcohol again, at least not while they are on Antabuse. It should be noted that not all persons respond in the same to way Antabuse; some patients can drink some amount of alcohol while on Antabuse, while others will react strongly to even very small amounts. Antabuse works by allowing an accumulation of acetaldehyde in the patient's system. Acetaldehyde is an extremely potent toxin that produces hypotension and nausea. The hypotension may produce shock, which can produce death. The drug is active for 3 to 5 days after last ingestion.

One-to-one psychotherapy on an outpatient basis has not been shown to be successful in treating alcoholics. Group therapy programs such as those offered by AA seem to be considerably more effective. Such groups have a structured program with built-in rewards and reinforcements as well as built-in restrictions. AA gives alcoholics someone or something more powerful than themselves to lean on. Alcoholics know that if their resistance to taking a drink begins to slip, they can simply call their AA partner (called a sponsor) and they will receive help immediately. Perhaps AA groups are more successful in treating alcoholics because their members were once active alcoholics themselves. Not only do these people have greater empathy for the alcoholic, but they also have a personal understanding of the problems faced by the alcoholic. AA also has a group called Al-Anon, which helps the families of alcoholics learn to deal effectively with their alcoholic family member.

Regardless of the method, treating the alcoholic is a difficult task.

ABUSE OF OTHER DRUGS

Patients who abuse drugs other than alcohol also come from all socioeconomic levels. Male addicts, however, outnumber female addicts 3:1. Most of these addicts show basic similarities in personality structure and could be described as rather unstable, immature, passive, and dependent individuals. Their self-esteem is usually poor, and they seem to lack a purpose in life. They tend not to become involved in social activities and have strong self-destructive tendencies. Many are self-centered and seem to relish playing the role of martyr. Such individuals have difficulty tolerating stress, anxiety, or pain, and many have poor interpersonal relationships. Drug addicts have significant feelings of futility and have either real or imagined deprivations. Such psychologic maladjustments, along with a ready access to drugs and peer acceptance of taking them, very often set the stage for such individuals to become addicts.

Before becoming addicted to a narcotic, individuals have usually experimented with other types of drugs. Sometimes addicted patients were exposed to drugs accidentally. For example, when hospitalized, patients may routinely receive medication for pain. Not only is the pain relieved, but the medication causes the patients to feel good and to forget or ignore many or most of their problems. After being released from the hospital, they may then start looking for some drug to take in order to feel as they did when they got the pain medication in the hospital. An individual may become psychologically addicted after the very first dose. Physical addiction may occur after a short period of time if the drug is used on a regular basis. When drug abusers begin to have difficulty obtaining the high they once did, they will begin to experiment with new drugs and combinations of drugs. This is, of course, related to the fact that after regular use of a drug, an individual's body develops a tolerance for that drug and it takes a larger and larger dose to produce the same "high." Many drug abusers say that the first high from a drug is the ultimate.

After a while, the drug abuser begins to take the drug not to feel good but primarily to keep from feeling bad and to prevent withdrawal symptoms. At this stage, many drug abusers begin to feel "sick" a great deal of the time. They have headaches and pains, gastrointestinal problems, and stomach cramps. The symptoms of these problems are similar to the symptoms reported when an individual has the flu. In addition to these problems, addicts often have to stop working because they are either too high or too sick to function. As the addict's tolerance increases and larger and larger doses of the drug are required to get high, an overdose is likely to occur. This happens when the individual exceeds his or her personal tolerance level or threshold for that particular drug.

Sometimes accidental overdoses occur because the strength of drugs such as heroin and cocaine is not carefully controlled from bag to bag. For example, most heroin is only 5 percent pure, but someone might accidentally get a bag of heroin that is 50 percent pure and consequently overdose. Individuals also sometimes get into difficulty because of the additives, such as strychnine, that are sometimes used to dilute, or "cut," the drug. Occasionally, suspected informers are intentionally overdosed by their suppliers.

When an individual develops a tolerance to a particular drug, he or she also develops a *cross tolerance* for other drugs in the same generic family. For example, an addict who has built up a tolerance for Demerol will not be able to obtain a high using heroin and vice versa.

Because of the cost of many of these drugs, addicts are often forced to steal to support their habit. Women frequently become prostitutes. One bag of heroin costs between $15 and $25, and because some addicted people take as many as 10 to 15 bags a day, it is easy to see that one can develop a $200 to $400 per day habit rather easily. Persons addicted to cocaine have told the authors their habits run as much as $500 to $700 dollar a day.

Although many people believe that it is the "doped-up" individual who commits crime, the truth of the matter is almost the reverse. An individual who has had a "fix" is highly·unlikely to commit any type of crime. While under the influence of drugs, addicts find their needs are at least temporarily satiated and they are usually not interested in anything, including food, sex, or more drugs. It is only when addicts are faced with the possibility of being without drugs that they turn to crime as a means of insuring their supply. Because addicts frequently spend all their money, time, and effort supporting their addiction, they do not eat well and consequently usually develop significant malnutrition.

Adults may develop other serious problems due to the side effects that often occur as a result of taking drugs. For example, heroin addicts who take their drug intravenously may develop infectious hepatitis from using contaminated needles; and, as we all know, use of contaminated needles is one of the most certain ways of contracting the AIDS virus. Persons ingesting cocaine nasally may experience deterioration or necrosis of the tissues in the nasal area. Other possible complications include overdose, local infection, respiratory infection, severe constipation, and severe malnutrition (which generally weakens the body's defense system). The "rush" that the addict gets immediately after taking a drug has been compared to a sexual orgasm, and for most addicts it seems to erase any fear or consideration of possible side effects. After a "fix," addicts may appear to be in a state somewhere between sleep and wakefulness. Life has no problems. They are relaxed, content, and experiencing feelings of extreme well-being.

While Demerol is the drug most abused by physicians and nurses, other types of drugs are abused by the general population. Narcotics and analgesics are frequently abused, as are central nervous system stimulants such as the amphetamines, hallucinogenic drugs (such as LSD), barbiturates (such as Seconal and phenobarbital), and some of the minor tranquilizers (such as Valium and Librium). Marijuana is one of the most commonly abused drugs after alcohol. The 1985 National Household Survey on Drug Abuse for the National Institute on Drug Abuse, reviewing nonmedical drug use, shows that alcohol has been used at least once by 57 percent of people surveyed, cigarettes by 45 percent, marijuana by 24 percent, inhalants by 9 percent, stimulants by 6 percent, analgesics by 6 percent, cocaine by 5 percent, tranquilizers by 5 percent, sedatives by 4 percent, and hallucinogens by 3 percent. A review of several studies of the incidence of drug abuse not including alcohol suggests that 5 to 7 percent of the population abuses drugs in such a way as to meet *DSM-III-R* criteria for legitimate diagnosis of addiction or abuse.

When using alcohol, individuals have a fairly good idea of what to expect when they drink. Unfortunately, the same is not true for people who abuse other drugs. Individuals on amphetamines or hallucinogens may have a good trip—but are just as likely to have a bad trip. Even when they have a good trip, they may become quite depressed afterwards, and many have strong suicidal impulses.

TREATMENT

Abusers of other drugs enter treatment in much the same manner as alcoholics. They may be seen by a physician because of an overdose or other medical complications or because they are brought to the treatment center by friends. Occasionally, addicts will seek help on their own. In general, the prognosis for any drug addict is not good, and the prognosis for heroin addicts is very poor. The cure rate for heroin addiction is said to be about 1 percent.

RECOGNIZING SIGNS AND SYMPTOMS

Hospitalized patients who are suspected drug abusers should be observed carefully for the signs and symptoms of withdrawal. These may begin approximately 12 to 16 hours after the patient's last "fix." These signs and symptoms include red or teary eyes, yawning, a runny nose, restlessness, and, within about 48 hours, flulike symptoms that may include abdominal cramps. In some cases, patients are quite hostile and paranoid and will refuse treatment if possible. Any time one observes a large number of needle marks ("tracks") on a patient's arms and hands or legs, the possibility of drug abuse should be considered, especially if the patient has other characteristics associated with drug abuse.

OVERDOSES

In treating drug addicts who have overdosed, the so-called ABCs of an overdose should be observed. A is to establish an open airway; B is to breathe the patient, giving mouth-to-mouth resuscitation if other equipment is not available; and C is to provide cardiopulmonary resuscitation, often known as "pumping." Some authorities add a D, the administration of an antagonistic drug, which for narcotic overdoses is usually Nalline. In cases of barbiturate overdoses, the physician will administer an anticonvulsant drug.

After the immediate medical crisis has passed, the treatment of drug-overdosed individuals is very similar to that of alcoholics. It is important to remember that addicts are usually psychologically immature individuals who are probably not accustomed to making decisions and who are fairly dependent. Be candid with the addicts, but not judgmental. Addicts need patience and understanding but also need structure and consistency. Addicts can also be quite manipulative and may resort to trickery in order to get the medication they need. Addicts may, for example, prick a finger and place a drop of blood in their urine in order to fake a urinary tract infection. Since urinary tract infections are quite painful, that trick could be good for several analgesics. Both alcoholics and other drug addicts like to make others responsible for their behavior. It is necessary, therefore, to be sure that a staff member does not accept responsibility for the addict's behavior.

METHODS OF TREATMENT

Methadone maintenance programs, along with a variety of other programs emphasizing individual, group, and family therapy, have been used to help heroin addicts. Methadone is a drug that is similar to heroin but that does not produce euphoria. Addicts do not stay high and are therefore better able to function. Essentially, methadone maintenance programs allow addicts to function by substituting one addictive agent for another that has less incapacitating properties. Methadone is legal, and over a long period of time, physicians may be able to decrease the amount of the drug used by patients. Hopefully, addicts would eventually need neither heroin nor methadone. Methadone is fairly inexpensive and can also be used to entice patients into therapy groups by insisting that they go to group therapy in order to obtain the methadone.

The goal of most therapy groups, whatever the individual's drug of choice, is to help addicts develop a different perspective of the world, become better educated about the ill effects of drugs on their physical and psychologic well-being, appreciate that life is possible without drugs or alcohol, learn how to establish and maintain positive interpersonal relationships, develop more positive feelings of self-esteem, and engage in lifestyle changes that will support a drug-free existence. Therapeutic communities and halfway houses often provide an extended therapeutic opportunity to help addicts make the transition from being drug-dependent individuals to being productive members of society.

Finally, one should not forget that psychologic problems are often associated with alcohol and drug abuse and dependencies. Anxiety, depression, and various psychosomatic complaints are often a part of the symptom picture. They should be properly diagnosed and addressed if treatment is to be successful.

SUMMARY

Drug- and alcohol-dependent individuals are generally difficult to treat. They often lack motivation and use a great deal of denial about the amount of drug or alcohol use. There are often psychologic as well as physical complications. The etiology of drug and alcohol abuse is not always clear, and relatively little is known about exactly why people become addicted. Treatment activities often must be carried out against the patient's will; even if the patient "recovers," relapse is more the rule than the exception. Still, some addicts are rehabilitated, and it is probably these successes and the hope of being able to do more that keep treatment teams involved in rehabilitation efforts.

ANNOTATED BIBLIOGRAPHY

Allebeck, P., and Allgulander, C.: *Suicide among young men: Psychiatric illness, deviant behaviour and substance abuse.* Acta Psychiatrica Scandinavica, 1990, 81:565–570.

A longitudinal study analyzing the role of psychiatric illness as opposed to social and behavioral risk factors for suicide.

Earley, P.H.: *The changing face of addiction: Is everything I do an addiction?* Insight, 1992, 12(3):2–7.

Explores the growth of the addiction movement, and provides information on what is and is not an addictive disease.

Foerster, D.W.: *Turning back: The anatomy of relapse.* Insight, 1992, 12(3):24–27.

Provides a definition and insight into the process of relapse from an addictive disease.

Haldeman, K.: *Are elderly alcoholics discriminated against?* Journal of Psychosocial Nursing and Mental Health Services, 1990, 28(5):6–11.

Discusses the prevalence of alcoholism in the elderly and the lack of programs designed to meet the need of this population.

Harvey, J.S.: *Why does it happen? The latest research in addiction.* Insight, 1992, 12(3):10–13.

Explores the cause of addiction and questions why some people become addicted while others do not.

Margolis, R.: *Leaps of faith: A model for recovery.* Insight, 1992, 12(3):18–23.

Discusses recovery of addicts, with emphasis on 12-step programs such as AA.

Posig, M.T.: *A conspiracy of silence: Women and recovery.* Insight, 1992, 12(3):8–9.

Discusses the lack of equality in treatment for men and women in terms of recognition, treatment, and understanding.

Rubio-Stipec, M., Bird, H., Canino, G. Bravo, M., and Alegria, M.: *Children of alcoholic parents in the community.* Journal of Studies on Alcohol, 1991, 52(1):78–88.

Provides information on how alcoholism and adverse family conditions increase the risk of maladjustment in children.

Wesner, R.B.: *Alcohol use and abuse secondary to anxiety.* Psychiatric Clinics of North America, 1990, 13(4):699–713.

Discusses the prevalence and complications of using alcohol to overcome feelings of anxiety. Offers case examples and treatment plans.

REFERENCES

Jellinek, E.M.: *The Disease Concept of Alcoholism.* College and University Press, New Haven, CT, 1960.

National Household Survey on Drug Abuse. National Institute on Drug Abuse. Alcohol, Drug Abuse, and Mental Health Administration, Washington, DC, 1985–1986.

True or False. Circle your choice.

T   F   1. Alcohol abuse has been said to be the third-largest health problem in the United States.

T   F   2. Some authorities report that an alcoholic has ambivalent feelings about living and dying and that chronic alcoholism represents a slow form of suicide.

T   F   3. Most alcoholics have aggressive and independent personality traits.

T   F   4. Three out of four American adults drink to some extent.

T   F   5. Alcoholics use the defense mechanism of denial most frequently and have difficulty accepting responsibilities for their drinking problem.

T   F   6. In the prodromal phase of alcoholism there is a loss of control and the individual is unable to abstain from drinking.

T   F   7. Alcoholics may go into active delirium tremens any time from 1 to 8 days after their last drink.

T   F   8. One-to-one psychotherapy is quite successful in treating alcoholism.

T   F   9. Most authorities believe that all alcoholics begin to drink for the same reason.

T   F   10. In the prealcoholic phase, drinking takes the place of the development of adequate coping mechanisms.

Short Answer. Answer the following questions as briefly and specifically as possible.

1. When are individuals diagnosed as being alcoholics?

_____

_____.

2. Describe the general physical appearance of chronic alcoholics.

_____

_____.

3. What appears to be the major key in the successful treatment of alcoholism?

_____

_____

_____.

303

4. List three effects that alcohol has on the body.

   a. _____.

   b. _____.

   c. _____.

5. Describe the behaviors that exist in the chronic phase of alcoholism as proposed by Jellinek.

   _____

   _____

   _____

6. What is the most frequent way an alcoholic receives treatment?

   _____

   _____

   _____

Multiple Choice. Circle the letter or number that you think represents the best answer.

1. The best definition of an alcoholic is:
   a. A person who consumes alcohol every day.
   b. A person who regularly goes on "benders."
   c. A person who drinks to escape problems.
   d. A person who has developed a dependency on alcohol that causes him or her serious problems in living.

2. The neurotic person uses alcohol:
   a. To build confidence.
   b. To escape responsibility.
   c. As a substitute for sex.
   d. To relieve anxiety.
   e. To consciously get mothering from others.
       (1) a, b, and d.
       (2) b and c.
       (3) a, b, c, and d.
       (4) c, d, and e.
       (5) All of the above.

3. The person with acute alcoholic hallucinosis most frequently experiences:
   a. Auditory hallucinations.
   b. Visual hallucinations.
   c. Tactile hallucinations.
   d. Olfactory hallucinations.

4. The defense mechanisms most commonly used by the alcoholic include all of the following except:
   a. Rationalization.
   b. Projection.
   c. Denial.
   d. Sublimation.
5. Alcohol is:
   a. A central nervous system stimulant.
   b. A central nervous system depressant.
   c. A fat oxidizer.
   d. A major tranquilizer.
   e. A volatile anesthetic agent.
6. When patients are taking Antabuse and consume alcohol in any quantity, they experience:
   a. Nausea, palpitations, and vomiting.
   b. Elation, grandiosity, and impotence.
   c. Headaches, dermatitis, and nocturnal sweats.
   d. Hepatitis and gastritis.
7. The primary site for detoxification of alcohol is:
   a. The kidneys.
   b. The stomach.
   c. The intestines.
   d. The liver.
   e. The brain.
8. A patient is admitted with DTs. Symptoms one might observe are:
   a. Restlessness, tremors, and confusion.
   b. Depression, withdrawal, and tearfulness.
   c. Suspiciousness, depression, and unpredictability.
   d. Manipulation, stubbornness, and negativism.
9. The drug that is used specifically to help alcoholics refrain from drinking is:
   a. Morphine.
   b. Dilantin.
   c. Antabuse.
   d. Chlorpromazine.
   e. Librium.
10. Which of the following behavior patterns best describes the addicted individual?
    a. Ability to tolerate anxiety.
    b. Concern for the welfare of others.
    c. Inability to tolerate frustration.
    d. Inability to derive pleasure.

11. Care of a drug addict should involve observing the patient for immediate withdrawal symptoms, which would include:
    a. Lacrimation, muscle twitching, rhinorrhea, and insomnia.
    b. Drowsiness, confusion, lability, and hallucinations.
    c. Tremors, euphoria, nausea, and palpitations.
    d. Inappropriate affect, restlessness, and impotence.
12. The most difficult problem in dealing with drug addicts is:
    a. Combating withdrawal symptoms.
    b. Keeping them free of their dependence on drugs.
    c. Obtaining family cooperation.
    d. Teaching them the danger of resorting to stronger drugs.

21

Geriatric Psychiatric Care

LEARNING OBJECTIVES

Student will be able to:
1. Identify several factors involved in the elderly's loss of self-esteem.
2. Identify major diseases occurring in the elderly.
3. Identify basic principles of working with the elderly.
4. Identify some of the basic needs of the elderly.

Since aging begins at the moment of conception, it seems it should be considered a natural process of living. Unfortunately, that is not the case in our society. Americans, as well as most people in the Western world, have become so engrossed with the idea of youthfulness that to become old is often seen as a fate worse than death itself. Billions of dollars are spent each year on beauty aids, cosmetic surgery, and other "miracle" treatments by individuals seeking to prevent, or at least cover up, the telltale signs of aging.

This emphasis on youthfulness is not the only factor causing the elderly to feel they are no longer valued members of our society, but it seems to be the major culprit. The mere presence of the elderly seems to make younger generations uncomfortable, for their existence serves as a constant reminder that aging does indeed occur. Perhaps this is part of the reason so many elderly are abandoned by their families and their society. One wonders what attitudes will prevail in the late 1990s, when it is predicted that more than half of our country's population will be over age 55, with one third being 65 years of age or older.

In addition to the normal day-to-day problems of living, the elderly must cope with special situations associated with old age and retirement. They tend to suffer a significant loss of self-esteem and therefore develop negative feelings about themselves. This loss of self-worth occurs for a variety of reasons, but retirement seems to be a major contributor. Our society values workers and often disregards nonproductive or unemployed individuals.

Retirement is viewed as the time in life when one is supposed to sit back, relax, and reap the benefits of years of hard work. Unfortunately, the mere act of reaching age 65 does not automatically change the work habits and attitudes an individual has developed over a lifetime. Many persons in Western cultures equate one's worth as a human being with what one contributes to society as a worker, and therefore to retire is to become worthless.

Retirement can also bring about a drastic reduction in income, which in turn contributes to the loss of self-esteem. Older individuals may no longer be able to afford to live independently of their children or may be forced to live in substandard housing. Inadequate nutrition may result from poor eating habits necessitated by a lack of money. Most often there is little, if any, money left over for entertainment, recreational activities, or hobbies. Frequently, the older individual settles down into a life of drudgery and boredom.

Activities are further restricted by loss of hearing, poor eyesight, and other physical ailments that occur with greater frequency as individuals grow older. Poor health, coupled with the loss of family and friends, forces one to face the inevitability of death. Some older individuals have a greatly decreased ability to tolerate emotional stress and few resources or opportunities to compensate for their losses. In such cases, interest in living begins to diminish. Perhaps this loss of interest is a contributing factor to the results of a recent survey, which indicates that people live only an average of 60 months past retirement.

All people, regardless of age, need to love and be loved, to have sufficient economic resources to meet basic physical needs, to feel a sense of achievement, and to receive recognition from others. Because elderly people begin to lose many of these satisfactions, a healthy adjustment to aging requires the ability to appraise circumstances realistically, making the most of the negative aspects and capitalizing on the positive. An elderly widow may not like the fact that she can no longer afford to live alone and must now live with a married daughter. On the other hand, she can make the most of the situation by offering to help with appropriate household chores and child care. By contributing in this manner, the grandmother may feel that she is a part of the family rather than a guest.

Emotional adjustment to old age is usually a continuation of lifelong adjustment patterns. People often believe that they are going to change their ways when they get old. Instead of being cantankerous, they say they are going to become sweet and loving. There is little chance such a change will occur. Basic personality traits and ways of handling stress are formed early in life and, if anything, the aging process exaggerates these traits and behaviors as the elderly person experiences the stress of losing authority, independence, and usefulness. The fact that people behave in ways that get them what they want is also not necessarily altered by age. The elderly may scream, yell, have temper tantrums, or become depressed or withdrawn in much the same way as they did early in life, if such behaviors helped to get what they wanted. On the other hand, they may be calm, quiet individuals who look at any new situation in an objective, problem-solving manner, just as they did as well-adjusted young adults.

In mentally healthy individuals, the final years of life are years in which they have an opportunity to acknowledge their contributions to themselves, their families, and their society. They recognize that whatever they have done with their lives must now be accepted because they cannot live their lives over again. For individuals who have been reasonably successful and who have developed healthy self-concepts, these tasks may be accomplished fairly easily. For individuals who have not been successful and thus do not feel reasonably fulfilled, aging is likely to bring a great deal of stress in the form of regret, guilt, and remorse. When elderly individuals cannot resolve such feelings, they often experience neurotic or psychotic disorders. Others may show significant behavioral disorganization as a result of neurologic impairment or disease processes.

Despite the many potential problems, most elderly people in this country are alert, competent, and functioning with reasonable independence in their communities. As Caldwell (1975) says, "Advanced age is reached only by those who have proved themselves capable of survival." Available data suggest that only 5 percent of the elderly need custodial care and that only 1 percent are found in mental hospitals, taking up about 30 percent of all public mental health beds. Included in that 30 percent are patients who (1) have been in mental facilities all their lives, (2) have been admitted off and on throughout their lives and cannot cope with the added stresses of old age, and (3) have become ill for the first time. Another 10 percent of our elderly population seek care for physical and mental disorders on an outpatient basis from community clinics. Several million more elderly people live under economic and environmental conditions that contribute to emotional breakdown. Although the elderly now account for only 12.7 percent of our total population, approximately 20 percent (Butler, 1989) of all suicides in this country are committed by elderly individuals (these figures vary from 20 to 35 percent, depending on the study).

Of the elderly patients confined to mental health institutions, most suffer from senile brain atrophy or brain changes that occur due to arteriosclerosis. Cerebral arteriosclerosis is a condition marked by a thickening and hardening of the arteries of the brain. When this occurs, less blood and oxygen reach the brain and the patient experiences periods of confusion and varied levels of consciousness. The patient may also be forgetful and complain of headaches, dizziness, and weakness. Such patients seem to have little emotional control and are often irritable and argumentative with family members, other patients, and staff. They may wander about aimlessly, having a noticeable shuffling gait and a tendency to lean backward as they try to maintain their balance.

The cause of senile brain atrophy is unknown, but in the course of the disease, calcium deposits appear in brain tissues. The size and weight of the brain decreases, and the amount of cerebrospinal fluid increases. Patients becomes progressively more and more confused. They have trouble remembering recent events but can recall in detail experiences of the past. Emotional instability is common, and tears or rage come quickly with little justification.

Another major problem for the elderly, and not so elderly, has been the increase in the number of cases of Alzheimer's disease and Alzheimer's-type dementias (called primary degenerative dementia of the Alzheimer type in the third revised edition of the *Diagnostic and Statistical Manual of Mental Disorders* [DSM-III-R]). Research is still lacking in terms of a definitive explanation for the cause of Alzheimer's disease, and treatment is equally lacking. This disease is characterized primarily by a gradual and progressive loss of cognitive, or thinking and problem-solving, ability; loss of memory; poor judgment; disorientation; and behavior and personality changes. Memory impairment is usually noticed first, with the more obvious cognitive interruption not showing up until the middle stages of the disease. In the late stage of the disease, patients become mute and inattentive and cannot care for themselves. Death usually occurs within about 5 years of onset.

Elderly patients may also experience any of a number of psychiatric disorders. Depression is common, and neurotic and paranoid reactions occur frequently. All forms of therapy are used in treating these disorders, and elderly patients respond to therapy in about the same manner as any other age group.

Staff members working with elderly patients must be careful to distinguish between individual mannerisms, temporarily stressful situations, and true psychotic or neurotic disorders. Is Mr. Jones, who walks up and down the hall talking to himself, confused because of a psychiatric disorder, disoriented because he was suddenly moved to unfamiliar surroundings in the middle of the night, still oversedated from his sleeping pill, or just a person who has always walked around mumbling to himself as he thought things over? Various physical factors, such as infection, dehydration, hunger, or traumatic injuries (for example, broken bones), may cause elderly patients to become temporarily confused. Restraining such patients often makes matters worse. Staff members must try to discover and understand the cause of behavior and help the patient to control it with as little loss of freedom and dignity as possible.

Extreme caution should be used when ordering or administering medications to elderly patients. Often a smaller amount of a given drug is indicated due to such factors as increased sensitivity to medications, decreased body weight, impaired circulation, and liver dysfunction. The likelihood of adverse drug reaction or overmedication (especially with barbiturates) is increased because kidney function is decreased and, therefore, drugs are not excreted from the system as quickly as in a younger person.

Working with elderly patients requires that certain basic principles of care be followed. Staff members should allow them to maintain as much independence as they can safely handle. Feelings of frustration, which contribute to fears, anxieties, restlessness, and agitation, are much like the frustration experienced by teenagers. Teenagers long for independence from adult authority, yet are afraid to give up the security of having someone on whom to rely. Elderly patients, while wanting to maintain their independence, also long for the security of depending on others. Elderly persons may also be compared to toddlers in that both groups cannot quite accomplish all the functions necessary to allow complete freedom. Toddlers can get their shoes on but cannot tie the laces. Elderly persons may have the same problem due to arthritic changes that make it difficult to bend over and to use their hands. Both situations cause feelings of frustration and probably angry outbursts at anyone nearby.

Despite some similarities, elderly patients should not be treated as if they were children. This mistake is often made by well-meaning family members and friends. When bossed around in an authoritarian, condescending, or parent-to-child manner, their response may become obstinate and contrary.

Correct names should be used. Despite what many people believe, few of the elderly enjoy being called "granny" or "gramps." Names are important to people, and being addressed correctly conveys respect. Most elderly patients especially dislike being given pet names by staff members. An individual struggling to maintain self-identity and respect has no wish to become a mascot.

The feeling of being accepted is needed as much by the elderly as by younger persons. Personal habits, such as dressing in a certain sequence or always drinking coffee from a saucer, should be permitted. However, staff members should try to correct unsanitary or self-defeating habits by encouraging more appropriate behaviors and by restructuring the environment to eliminate the need for some of the inappropriate behavior. For example, if Mr. Green insists on taking a short walk despite the fact that he can hardly walk, a staff member might try to find an easily accessible place, provide him with a cane or walker, and walk with him. If he is clearly not able to walk very far, he might agree to a shorter walk if the staff member will get a picture book of world travels to show to and discuss with him.

Loneliness is a major problem for older people, even those who are hospitalized. They greatly need someone they can trust and who will be supportive. Sometimes a simple pat on the arm, a gentle hug, or a back rub can communicate a sense of warmth and affection. Most elderly patients need this type of human closeness and should not be rejected when they reach out to a staff member for comfort.

Elderly persons need to be encouraged to talk about their feelings, fears, and worries. If they want to talk about old memories, they should be permitted to do so. Sometimes elderly patients have difficulty remembering recent events due to organic brain changes, but more often they dwell in the past as a means of dealing with the painfulness of the present. They may also be attempting to understand their present situation by reviewing past events in their lives. However, if elderly patients continually live in the past, staff members should attempt to focus their attention on daily events.

Patients and their families should be encouraged to maintain close communication. Fortunately, the pattern of hospitalizing mentally ill patients in their own community instead of sending them to large, distant state hospitals is well established. This fosters a continuing relationship with family and friends and helps the rehabilitation process. Many elderly patients do not need to be hospitalized if they can participate in day-care programs and return to their homes at night. Thus many communities have day-care treatment centers for elderly persons.

Older individuals need to be encouraged to participate in activities that bring them in contact with other people. Staff members should help patients choose activities that they not only enjoy but that bring satisfaction and a sense of purpose while helping to fill the long hours of the day. They must practice their socialization skills in order to keep them. Socialization is also important because it helps patients to maintain a satisfactory orientation to their environment. They learn names and places and make friends. A few other things can be done to help keep patients oriented. Placing a large clock in the person's room and a cube calendar that can have the date changed each day is helpful. Patients are more aware of the year, month, day, and time if such devices are available. To help with orientation to place, patients may be taken for walks or wheelchair rides or placed by windows so that the front, side, or back of buildings can be pointed out.

Older patients do not like to be rushed. They rise early and their days are long, so they should not be pushed. They also fare much better in a calm, consistent environment that functions at a moderately slow pace and follows a well-established routine.

The physical needs of the elderly are of primary importance, and the staff should ensure that these needs are met. Most will readily report physical problems to staff members, but patients who are confused must be carefully observed. They may be unable to report problems accurately.

It is imperative for elderly patients to stay active and to participate in physician-approved exercise programs. Physical activity promotes good health by increasing circulation, stimulating appetite, helping regulate bowel function, and preventing such complications of inactivity as joint immobility, muscle stiffness, bedsores, and pneumonia. Fresh air is good for the elderly; if they are dressed warmly, being outside on cold winter days is not harmful.

Staff members should be constantly alert for potential hazards in the environment. Individuals having problems with dizziness should be assisted when walking, climbing stairs, or getting in or out of the bathtub. In order to minimize stumbling by those with impaired vision, furniture should not be rearranged. Floors should not be slippery, and carpets and tiles should be kept in good repair. Throw rugs should never be used because they slide easily and may cause a fall. If elderly patients are confused or groggy, they should not be allowed to smoke alone. A staff member should sit with them and use that time to interact with them.

Staff members should be aware that patients may need help with personal hygiene, especially if they are confused or forgetful. The degree of help needed will vary. Some patients will need total care, while others will need only minor assistance, such as fastening a dress with buttons up the back or tying shoelaces. Patients should be allowed to do all they can for themselves even when it would be much quicker and simpler for a staff member to assist.

It is usually not necessary for elderly patients to take a complete bath every day. The face, underarms, and perineum do, however, need daily washing. Since the skin has a tendency to be dry, frequent washing will increase dryness. Soap must be thoroughly rinsed to avoid itching and skin irritation. Elderly patients may prefer showers because it is hard to get in and out of a bathtub, and they are often afraid of falling. For patients who tire easily or are unsteady on their feet, a chair can be placed in the shower stall so that they can shower in a sitting position. Remember, elderly patients are usually very modest, and their right to personal privacy and dignity should be respected whenever possible.

A well-balanced diet is essential to health; however, physical changes may lead to problems in this area. Ill-fitting dentures and tough, undercooked meats and foods may make chewing difficult, if not impossible. Dentures must be worn consistently in order to avoid a misfit. Conversely, any time a patient consistently does not wear dentures, it usually means they hurt and are not properly fitted. Most elderly patients do not like to eat alone, and appetite may decrease as activity level decreases. Constipation may cause discomfort and lead to a poor appetite. Plenty of fluids, fruits, and vegetables should be included in the diet to aid digestion. If a patient is used to taking a mild laxative on a routine basis, there is probably no harm in allowing this practice to continue. If there is a problem, the patient's physician should be consulted. Elderly individuals often eat slowly and need to be allowed to finish their meals at a leisurely pace. Most seem to prefer small meals served frequently rather than three large meals a day.

Staff members must be alert to behavioral changes that indicate physical problems. If Mr. Jones does not answer when his name is called, he may not be acting stubborn, but may actually have a hearing problem due to a build-up of ear wax. A patient who stumbles over objects may need glasses. A male patient who urinates frequently may have an enlarged prostate. Bunions, corns, ingrown toenails, or ill-fitting shoes may be the real reason a patient refuses to go outside for a walk.

If patients do not sleep well at night, their sleeping pattern during the day should be observed. If they have been taking a daytime nap, the length of that nap might be shortened, bedtime delayed, activities increased, and relaxation methods, such as a warm bath or warm milk, used just before bedtime. If sleeping pills are used, patients may be groggy and sleepy during the day and awaken just in time to go to bed again. This pattern is not uncommon and should be considered if a patient has difficulty sleeping.

Working with the elderly is not easy, and staff members who do this work need a great deal of patience. In not too many years, today's staff members will be elderly patients themselves. It is not a matter of if, but a matter of when. One might strive to be the kind of staff member one would like to have when one becomes the patient.

ANNOTATED BIBLIOGRAPHY

Beck, C., Heacock, P., Mercer, S.,Walton, C.G., and Shook, J.: *Dressing for success: Promoting independence among cognitively impaired elderly.* Journal of Psychosocial Nursing and Mental Health Services, 1991, 29(7):30–35.

Presents ideas on how to encourage cognitively impaired elderly patients to take more responsibility for personal care.

Curl, A.: *Agitation and the older adult.* Journal of Psychosocial Nursing and Mental Health Services, 1989, 27(12):12–14.

Focuses on agitation caused by delirium, dementia, parkinsonism, and depression and the appropriate management of these behaviors by nursing staff.

Dellasega, C.: *Meeting the mental health needs of elderly clients.* Journal of Psychosocial Nursing and Mental Health Services, 1991, 29(2):10–14.

Preliminary investigation exploring the availability of mental health resources for the elderly on the local level, with emphasis on outpatient services available and long-term care facilities.

Haldeman, K.: *Are elderly alcoholics discriminated against?* Journal of Psychosocial Nursing and Mental Health Services, 1990, 28(5):6–11.

Discusses the prevalence of alcoholism in the elderly and the lack of programs designed to meet the needs of this population.

Kroessler, D.: *Personality disorders in the elderly.* Hospital and Community Psychiatry, 1990, 41(12):1325–1329.

A review of the literature on the prevalence of personality disorders in the elderly.

Masters, J.C., and O'Grady, M.: *Normal pressure hydrocephalus: A potentially reversible form of dementia.* Journal of Psychosocial Nursing and Mental Health Services, 1992, 30(6):25–28.

Discusses the symptoms, diagnosis, etiology, treatment, and nursing care for normal pressure hydrocephalus (NPH), a form of dementia that has proven to be reversible.

Puntil, C.: *Integrating three approaches to counter resistance in a noncompliant elderly client.* Journal of Psychosocial Nursing and Mental Health Services, 1991, 29(2):26–30.

Discusses how resistance is used by the elderly patient and how nurses can work through the resistance.

Roberts, B.L.: *Nursing research in geriatric mental health.* Journal of Advanced Nursing, 1990, 15:1030–1035.

Review of the literature focusing on the mental and cognitive health of older adults.

Smyer, T., and Hillman, M.: *The public library system: social services resource for the geriatric population.* Journal of Psychosocial Nursing and Mental Health Services, 1991, 29(3):22–25.

Discusses how libraries can meet both the informational and recreational needs of the elderly.

Tillman-Jones, T.K.: *How to work with the elderly patients on a general psychiatric unit.* Journal of Psychosocial Nursing and Mental Health Services, 1990, 28(5):27–31.

Focuses on the care of the elderly on a psychiatric unit with regard to assessment, planning, treatment, and evaluation.

Zerhusen, J.D., Boyle, K., and Wilson, W.: *Out of the darkness: Group therapy for depressed elderly.* Journal of Psychosocial Nursing and Mental Health Services, 1991, 29(9):16–21.

Research study examining the benefits of nurses' facilitating cognitive group therapy with nursing home residents suffering from depression.

REFERENCES

Butler, R.N.: Psychosocial aspects of aging. In Kaplan, H.I., and Saddock, B.J. (eds.): *Comprehensive Textbook of Psychiatry,* ed. 5, Vol. 2, Williams & Wilkins, Baltimore, 1989, pp. 2014–2019.

Caldwell, E.: *Geriatrics: A Study of Maturity.* Delmar Publishers, Albany, NY, 1975.

True or False. Circle your choice.

T F 1. Most elderly patients hospitalized for psychiatric problems suffer from senile brain atrophy or brain changes that occur due to arteriosclerosis.

T F 2. Calling the elderly "granny" or "gramps" tends to make them feel more at home.

T F 3. It is necessary to encourage the elderly to hurry because they tend to be so slow.

T F 4. Many elderly people feel that they are no longer valued members of our society.

T F 5. Life situations often cause elderly individuals to suffer a significant loss of self-esteem and, therefore, to develop negative feelings about themselves.

T F 6. Emotional adjustment changes drastically with increasing age.

T F 7. The majority of elderly people are alert, competent, and functioning in their communities.

T F 8. Depression is a common psychiatric disorder seen in the elderly.

T F 9. It is important for the elderly to maintain their independence whenever possible.

T F 10. Whenever elderly patients begin acting like children, they should be treated as children.

T F 11. Twenty to thirty-five percent of all suicides in this country are committed by elderly individuals.

Short Answer. Answer the following questions as briefly and specifically as possible.

1. What is a major factor contributing to the elderly individual's loss of self-worth and self-esteem.

   _____.

2. What are some of the main factors that should be considered before administering medications to elderly patients?

   _____.

3. What is one of the main reasons that elderly patients have difficulty remembering recent events?

   _____.

317

4. What are some basic things that mental health workers can do to keep elderly patients well oriented?

_____.

5. Why is it necessary for the elderly patient to stay active?

_____

_____

_____.

Multiple Choice. Circle the letter that you think represents the best answer.
1. People become old:
   a. At the same rate.
   b. When they reach age 65.
   c. When they reach age 75.
   d. At a very individual rate.
2. The basic attitude of Western cultures toward the elderly is that:
   a. They should be held in esteem.
   b. They are of lesser importance.
   c. Their opinions should be sought.
   d. Their skills are valuable.
3. Changes in self-image are brought about by:
   a. Loss of vigor and vitality.
   b. Loss of independence.
   c. Loss of physical stamina.
   d. All of the above.
4. Mental health workers can help increase elderly patients' self-esteem by:
   a. Calmly accepting them and their behavior.
   b. Being critical of their behavior.
   c. Firmly stating what behavior is acceptable.
   d. Ignoring them until they behave in an acceptable way.
5. If an elderly patient complains that everyone is mumbling these days, which of the following is most likely to be true?
   a. He or she is just being cranky.
   b. He or she is probably becoming emotionally disturbed.
   c. His or her hearing is becoming less acute.
   d. None of the above.
6. Staff members must come to an understanding of their own feelings about the aged and aging because:
   a. They can be more therapeutic.
   b. Feelings are difficult to hide.
   c. Anxiety about aging is easily transmitted.

     d. All of the above.

7. A person's identity is reinforced when he or she wears:
     a. His or her own clothes.
     b. A hospital gown.
     c. A uniform.
     d. A friend's clothing.

8. The elderly person will probably eat better if:
     a. Food servings are large.
     b. Hard rolls are included.
     c. The foods are chewy.
     d. Food servings are small.

9. A general precaution to remember when considering the safety of the elderly is:
     a. Confine elderly individuals to a small area.
     b. Keep their clothing loose fitting and long.
     c. Have sufficient light.
     d. Use open heaters in the bathroom.

10. The most common accident to the elderly involves:
      a. Falls.
      b. Burns.
      c. Cuts.
      d. Bruises.

Crisis Intervention

LEARNING OBJECTIVES

Student will be able to:
1. Define *crisis*.
2. Identify the goal of crisis intervention.
3. Identify ways a crisis may be precipitated.
4. Define *social crisis*.
5. Identify the four phases of a crisis.
6. Identify the steps in crisis intervention.

Mental health authorities define *crisis* as a state of psychological disequilibrium brought about by a conflict, problem, or life situation that an individual perceives as a threat to self and cannot effectively handle by using previously successful problem-solving and coping techniques. The crisis develops not because of the event itself but because of the person's inability to cope with the event. When this situation occurs, individuals become increasingly anxious and tense and feel that their self-esteem and well-being are seriously threatened.

Without swift and effective intervention, these feelings usually intensify rapidly and the individual may become behaviorally disorganized, have difficulty thinking in a rational manner, and experience feelings of anger, depression, helplessness, and guilt.

Clients in crisis are likely to repeat over and over again phrases such as: "I don't know what to do"; "I feel so helpless"; "What's happening to me?"; "I can't believe this"; "This just can't be true."

Therefore crisis intervention is usually conducted in an outpatient setting on a short-term basis and uses problem-solving techniques to help clients resolve stress-provoking problems. The goal of this type therapy is to help clients return to a level of functioning that is at least equal to their precrisis state. It is hoped that crisis therapy will also enable clients to learn new coping and adaptive behaviors, thus actually improving levels of mental health.

A crisis state may be precipitated by two types of events. Developmental or maturational crises are those that occur at foreseeable stages in the lives of most individuals. As discussed in earlier chapters, each stage of development has its own developmental task. In order to carry out these tasks, certain traits and behaviors must be strengthened while others must be restrained. Such changes often produce a great deal of stress, especially during the transition period between two developmental stages.

For example, many middle-aged couples become depressed when their long-awaited freedom from dependent children is replaced with greater emotional and financial responsibility for elderly parents. Learning to find workable solutions to this problem is one of the predictable developmental tasks of the middle years of life. This type of crisis can often be prevented by anticipatory guidance, an education process that alerts individuals and their families to behavioral changes that they are likely to experience in current stages of development. This allows clients to foresee problem areas and to develop ways to adapt in a positive manner. Anticipatory guidance also helps individuals and their families to distinguish between normal experiences and unusual ones. The anxiety normally produced when an individual faces an unknown situation is thus reduced.

A second circumstance that may produce a crisis state is called a situational event. This kind of crisis is precipitated by an unexpected event that suddenly disrupts a person's life and threatens his or her emotional security. Some examples of events that may lead to situational crises are loss of a loved one through death or divorce, loss of a job, a move to a new city or a new job, graduation from school, marriage, or an unwanted pregnancy.

Even a long-awaited promotion or career change may cause trouble because of added stress. Such events produce new situations with increased demands and challenges that the individual must meet.

A person may experience both types of stress-producing situations at the same time. Many middle-aged women trying to adjust to the empty nest syndrome find themselves also adjusting to the loss of a mate through divorce and the economic need to return to the work force. It is understandable that persons experiencing multiple stressful events in close succession are likely to have difficulty coping in a positive manner.

Some authorities break situational crises into two subtypes: those discussed above and social crises. *Social crisis* is defined as an unanticipated crisis that involves multiple losses or extensive environmental changes or both. These may include fires, floods, war, murder, and racial persecution. This type of crisies does not usually occur in everyday life, but when it does, stress levels become so high that the coping mechanisms of everyone involved are seriously threatened.

Every individual reacts to stressful events in different ways. Some seem to be able to handle an extraordinary amount of stress, while others find minor occurrences upsetting. A degree of stress resulting from routine changes and challenges is unavoidable in day-to-day living. This type of stress is not necessarily bad, because it motivates us to complete our daily tasks, such as working or studying, in a satisfactory manner. The individual in crisis is rarely the only person affected by a given situation. The individual's support system of significant others (family, special friends, neighbors) is invariably involved and should also be assumed to be in a state of crisis.

The development of a crisis seems to follow four different, overlapping phases. The first phase is denial and usually lasts only for a few hours. Denial is a mental mechanism to temporarily defuse or diminish overwhelming anxiety. In mentally healthy persons, reality is quickly recognized, leading to an understanding of what is occurring. An example of denial is a wife's refusal to believe that the husband she kissed good-bye that morning has died in an automobile accident on the way to work. She may insist that the police and medical personnel have mistaken his identity. As she is given more details concerning the accident, she will begin to confront the reality of her situation.

In the second phase, anxiety increases as the individual tries to continue daily activities while also searching for ways to handle the increased tension. The new widow somehow manages to make the funeral arrangements for her late husband and to get through the formalities.

The third stage is one of disorganization, when individuals in crisis seem to "go to pieces." They are unable to think clearly and neglect many of the activities of daily living. They are also preoccupied with the event. Persons in this stage are conscious of extreme anxiety because coping mechanisms have failed and there may even be fears of insanity. In this stage individuals may seek professional help to deal with the situation. The young widow at this stage may become unable to cope with household tasks, such as cooking meals, preparing the children for school, and cleaning. She may neglect her personal appearance, while dwelling on her husband's death and her inability to live without him. Decisions may become difficult or impossible for her to make.

With professional help, the fourth and final stage should be one of reorganization and the development of new skills that allow individuals to return to a functional lifestyle. A functional lifestyle allows the individual to face and master the challenges of day-to-day living. If there is no improvement, anxiety will continue to increase until the patient experiences a state of panic and, possibly, generalized personality disorganization.

For the individual whose usual defense mechanisms are already functioning poorly, the extreme levels of stress and anxiety experienced during crisis are strong motivators for change. During this period, persons are more likely than at any other time to change their behavior and develop new problem-solving and coping techniques.

Because the acute stage of a crisis usually lasts approximately 4 to 6 weeks, clients who have not resolved the crisis, or have not learned to cope satisfactorily in that length of time, may be referred to other professionals or to mental health agencies that are equipped to provide long-term therapies. Aquilera and Messick (1978) state that effective resolution of a crisis situation is more likely to occur if the individual's perception of the precipitating event is realistic, if there are significant others in the client's environment who are available and willing to help, and if positive coping mechanisms to deal with the stressful events in life have previously been developed and can be called on. Resolution is also affected in a positive way by the therapist who is able to establish rapport quickly and who conveys to the client a warm and caring attitude.

The first step in crisis intervention is to collect information about the nature of the crisis and the effect it is having on the patient and his or her family and friends. In the initial interview the mental health professional should identify the precipitating event and the patient's perception of that event, learn the patient's positive characteristics and coping mechanisms, and determine the strength of support the patient can expect from family and friends.

People usually seek help within 2 weeks of the precipitating event. Often the event may have occurred as recently as the day before the patient asks for help. In this first stage of intervention, open-ended questions such as the following will help the mental health professional obtain useful information:

> What has happened that brought you here for help at this time?
> When did it happen?
> Tell me how you feel.
> How is this situation affecting your life?
> How is it affecting those around you?
> Have you ever faced a problem like this before?
> When you are anxious or tense, what do you do to feel better?

Have you tried that this time?
What do you think might help you feel better?
Do you live with someone? Who?
Do you have a friend that you trust?
Do you have someone that you feel understands you?

Questions such as these may help the patient and family put their thoughts and feelings in order at a time when they are likely to be disorganized. It may also be helpful to have clients give an account of activities for the weeks preceding the intervention if they have difficulty identifying the event that precipitated the crisis. Talking about the situation should help lower patients' state of tension, helping them to see the situation more clearly. At this point the nurse or therapist may find it helpful to reassure patients that seeking help is both a sign of strength and a step toward resolution of the problem. False reassurance should never be given. Instead, the therapist should express belief in patients' ability to learn to cope, while encouraging patients to help themselves in every way possible.

Planning is the second stage of the intervention process. All available data from the patient, family, and any other professional sources should be reviewed and evaluated. A solution or solutions should be outlined and alternatives provided. The skills the patient will need to work through the problem should be identified and supportive community resources pointed out.

The third stage of crisis intervention is to implement the plan developed in the second stage. First, the mental health professional should discuss his or her perception of the problem with the patient to see if their perceptions correspond, making corrections as needed. As both explore the precipitating event and the resulting crisis, the patient should be encouraged to verbalize feelings about the situation.

Next, possible solutions to the problem may be discussed. It will be helpful to identify any of the patient's coping skills that will assist in resolving the crisis. It will also be beneficial to identify the availability of supportive individuals in the person's environment. The mental health worker and patient may even role play the new problem-solving techniques to allow the patient to become more comfortable with them in a controlled environment.

Sometimes the best approach to alleviating a crisis situation is to change the client's physical or interpersonal environment. A middle-aged woman who faces the prospect of serious surgery, and who also is responsible for her healthy but sometimes slightly confused elderly mother, may have to make other living arrangements for the mother, despite the latter's strenuous objections. The mother may have to live temporarily with another son or daughter, or if this is not a feasible solution, the client may need help in finding a home for senior citizens that provides the level of care her mother needs. If this type of care is too expensive for the daughter to finance alone, she will need to be referred to social agencies that can help her apply for funds to defray the additional cost.

Anticipatory guidance is also an effective way of dealing with many situational crises. Stages of grief have been identified for those who are seriously ill or dying, and these stages also apply to the feelings associated with the loss of a spouse through death or divorce, or diminished feelings of self-worth due to the loss of a job.

Education concerning these stages may be a very effective way of helping the client deal with the situations and the emotions involved. In all crisis counseling it is extremely important to establish a rapport with patients and to provide a therapeutic climate in which patients feel comfortable in voicing their feelings and concerns.

The final stage of crisis intervention process is evaluation. In this stage the mental health worker and the patient have the opportunity to compare the goals they set in the planning stage with the actual behavioral changes in the patient's lifestyle. In the evaluation process, other unmet needs may be identified and appropriate patient actions or referrals to other helping agencies can be initiated.

It should be kept in mind that the goal of successful crisis intervention is at least to return patients to their precrisis level of functioning, hopefully with improved adaptive capabilities, within a relatively short time. Such short-term therapy in an outpatient setting allows community mental health workers to reach a greater number of patients more quickly and, in this manner, prevent more severe mental problems that might require long-term hospitalization.

ANNOTATED BIBLIOGRAPHY

Cowles, K.V., and Rodgers. B.L.: *When a loved one has AIDS: Care for the significant other.* Journal of Psychosocial Nursing and Mental Health Services, 1991, 29(4):6–12.

> *Addresses the needs of family members, friends, and partners upon learning a loved one has AIDS. These needs include support and reassurance, assistance in adjusting to personal relationship changes, and help in becoming involved in some form of AIDS-related work.*

Koontz, E., Cox, D., and Hastings, S.: *Implementing a short-term family support group.* Journal of Psychosocial Nursing and Mental Health Services, 1991, 29(5):5–8.

> *Focuses on the crisis the family experiences when the patient is admitted to the hospital due to mental illness, and discusses the use of a family support group to provide education and support to these families.*

McArther, M.J.: *Reality therapy with rape victims.* Archives of Psychiatric Nursing, 1990, 4(6):360–365.

> *Discusses the use of reality therapy groups with rape victims to provide a supportive arena in which the victim can tell her story, diminish her desire to withdraw from others, and recognize control over her behavior.*

Rew, L., Agor, W., Emery, M., and Harper, S.: *Intuitive skills in crisis management.* Nursing Connections, 1991, 4(2):3–12.

> *Discusses the nurse's use of analytic reasoning and intuition to manage the complex, rapidly changing, and often unpredictable circumstances surrounding crises.*

Stanley, S.R.: *When the disaster is over: Helping the healers to mend.* Journal of Psychosocial Nursing and Mental Health Services, 1990, 28(5):12–16.

> *Describes a postdisaster crisis stabilization program and discusses the stages of disaster, role conflict, expected reactions, and self-help techniques.*

Van Servellen, G., Nyamathi, A., and Mannion, W.: *Coping with a crisis: Evaluating psychological risks of patients with AIDS.* Journal of Psychosocial Nursing and Mental Health Services, 1989, 27(12):16–21.

> *Presents a framework for assessing levels of functioning and an assessment tool that may assist in predicting overall coping status in persons with AIDS.*

Walker, V., and Gatzert-Snyder, S.: *When disaster strikes: The concerns of staff nurses.* Journal of Psychosocial Nursing and Mental Health Services, 1991, 29(6):9–13.

> *Discusses how the calamity of an earthquake affected patient care delivery and presents what nurses need to know to continue providing safe and efficient care in the midst of such adversity.*

REFERENCE

Aquilera, D.C., and Messick, M.: *Crisis Intervention: Theory and Methodology,* ed. 3, CV Mosby, St. Louis, 1978.

Short Answer. Answer the following questions as briefly and specifically as possible.

1. State the goal of crisis intervention therapy.

_____

_____

_____.

2. List and describe the four overlapping phases in the development of a crisis.

_____

_____

_____.

3. Define *crisis*.

_____

_____

_____.

4. Define *social crisis*.

_____

_____

_____.

5. List the four steps in crisis intervention.

_____

_____

_____.

Multiple Choice. Circle the letter or number that you think represents the best answer.

1. A crisis state may be precipitated by which of the following events?
   a. Developmental and maturational stages.
   b. Transition period between two developmental stages.
   c. Unanticipated external event.
   d. b and c.
   e. a, b, and c.

2. Which of the following situations could precipitate a crisis?
   a. Marriage.
   b. Career change.
   c. Pregnancy.
   d. Job promotion.
      (1) a and b.
      (2) b and c.
      (3) a, b, and c.
      (4) All of the above.
3. Which of the following are manifestations of a person in crisis?
   a. Anxiety and tension.
   b. Increased feelings of self-esteem.
   c. Feelings of anger and depression.
   d. Behavioral disorganization.
      (1) a and b.
      (2) b.
      (3) a, c, and d.
      (4) All of the above.
4. Which of the following is not a recognized phase in the development of a crisis?
   a. Disorganization.
   b. Reorganization.
   c. Denial.
   d. Anger.
5. The acute stage of a crisis usually lasts approximately:
   a. 4 to 6 weeks.
   b. 6 to 8 hours.
   c. 3 to 4 days.
   d. 4 to 6 days.
6. The initial step in crisis intervention is to:
   a. Try to resolve the problem.
   b. Collect information.
   c. Identify the strength of support.
   d. Identify the patient's positive characteristics.
7. The final stage of the crisis intervention process is:
   a. Evaluation.
   b. Anticipatory guidance.
   c. Implementing the plan of action.
   d. Exploring possible solutions.
8. Which of the following would not be considered a social crisis?
   a. Flood.
   b. War.

    c. Racial persecution.
    d. Loss of job.

True or False. Circle your choice.

T F   1. Sometimes the best approach to alleviating a crisis situation is to actually change the client's physical or interpersonal environment.

T F   2. It is all right to give false assurance to patients if it helps them get through the crisis.

T F   3. It is necessary to hospitalize a person in a crisis situation most of the time.

T F   4. The first phase in the development of a crisis is denial.

T F   5. Anticipatory guidance is an effective way of dealing with many situational crises.

T F   6. A certain amount of stress in life is unavoidable.

A
Answer Keys

CHAPTER 1

Attitude Inventory

1.	F	22.	F
2.	F	23.	F
3.	T	24.	F
4.	F	25.	T
5.	T	26.	T
6.	F	27.	F
7.	T	28.	T
8.	F	29.	T
9.	F	30.	F
10.	F	31.	F
11.	T	32.	F
12.	F	33.	T
13.	F	34.	F
14.	F	35.	F
15.	F	36.	F
16.	F	37.	F
17.	F	38.	F
18.	T	39.	F
19.	T	40.	F
20.	F	41.	T
21.	F		

True or False

1.	T	6.	T
2.	T	7.	F
3.	F	8.	F
4.	T	9.	F
5.	F	10.	F

Fill in the Blanks

1. f, d
2. e
3. c

4. a
5. g

Multiple Choice

1. (3)
2. (2)
3. (4)

4. (4)
5. (3)

CHAPTER 2

Fill in the Blanks

1. b
2. a
3. d

4. c
5. e

True or False

1. F
2. T
3. T

4. F
5. F

Multiple Choice

1. b
2. c
3. b
4. (4)
5. a
6. b
7. a
8. d
9. c
10. d

11. b
12. (5)
13. b
14. c
15. (5)
16. d
17. c
18. (4)
19. c

CHAPTER 3

Matching

1. g
2. c
3. e
4. a

5. i
6. d
7. b
8. f

True or False

1.	T	**4.**	F
2.	F	**5.**	F
3.	T	**6.**	T

Fill in the Blank

1.	c	**4.**	e
2.	a	**5.**	g
3.	b, f		

Multiple Choice

1.	(4)	**10.**	e
2.	(3)	**11.**	c
3.	d	**12.**	d
4.	c	**13.**	a
5.	a	**14.**	c
6.	(3)	**15.**	c
7.	c	**16.**	(2)
8.	(5)	**17.**	(4)
9.	e	**18.**	d

CHAPTER 4

Judgment Exercises

Answers may vary—discuss with classmates.

True or False

1.	F	**8.**	F
2.	T	**9.**	T
3.	F	**10.**	T
4.	F	**11.**	T
5.	T	**12.**	F
6.	T	**13.**	F
7.	T	**14.**	T

Matching

1.	d	**4.**	f
2.	c	**5.**	e
3.	a		

Short Answer

1. Willful neglect, abuse, harassment, or failure to attend adequately to a patient.
2. In a voluntary admission the patient admits himself or herself. Involuntary admission involves legal action in which it is determined by a judge or a doctor (depending on state law) that a person is to be admitted.
3. Tell the patient you do not know the answer but will attempt to find out and tell him or her.
4. To protect the patient from harming himself or herself or others.
5. A negligent act.

CHAPTERS 5, 6, AND 7

Matching

1.	d	6.	i
2.	a	7.	b
3.	h	8.	c
4.	e	9.	f
5.	f		

True or False

1.	F	8.	T
2.	F	9.	F
3.	T	10	F
4.	T	11.	F
5.	F	12.	T
6.	F	13.	F
7.	F		

Short Answer

1. Persistent and irrational fear of some object, place, or condition.
2. Rigid; perfectionistic; often obstinate.
3. Tendency to be self-indulgent; poor self-concept; exaggerated dependency needs.
4. Accept the patient.
5. In organic psychosis, pathology can be demonstrated, while functional psychosis is caused by psychologic stress.
6. Sexual disorders (paraphilia) involve sexual activity and arousal patterns that are not common to the general public, while sexual dysfunctions involve problems with carrying through the usual

sexual-response cycle from attraction, to desire, to arousal, to intercourse, to orgasm.

Multiple Choice

1.	a	12.	d
2.	b	13.	d
3.	d	14.	e
4.	d	15.	c
5.	b	16.	c
6.	c	17.	b
7.	d	18.	b
8.	a	19.	(3)
9.	a	20.	d
10.	c	21.	b
11.	(4)	22.	a

CHAPTER 8

True or False

1.	T	6.	T
2.	T	7.	F
3.	T	8.	T
4.	F	9.	F
5.	T	10.	T

Multiple Choice

1.	d	8.	(2) and (4)
2.	d	9.	b
3.	d	10.	c
4.	d	11.	(2)
5.	(4)	12.	d
6.	b	13.	d
7.	d		

CHAPTER 9

Matching I

1.	c	4.	b
2.	a	5.	f
3.	e		

Matching II

1.	e	6.	a
2.	d	7.	c
3.	f	8.	d
4.	e	9.	a
5.	b		

True or False

1.	F	4.	T
2.	T	5.	F
3.	F	6.	F

Short Answer

1. Help calm the patient, control severe agitation, and decrease hallucinations.
2. Caution the patient to increase fluid intake to help prevent dry mouth, as well as to decrease intake of fatty foods and increase intake of salads to prevent excessive weight gain and constipation.
3. Tricyclic compounds and MAO inhibitors.
4. Dry mouth, fatigue, weakness, blurring vision, constipation, parkinsonian syndrome, and increased perspiration.

Multiple Choice

1.	(4)	5.	c
2.	(5)	6.	(5)
3.	d	7.	(3)
4.	(2)		

CHAPTER 10

True or False

1.	F	4.	F
2.	F	5.	T
3.	T	6.	F

Short Answer

1. Helps the patient to forget painful life experiences; perceived by the patient as a form of punishment.
2. ECT may place a great deal of strain on the patient's heart.
3. Depressed patients.
4. To prevent the patient from aspirating during treatment.

Multiple Choice

1. a
2. d
3. (2)

4. a
5. (3)

CHAPTER 11

True or False

1. T
2. T
3. F

4. T
5. F
6. T

Short Answer

1. **a.** The patient must want to get better.
   b. The patient must come to a better understanding of what is causing the problems and learn methods of dealing with them more effectively.
   c. The patient must be in an environment that makes change possible.
2. The patient must be in an environment that makes change possible.
3. To help patients gain insight and/or understanding into their problems so they can learn to deal with them more effectively.

Multiple Choice

1. c
2. (1)
3. (4)
4. b

5. c
6. (3)
7. c

CHAPTER 12

True or False

1. T
2. F
3. T
4. T
5. T

6. F
7. T
8. F
9. T

Matching

1.	(3)	**4.**	d
2.	(3)	**5.**	d
3.	b		

Short Answer

1. Confront the patient with the behavior.
2. Plan a program of activities that will not permit the patients so much free time that they become bored.
3. When the patient feels threatened and unable to do anything else.
4. Patients are usually calmer when they do not have an audience.

CHAPTER 13

True or False

1.	T	**6.**	F
2.	F	**7.**	F
3.	F	**8.**	T
4.	T	**9.**	T
5.	F	**10.**	F

Multiple Choice

1.	(4)	**7.**	(3)
2.	a	**8.**	b
3.	(3)	**9.**	b
4.	(3)	**10.**	c
5.	(2)	**11.**	e
6.	a		

CHAPTER 14

True or False

1.	T	**5.**	T
2.	F	**6.**	F
3.	T	**7.**	T
4.	T		

Multiple Choice

1.	c	**4.**	c
2.	c	**5.**	c
3.	c	**6.**	e

CHAPTER 15

True or False

1.	T	6.	F
2.	T	7.	F
3.	F	8.	T
4.	F	9.	T
5.	T	10.	F

Multiple Choice

1.	d	4.	d
2.	(1)	5.	c
3.	b	6.	c

CHAPTER 16

Judgment Exercises

Answers may vary—discuss with classmates.

Short Answer

1. 10 to 20.
2. Persons who have previously attempted suicide, the terminally ill, the elderly, the alcoholic, the severely emotionally ill, and people who associate with persons who have made suicide attempts.
3. The need for help and the recognition that something is wrong and a change is necessary for survival.
4. One's acute awareness and alertness.
5. Any three of the following:
   a. Continuously talking about suicide.
   b. Showing the vegetative signs of depression.
   c. Having extreme difficulty sleeping.
   d. Dwelling on sad thoughts.

True or False

1.	T	9.	F
2.	F	10.	F
3.	F	11.	F
4.	T	12.	T
5.	T	13.	F
6.	T	14.	T
7.	T	15.	T
8.	F		

Matching

1.	a, b	4.	e
2.	c	5.	a
3.	d	6.	e

Multiple Choice

1.	c	4.	(3)
2.	(4)	5.	(4)
3.	(3)		

CHAPTER 17

True or False

1.	F	4.	F
2.	F	5.	T
3.	T	6.	T

Multiple Choice

1. b
2. b
3. (2)

Short Answer

1. Two of the following: schizophrenia, senile dementia, manic-depressive psychosis.
2. May first exhibit loud talk, rapid pacing, grandiose ideas.
3. Delusions, illusions, hallucinations.
4. An illusion is a false interpretation of a real sensory impression.
5. A hallucination is an idea or perception that does not exist in reality.

CHAPTER 18

Multiple Choice

1.	(5)	5.	(1)
2.	(2)	6.	b
3.	e	7.	b
4.	(5)	8.	b

True or False

1.	F	4.	F
2.	T	5.	F
3.	T		

Short Answer

1. J = judgment
   O = orientation
   C = confabulation
   A = affect
   M = memory
2. Be as brief as possible.
3. Five of the following:
   Wear large name tags.
   Put patients' names on their room doors.
   Put up large calendars with big numbers.
   Use big clocks and place several around patient areas.
   Show patients around the unit and help them only as much as they need it; do not be overly helpful because this increases dependency.
   Let patients bring favorite and familiar things from home; this will help their new room to become "theirs."
4. The patient may not remember what he or she said or did and thus feels that he or she is being unfairly punished.
5. Routine and structure.

CHAPTER 19

Multiple Choice

1.	d	4.	c
2.	c	5.	d
3.	d	6.	a

Short Answer

1. Make sure the patient is stabilized; establish trust; promote improved nutrition; promote effective coping; promote improved perception of body image; and promote feelings of self-worth.
2. Promote effective coping; identify binge triggers; promote guilt reduction; and involve the patient in discharge planning.
3. Display nonjudgmental acceptance; teach good nutrition; establish realistic nutritional goals; encourage social interaction; and promote a sense of well-being.

True or False

1.	T		4.	F
2.	F		5.	T
3.	F		6.	F

CHAPTER 20

True or False

1.	T		6.	F
2.	T		7.	T
3.	F		8.	F
4.	T		9.	T
5.	T		10.	T

Short Answer

1. When they have lost control of their drinking to the extent that interpersonal, family, and community relationships have become seriously threatened or disturbed.
2. Tend to be pale, skinny, and poorly nourished; may have dilated blood vessels in their faces and bulblike, fleshy noses.
3. The process of being able to accept the fact that one is an alcoholic.
4. a. Depresses bone marrow and thus the production of red blood cells.
   b. Causes brain tissue changes.
   c. Causes formation of scar tissue in the liver (cirrhosis)
5. Marked by frequent "benders"; usually a daily intake of alcohol in response to the physical craving.
6. Through recognition of the alcoholic status by someone in the general hospital when the patient is admitted for some other reason.

Multiple Choice

1.	d		**7.**	d
2.	(1)		**8.**	a
3.	b		**9.**	c
4.	d		**10.**	c
6.	b		**11.**	a
6.	a		**12.**	b

CHAPTER 21

True or False

1.	T		**7.**	T
2.	F		**8.**	T
3.	F		**9.**	T
4.	T		**10.**	F
5.	T		**11.**	T
6.	F			

Short Answer

1. Retirement.
2. Factors such as increased sensitivity to medications, decreased body weight, impaired circulation, and liver dysfunction.
3. Organic brain damage.
4. Placing a large clock and a cube calendar in the room.
5. Activity promotes good health by increasing circulation, stimulating appetite, helping regulate bowel function, and preventing such complications of inactivity as joint immobility, bedsores, and pneumonia.

Multiple Choice

1.	d		**6.**	d
2.	b		**7.**	a
3.	d		**8.**	d
4.	a		**9.**	c
5.	c		**10.**	a

CHAPTER 22

Short Answer

1. The goal of crisis intervention therapy is to help clients return to a level of functioning that is at least equal to their precrisis state.
2. The first phase is denial and usually lasts for only a few hours.

Denial is a mental mechanism used by the mind to temporarily defuse overwhelming anxiety. In the second phase, anxiety increases and the individual tries to continue his or her daily activities while attempting to find a way to handle the increased tension. The third phase is one of disorganization, where the individual in crisis just seems to "go to pieces." The fourth phase is one of reorganization and the development of new skills that allow the individual to function at a precrisis level.

3. Mental health authorities define *crisis* as a state of psychological disequilibrium brought about by conflict, problems, or life situations that an individual perceives as a threat to self and cannot effectively handle by using previously successful problem-solving and coping techniques.

4. A *social crisis* is defined as an unanticipated crisis that involves multiple losses and/or extensive environmental changes, such as fires, floods, war, murder, and racial persecution.

5. Collecting information, planning, intervention, and evaluation.

Multiple Choice

1.	e	5.	a
2.	(4)	6.	b
3.	(3)	7.	a
4.	d	8.	d

True or False

1.	T	4.	T
2.	F	5.	T
3.	F	6.	T

A Patient's Bill of Rights

1. The patient has the right to considerate and respectful care.
2. The patient has the right to and is encouraged to obtain from physicians and other direct caregivers relevant, current, and understandable information concerning diagnosis, treatment, and prognosis.

   Except in emergencies when the patient lacks decision-making capacity and the need for treatment is urgent, the patient is entitled to the opportunity to discuss and request information related to the specific procedures and/or treatments, the risks involved, the possible length of recuperation, and the medically reasonable alternatives and their accompanying risks and benefits.

   Patients have the right to know the identity of physicians, nurses, and others involved in their care, as well as when those involved are students, residents, or other trainees. The patient also has the right to know the immediate and long-term financial implications of treatment choices, insofar as they are known.
3. The patient has the right to make decisions about the plan of care prior to and during the course of treatment and to refuse a recommended treatment or plan of care to the extent permitted by law and hospital policy and to be informed of the medical consequences of this action. In case of such refusal, the patient is entitled to other appropriate care and services that the hospital provides or transfer to another hospital. The hospital should notify

---

These rights can be exercised on the patient's behalf by a designated surrogate or proxy decision maker if the patient lacks decision-making capacity, is legally incompetent, or is a minor.

345

patients of any policy that might affect patient choice within the institution.

4. The patient has the right to have an advance directive (such as a living will, health care proxy, or durable power of attorney for health care) concerning treatment or designating a surrogate decision maker with the expectation that the hospital will honor the intent of that directive to the extent permitted by law and hospital policy.

   Health care institutions must advise patients of their rights under state law and hospital policy to make informed medical choices, ask if the patient has an advance directive, and include that information in patient records. The patient has the right to timely information about hospital policy that may limit its ability to implement fully a legally valid advance directive.

5. The patient has the right to every consideration of privacy. Case discussion, consultation, examination, and treatment should be conducted so as to protect each patient's privacy.

6. The patient has the right to expect that all communications and records pertaining to his/her care will be treated as confidential by the hospital, except in cases such as suspected abuse and public health hazards when reporting is permitted or required by law. The patient has the right to expect that the hospital will emphasize the confidentiality of this information when it releases it to any other parties entitled to review information in these records.

7. The patient has the right to review the records pertaining to his/her medical care and to have the information explained or interpreted as necessary, except when restricted by law.

8. The patient has the right to expect that, within its capacity and policies, a hospital will make reasonable response to the request of a patient for appropriate and medically indicated care and services. The hospital must provide evaluation, service, and/or referral as indicated by the urgency of the case. When medically appropriate and legally permissible, or when a patient has so requested, a patient may be transferred to another facility. The institution to which the patient is to be transferred must first have accepted the patient for transfer. The patient must also have the benefit of complete information and expla-

nation concerning the need for, risks, benefits, and alternatives to such a transfer.

9. The patient has the right to ask and be informed of the existence of business relationships among the hospital, educational institutions, other health care providers, or payers that may influence the patient's treatment and care.

10. The patient has the right to consent to or decline to participate in proposed research studies or human experimentation affecting care and treatment or requiring direct patient involvement, and to have those studies fully explained prior to consent. A patient who declines to participate in research or experimentation is entitled to the most effective care that the hospital can otherwise provide.

11. The patient has the right to expect reasonable continuity of care when appropriate and to be informed by physicians and other caregivers of available and realistic patient care options when hospital care is no longer appropriate.

12. The patient has the right to be informed of hospital policies and practices that relate to patient care, treatment, and responsibilities. The patient has the right to be informed of available resources for resolving disputes, grievances, and conflicts, such as ethics committees, patient representatives, or other mechanisms available in the institution. The patient has the right to be informed of the hospital's charges for services and available payment methods.

Index

Page numbers followed by a "t" indicate tables.

AA. *See* Alcoholics Anonymous
Abstract statement, 127
Acetophenazine (Tindal), 147t
Acute schizophrenic reaction, 86
Adapin. *See* Doxepin
Adjustment mechanism(s). *See* Defense
    mechanism(s)
Admission
  involuntary, 51
  voluntary, 51
Adolescence
  dependence-independence conflict in, 20
  masturbation during, 20–21
  parent-child relationship during, 20
  peer approval during, 21
  personality development during, 20–21
  suicide during, 231
Adventure therapy, 178
Affect
  definition of, 258
  flat, 258
  impairment due to neurologic deficit,
    255–259
Affective instability, 101
Aggressive patient(s), behaviors of
  agitated, 189–191
  antagonistic, 193–194
  demanding, 192
  intimidating, 193–194
  lying, 192–193
  physically abusive, 193–194
  physically destructive, 189–191
  sexually aggressive, 196–197
  stealing, 192–193
  uncooperative, 194–196
  verbally abusive, 187–189
  violent, 189–191
Aging. *See* Elderly patient(s)
Agitated behavior, 189–191, 205–206
Agoraphobia, 72
AIDS, disclosure of illness to sexual
    partners, 53
Akathisia, as side effect of major
    tranquilizers, 145

Al-Anon, 296
Alcohol abuse, 283–296
  alcoholic process, 290–291
  comparison with drug abuse, 285–286t
  factors influencing, 287–289
  physiologic effects of alcohol, 289
  recognizing tendencies toward, 289–290
  signs and symptoms of, 293–294
  treatment of, 291–296
    methods of, 294–296
    ways of entering treatment, 292–293
  withdrawal symptoms, 293–294
Alcohol idiosyncratic intoxication, 293
Alcohol-dependent patient(s), 284–286
Alcoholic hallucinosis, 291, 293
Alcoholics Anonymous (AA), 289, 296
Alcoholism. *See* Alcohol abuse
Allergic reaction(s)
  to barbiturates, 153
  to major tranquilizers, 145–146
Alprazolam (Xanax), 149t
Alurate. *See* Aprobarbital
Alzheimer's disease, 310
Ambulatory mentally ill, 54
Amitriptyline (Elavil), 151t
Amnesia
  continuous, 80
  generalized, 80
  localized, 80
  in multiple personality disorder, 79
  psychogenic, 79–80
  in psychogenic fugue, 80
  selective, 80
Amobarbital (Amytal), 154t
Amoxapine (Asendin), 151t
Amphetamine abuse, 298
Amytal. *See* Amobarbital
Analgesic abuse, 298
Ancillary therapy, 224
Anectine. *See* Succinylcholine chloride
Anesthesia, before electroconvulsive
    therapy, 155, 165
Anniversary reaction(s), 74

Anorexia nervosa, 266–267
  history in, 267
  nursing interventions in, 268–270
  prognosis and outcome in, 270–271
  signs and symptoms in, 267–268
Antabuse. *See* Disulfiram
Antagonistic behavior, 193–194
Anticipatory guidance, 322, 326
Anticonvulsant(s), 154–155
  nursing considerations in, 158–159
  in treatment of alcoholics, 294
Antidepressant(s), 151t, 233
  cyclic, 151–153, 151t
  dosage of, 151t
  MAO inhibitors, 150–152, 151t, 157–158
  nursing considerations in, 157–158
  patient teaching for use of, 152–153
  route of administration of, 151t
  side effects of, 150, 152
Anti-emetic(s), 147t
Antihistamine(s), 149t
Antiparkinson(s), 155
  indications for, 145
  nursing considerations in, 159
Antipsychotic(s), 147t
Antisocial personality disorder, 97–100
Anxiety, 39
  during crisis, 321–326
Anxiety attack, 70
Anxiety disorder(s)
  generalized anxiety disorder, 68–71
  not otherwise specified, 68–71
  obsessive-compulsive disorders, 72–74
  phobic disorders, 71–72
  post-traumatic stress disorder, 74
Anxious patient(s), behaviors of, 135–136,
    203–205
  agitated, 205–206
  compulsive, 206–207
  phobic, 207–208
  restless, 205–206
Appearance of patient. *See* Personal
    appearance/hygiene
Apprehensive expectation, 68
Aprobarbital (Alurate), 154t
Argument(s)
  among patients, 193–194
  between staff and patient, 188, 190, 214
Arson, 99
Art therapy, 178
Artane, 155
Arteriosclerosis, 309–310
Asendin. *See* Amoxapine
Assertiveness training, 104
Atarax. *See* Hydroxyzine
Ativan. *See* Lorazepam
Attention span, 126, 256
Attitude(s), toward mental illness, 3–7
  Mental Health Attitude Inventory, 3–4
Attitude Inventory, 3–4

Authority figure, patient seeing staff as,
    129
Autonomic reaction(s)
  hyperactivity in anxiety disorders,
    70–71
  side effect of major tranquilizers, 145
Autonomy, development in toddler period,
    16
Auxiliary therapy(ies), 178–179
Aventyl. *See* Nortriptyline
Avoidant personality disorder, 97, 104

Barbiturate(s), 153–154, 154t, 158
  abuse of, 298–299
Basic concept(s)
  defense mechanisms, 31–32
    compensation, 35
    conversion reactions, 34–35
    denial of reality, 33–34
    displacement, 39
    fantasy, 36–37
    introjection, 37
    projection, 35–36
    rationalization, 33
    reaction formation, 37–38
    regression, 38
    repression, 32–33
    restitution, 39
    sublimation, 38–39
  mental health continuum, 27–31
  neurosis, 39–42, 41t
  psychosis, 39–42, 41t
Behavior(s)
  acceptable by society, 30
  agitated, 189–191, 205–206
  antagonistic, 193–194
  of anxious patient, 135–136
  bizarre, 247–250
  body, 132
  charting of, 131–133
  of chemically dependent patient,
    283–301
  compulsive, 206–207
  crying, 222, 224, 258
  demanding, 192
  of depressed patient, 136, 221–225
  of elderly patient, 307–314
  general, 132
  inappropriate, 247–250
  intimidating, 193–194
  lying, 192–193
  of manic patient, 136
  manipulative, 195
  in neurologic disorder, 137
  as nonverbal communication, 122–123
  of patient with eating disorder, 265–278
  of patient with neurologic deficit,
    255–259

of patient who has lost contact with
  reality, 247–250
phobic, 207–208
physically abusive, 193–194
physically destructive, 189–191
in psychosis, 136–137
restless, 205–206
ritualistic, 73–74, 98, 206–207
sexually aggressive, 196–197
stealing, 192–193, 297–298
of suicidal patient, 229–238
of suspicious patient, 213–216
in terms of mental health continuum,
  27–31
uncooperative, 194–196
verbally abusive, 187–189
violent, 189–191
Behavior therapy, 176–178
Benadryl, 155
Benzodiazepine(s), 149t
Bicyclic antidepressant(s), 151t
Bill of rights, patient's, 345–346
Binge eating. See Bulimia nervosa;
  Compulsive overeating
Bipolar disorder(s)
  depressed, 81–82
  manic, 81–82
  mixed, 81–82
Bizarre behavior, 247–250
"Blaming" theme, 36
Blurred vision, as side effect of major
  tranquilizers, 146
Body behavior, 132
Body dysmorphic disorder, 75, 77
Body image, improving perception of, in
  anorexia nervosa, 270
Body language, 122–123
Borderline personality disorder, 97,
  101–102
Brain, senile atrophy of, 309–310
Brain-damaged patient(s), 255–259
Brainwashing, 37
Brevital, 155
Bulimia nervosa, 271–274
  history in, 271–272
  nursing interventions in, 272–274
  prognosis and outcome in, 274
  signs and symptoms of, 272
Bum, 284
BuSpar. See Buspirone
Buspirone (BuSpar), 154t
Butabarbital (Butisol), 154t
Butaperazine (Repoise), 147t
Butisol. See Butabarbital
Butyrophenone(s), 147t

Care plan, patient participation in, 128
Catastrophizing, 205
Catatonic excitement, 88

Catatonic schizophrenia, 86, 88, 144
Catatonic stupor, 88
Centrax. See Prazepam
Cerebral arteriosclerosis, 309–310
Charting patient information, 130–135
Chemically-dependent patient(s), 283–301
  alcohol abuser, 284–296
  drug abuser, 296–300
Child abuse
  in antisocial personality disorder, 99
  duty to report, 53–54
  multiple personality disorder and, 79
  in pedophilia, 110
Chloral hydrate (Noctec, Somnos), 154t
Chlorazepate dipotassium (Tranxene), 149t
Chlordiazepoxide (Librium), 149t, 157, 298
  in treatment of alcoholics, 294
Chlorpromazine (Thorazine), 147t
Chronic phase of alcoholism, 291, 294
Chronic schizophrenic reaction, 87
Cirrhosis, 289, 294
Civil rights, patient's, 54, 345–346
Clairvoyance, 98
Clarification, in staff-patient
  communication, 130
Cocaine, 283, 297–298
Cogentin, 155
Command hallucination, 248
Communication
  goal of conversation, 126
  nonverbal, 121–123, 129
  privileged, 53
  recording, 130–135
    of behavior of patient, 131–133
    of physical symptoms of patient,
      134–135
  reporting, 130–135
  skills in, 121–137
  staff-patient relationships and, 123–126
  techniques of, 126–130
  verbal, 121–122, 132
  written, 121–122
Compazine. See Prochlorperazine
Compensation, 35
Competency, legal declaration of, 54
Complainer, chronic, 107
Compulsion, 40
Compulsive behavior, 206–207
Compulsive disorder, 72–74
Compulsive overeating, 274–278. See also
  Obese patient(s)
Concept(s), basic. See Basic concept(s)
Conditioning, 176–178
Confabulation, 255–259
Confidentiality, 7, 51–52
  duty to report child abuse, 53–54
  duty to warn, 52–53
Confused patient(s), 255–259, 313
  after electroconvulsive therapy, 168–170
Consent. See Informed consent

Consumers' rights, 49
Contact with reality, 40, 247–250
Continuous amnesia, 80
Contract, patient, 273
Control, perceived lack of, 69
Conversion disorder, 75–77
Conversion reaction, 34–35
Convulsion. *See also* Electroconvulsive
    therapy
  Indoklon-induced, 155
Cooper's sign, 272
Coping, effective
  promoting in anorexia nervosa, 269–270
  promoting in bulimia nervosa, 273–274
Coping mechanism(s). *See* Defense
    mechanism(s)
Criminal behavior, 100, 297–298
Crisis
  definition of, 321
  developmental, 322
  phases in development of, 323
  precipitation of, 322
  social, 322–323
Crisis intervention, 321–326
  collecting information about crisis,
    324–325
  evaluation stage of, 326
  implementation of plan, 325
  planning stage of, 325
Cross tolerance, 297
Cross-dressing, 108
Crucial phase of alcoholism, 290–291, 294
Crying behavior, 222, 224, 258
Cult ideology, 231
Cyclic antidepressant(s), 151–152, 151t
  dosage of, 151t
  patient teaching for use of, 152–153
  route of administration of, 151t
  side effects of, 152
Cyclothymia, 81–82

Dating, staff-patient, 125
Day-care program(s)
  for elderly, 312
  for psychiatric patients, 6
Daydreaming, 36–37
Defense mechanism(s), 31–32
  compensation, 35
  conversion reactions, 34–35
  denial of reality, 33–34, 288, 292
  displacement, 39
  fantasy, 36–37
  introjection, 37
  malfunctioning, 39–42
  projection, 35–36, 92, 213
  rationalization, 33
  reaction formation, 37–38
  regression, 38
  repression, 32–33

restitution, 39
  sublimation, 38–39
Delirium tremens ("DTs"), 291–293
Delusion(s), 81
  care of patients with, 247–250
  definition of, 248
  drug therapy in, 144
  erotomanic, 90
  grandiose, 90–91
  jealous, 91
  persecutory, 91
  religious, 215
  in schizophrenic disorders, 87–89
  somatic, 91
  staff reactions to, 215–216
Delusional (paranoid) disorder, 77, 90–92
Demanding behavior, 192
Dementia, primary degenerative, 310
Demerol abuse, 297–298
Denial phase of crisis, 323
Denial of reality, 33–34, 288, 292
Dependence-independence conflict, in
    adolescence, 20
Dependent personality disorder, 97,
    104–105
Depersonalization disorder, 79–81
Depressed patient(s)
  with antisocial personality disorder, 100
  behaviors of, 136, 221–225
  elderly, 310
  electroconvulsive therapy in, 166
  episodes in bipolar disorders, 81–82
  physical appearance of, 223
  physical problems of, 221
  potential suicide, 231–232
  "vegetative" signs of, 82
Depressive disorder(s)
  depressive disorder, not otherwise
    specified, 82–83
  dysthymia, 82–83
  major depression
    recurrent, 82–83
    single episode, 82–83
Derelict, 284
Description, in written communication, 122
Desipramine (Norpramin), 151t
Desyrel. *See* Trazodone
Developmental crisis, 322
Diagnosis, 65
Diagnostic category(ies), 66–67
  anxiety disorders, 68–74
  delusional disorders, 90–92
  dissociative disorders, 78–81
  mood disorders, 81–83
  personality disorders, 95–107
  schizophrenic disorders, 86–90
  sexual disorders, 107–110
  somatoform disorders, 74–78

Diagnostic and Statistical Manual of Mental Disorders. See also Diagnostic category(ies)
DSM-III-R, 66
DSM-IV, 67
Diagnostically related group(s) (DRG), 65–66
Diazepam (Valium), 149t, 157, 298
Dibenzoxazepine(s), 147t
Dieting. *See* Eating disorder(s)
Dihydroindolone(s), 147t
Dilantin, 154–155
Discharge procedure, 51
Discipline, during preschool period, 17–18
Disorganization phase of crisis, 323
Disorganized schizophrenia, 86, 89
Displacement, 39
Dissociative disorder(s)
  depersonalization disorder, 79–81
  multiple personality disorder, 78–79
  psychogenic amnesia, 79–80
  psychogenic fugue, 78, 80
Disulfiram (Antabuse), 295–296
Diuretic abuse, 271
Divorce, 322
Dizziness, as side effect of minor tranquilizers, 148
Doriden. *See* Glutethimide
Doxepin (Adapin, Sinequan), 151t
DRG. *See* Diagnostically related group(s)
Drowsiness, as side effect of major tranquilizers, 146
Drug(s), therapeutic uses of
  anticonvulsants, 154–155, 158–159
  antidepressants, 150–153, 151t, 157–158
  antiparkinsons, 155, 159
  in elderly patients, 311
  general considerations, 156
  hypnotics, 153–154, 154t, 158
  major tranquilizers, 144–148, 147t, 156–157
  minor tranquilizers, 148–150, 149t, 157
  miscellaneous drugs, 155
  nursing considerations in, 144, 156–159
  sedatives, 153–154, 154t, 158
Drug abuse, 283–284, 296–300
  barbiturates, 153
  comparison with alcohol abuse, 285–286t
  intravenous, 298–299
  signs and symptoms of, 299
  tranquilizers, 148
  treatment of, 299–300
    methadone maintenance programs, 300
Drug overdose, 294, 297
  treatment of, 299–300
Drug tolerance, 297
  cross tolerance, 297
Drunkenness, public, 292
"DTs." *See* Delirium tremens

Due caution, 55
Duty
  to report child abuse, 53–54
  to warn, 52–53
Dyskinesia, as side effect of major tranquilizers, 145
Dysthymia, 82–83, 136

Eating disorder(s)
  anorexia nervosa, 266–271
  behavior of patients with, 265–278
  bulimia nervosa, 271–274
  compulsive overeating, 274–278
ECT. *See* Electroconvulsive therapy
Edema, as side effect of major tranquilizers, 145
Ego, 17–18
Elavil. *See* Amitriptyline
Elderly patient(s)
  behaviors of, 307–314
  depressed, 310
  drug therapy in, 153, 311
  exercise programs for, 313
  income of, 308
  nutritional status of, 314
  personal hygiene of, 313–314
  physical ailments of, 308–310, 314
  principles of care of, 311–314
  reactions to sedatives and hypnotics, 153
  safe environment for, 313
  self-esteem of, 307–308
  suicidal, 309
Electrocardiogram, 166
Electroconvulsive therapy (ECT)
  anesthesia before, 155, 165
  indications for, 166, 225
  legal issues in, 50, 168
  muscle relaxation before, 155, 165
  post-treatment procedures for, 170
  pre-treatment procedures for, 168–169
  procedural guidelines for, 168–170
  questions often asked by patients, 167
  tests prior to first treatment, 166
  theories about why it is effective, 165–166
  treatment procedures, 169–170
Electroencephalogram, 166
Empty nest syndrome, 322
Entitlement, 103
Equanil. *See* Meprobamate
Erotomanic delusion, 90
Ethchlorvynol (Placidyl), 154t
Ethical consideration(s), 56
Exercise
  excessive
    in anorexia nervosa, 266–268
    in bulimia nervosa, 271
  for obese patient, 277–278
  program for elderly, 313

Exhibitionism, 108–109
Extrapyramidal symptom(s), as side effect
    of major tranquilizers, 145

Fainting, as side effect of major
    tranquilizers, 145
Family therapy, 176
Family triangle period, 18–19
Fan obsession, 90
Fantasy, 36–37
Fault-finding, 36
Fetishism, 108–110
    transvestic, 108
Flashback, 74
Flat affect, 258
Flexibility, waxy, 88
Fluoxetine (Prozac), 151t
Fluphenazine (Permitil, Prolixin,
    Prolixin D), 147t
Food journal, 277
Forgetful patient(s), 255–259, 313
Formal thought disorder, 87
Frotteurism, 108, 110
Fugue, psychogenic, 78, 80
Functional psychosis, 85

Gain
    primary, 75
    secondary, 75
Generalized amnesia, 80
Generalized anxiety disorder, 68–71
Genetic factor(s), in alcohol abuse, 288
Genetic potential, 14
Geriatric patient(s). See Elderly patient(s)
Global amnesia. See Generalized amnesia
Glutethimide (Doriden), 154t
Goal(s), use in verbal communication, 126
"Going to pieces," 323
Gorging. See Bulimia nervosa; Compulsive
    overeating
Grandiose delusion, 90–91
Grandiose patient(s), 214
Grief, 326
Group therapy, 194
Guidance, anticipatory, 322, 326

Halazepam (Paxipam), 149t
Haldol. See Haloperidol
Hallucination(s), 74, 81
    in alcoholic patient, 291, 293
    care of patients with, 247–250
    command, 248
    definition of, 248
    drug therapy in, 144
    in schizophrenic disorders, 87–89
    suicide and, 232
Hallucinogen(s), 247, 298

Haloperidol (Haldol), 147t
Hand washing, ritualistic, 206–207
Headache
    after electroconvulsive therapy, 167, 170
    as side effect of minor tranquilizers, 148
Heroin, 283, 297–299
    methadone maintenance programs, 300
History
    in anorexia nervosa, 267
    in bulimia nervosa, 271–272
    in compulsive overeating, 275
Histrionic personality disorder, 97,
    102–103
Homeless population, 54
Homosexuality, 107–108
Hospitalization, 6
    admission procedures, 51
    discharge procedures, 51
    legal issues in, 51
Hostility, 88
Hydroxyzine (Atarax, Vistaril), 149t
Hypertension, as side effect of MAO
    inhibitors, 150
Hypnotic(s), 153–154, 154t
    nursing considerations in, 158
Hypochondriasis, 75, 77
Hypomania, 81–82
Hypotension, as side effect of major
    tranquilizers, 145
Hysterical paralysis, 40

Id, 14
Illusion(s), 74
    care of patients with, 247–250
    definition of, 248
Imipramine (Tofranil), 151t
Inappropriate behavior, 247–250
Incest, 110
Income, of elderly patients, 308
Incompetency, legal declaration of, 54
Incriminating statement(s), 130
Indefinite pronoun(s), 127
Independence, development in toddler
    period, 16
Indoklon, 155
Infancy
    parent-child relationship in, 15
    personality development during, 14–15
Informed consent, 55
    for electroconvulsive therapy, 168
Intimidating behavior, 193–194
Intravenous drug abuse, 298–299
Introjection, 37
Involuntary admission, 51
Isocarboxazid (Marplan), 151t

Jealous delusion, 91
"Jitters," 287

Job responsibility(ies), 50–51
JOCAM problem(s), 255–259
Judgment, impairment due to neurologic
    deficit, 255–259

Language
    of patient with neurologic deficit, 258
    in staff-patient communication, 126–130
Lappster, 284
Lawsuit. *See* Legal consideration(s)
Laxative abuse, 271
Legal consideration(s), 49–50
    adequate supervision of patients, 54–55
    charting and, 130–131
    confidentiality, 51–52
    due caution, 55
    duty to warn, 52–53
    in electroconvulsive therapy, 50, 168
    informed consent, 55
    job responsibilities, 50–51
    patient's bill of rights, 345–346
    patient's civil rights, 54
    patient's right to refuse treatment, 55
    reporting child abuse, 53–54
    voluntary and involuntary admissions,
        51
Librium. *See* Chlordiazepoxide
Lithium carbonate, 155
Lithium intoxication, 155
Localized amnesia, 80
Lorazepam (Ativan), 149t
Loxapine (Loxitane), 147t
Loxitane. *See* Loxapine
LSD, 247, 298
Ludiomil. *See* Maprotiline
Luminal. *See* Phenobarbital
Lying, 192–193

Magical thinking, 98
Major tranquilizer(s), 144–148, 147t,
    156–157
Malabsorption syndrome, 294
Maladjustment
    neurotic, 31
    psychotic, 31
Manic disorder, 136
Manic episode, 81–82
    care of manic patient, 247–250
Manipulative behavior, 195
MAO inhibitor(s), 150–151, 151t
    dosage of, 151t
    food and drug interactions of, 150
    nursing considerations in, 157–158
    patient teaching for use of, 152
    route of administration of, 151t
    side effects of, 150
Maprotiline (Ludiomil), 151t
Marijuana, 298

Marplan. *See* Isocarboxazid
Masochism, sexual, 108–109
Masturbation
    during adolescence, 20–21
    in fetishism, 109–110
    normality of, 107
    during preschool period, 19
Maturational crisis, 322
Mechanical restraint, 191
Mellaril. *See* Thioridazine
Memory, impairment due to neurologic
    deficit, 255–259
Menstruation, 20
Mental health, guidelines for evaluation of,
    28–29
Mental Health Attitude Inventory, 3–4
Mental health continuum, 27–31
Mental illness
    attitudes toward, 3–7
    causes of, 6
    among homeless, 54
Meprobamate (Equanil, Miltown), 149t
Mesoridazine (Serentil), 147t
Methadone maintenance program, 300
Miltown. *See* Meprobamate
Minor tranquilizer(s), 148–150, 149t, 157,
    294, 298
Misperception(s), 247–250
Moban. *See* Molindone
Molindone (Moban), 147t
Monoamine oxidase inhibitor(s). *See* MAO
    inhibitor(s)
Mood disorder(s)
    bipolar disorders, 81–82
    cyclothymia, 81–82
    depressive disorders, 82–83
    schizoaffective disorder, 89–90
Motor tension, in anxiety disorders, 70
Multiple personality disorder, 78–79
Muscle relaxation, before electroconvulsive
    therapy, 155, 165
Music therapy, 178

Nalline, 299
Narcissistic personality disorder, 97,
    103–104
Narcotic abuse, 296–300
Nardil. *See* Phenelzine
Negligent act, 50
Nembutal. *See* Pentobarbital
Neuroleptic(s), 147t
Neurologic deficit(s), behaviors of patients
    with, 137, 255–259
Neurosis, 39–42, 41t, 67
    depersonalization. *See* Depersonalization
        disorder
    depressive. *See* Dysthymia
    in elderly patient, 310
    hypochondriacal. *See* Hypochondriasis

Neurosis—*Continued*
  hysterical. *See* Conversion disorder
  neurotic behavior patterns, 67–68
  obsessive-compulsive. *See* Obsessive-
    compulsive disorder
  phobic. *See* Phobic disorder(s)
Neurotic maladjustment, 31
Noctec. *See* Chloral hydrate
Nonverbal communication, 121–123, 129
Norpramin. *See* Desipramine
Nortriptyline (Aventyl, Pamelor), 151t
Nursing considerations
  in anorexia nervosa, 268–270
  in bulimia nervosa, 272–274
  in compulsive overeating, 276–278
  in drug therapy, 144
    anticonvulsants, 158–159
    antidepressants, 157–158
    antiparkinsons, 159
    hypnotics, 158
    major tranquilizers, 156–157
    minor tranquilizers, 157
    sedatives, 158
Nutrition
  deficiencies
    in alcoholism, 291, 294
    in drug abusers, 298
  improved
    promoting in anorexia nervosa, 269
    promoting in obese patient, 276–277
  status of elderly patients, 314

Obese patient(s), 274–278
  definition of obesity, 274
  history of, 275
  nursing interventions for, 276–278
  prognosis and outcome in, 278
  signs and symptoms in, 275–276
Obsession, 40
Obsessive-compulsive disorder, 72–74
Obsessive-compulsive personality disorder,
  97, 105–106
Occupational therapy, 178
Oedipal conflict, 19
Open-ended question(s), 127–128, 324–325
Organic psychosis, 85
Orientation
  impairment due to neurologic deficit,
    255–259
  of patient to here and now, 127, 133
Outcome
  in anorexia nervosa, 270–271
  in bulimia nervosa, 274
  in compulsive overeating, 278
Outpatient program(s), 6
Overeating, compulsive, 274–278
Overmedication of elderly, 311
Oxazepam (Serax), 149t

"Pack rat," 106
Pain
  abuse of medication for, 296–297
  in somatoform pain disorder, 75, 78
Pamelor. *See* Nortriptyline
Panic disorder
  with agoraphobia, 72
  without agoraphobia, 72
Paradoxic excitement, as side effect of
  hypnotics, 153
Paralysis, hysterical, 40, 75
Paranoid patient(s)
  behaviors of, 213–216
  elderly, 310
Paranoid personality disorder, 96–97
Paranoid schizophrenia, 86, 88–89, 91–92
Paranoid stare, 88, 215
Paraphilia, 108
Parent-child relationship
  in adolescence, 20
  antisocial personality disorder and, 99
  in infancy, 15
Parnate. *See* Tranylcypromine
Passive-aggressive personality disorder,
  97, 106–107
Pathologic intoxication, 293
Patient(s). *See also* Staff-patient
    relationship(s)
  adequate supervision of, 54–55
  aggressive, 187–197
  anxious, 203–208
  bill of rights, 345–346
  brain-damaged, 255–259
  charting behavior of, 131–133
  charting physical symptoms of, 134–135
  chemically dependent, 283–301
  civil rights of, 54
  conflicts among patients, 193–194
  depressed, 221–225
  with eating disorder, 265–278
  elderly, 307–314
  with neurologic deficit, 255–259
  obese, 274–278
  privileges of, 195
  records/charts of, 130–135
  right to refuse treatment, 55
  suicidal, 229–238
  suspicious, 213–216
  who has lost contact with reality,
    247–250
Patient contract, for bulimic patient, 273
Patient teaching
  for drug therapy
    antidepressants, 152–153
    major tranquilizers, 146–148
    minor tranquilizers, 149–150
    sedatives and hypnotics, 153–154
  nurse's role in, 144
Paxipam. *See* Halazepam

Pedophilia, 108, 110
  exclusive type of, 110
  nonexclusive type of, 110
Peer-group pressure, 21, 37
Pentobarbital (Nembutal), 154t
Perfectionist, 106
Peripheral neuropathy, 294
Permissive parent, 17
Permitil. *See* Fluphenazine
Perphenazine (Trilafon), 147t
Persecutory delusion, 91
Personal appearance/hygiene, 131
  concerns of patient with eating disorder,
    265–278
  of depressed patient, 223
  of elderly patient, 313–314
Personality, stages in development of
  adolescence, 20–21
  infancy, 14–15
  preschool period, 17–19
  school-age period, 19–20
  toddler period, 16–17
Personality decompensation
  mild, 40
  severe, 40
Personality disorder(s), 95–97
  antisocial personality disorder, 97–100
  avoidant personality disorder, 97, 104
  borderline personality disorder, 97,
    101–102
  dependent personality disorder, 97,
    104–105
  histrionic personality disorder, 97,
    102–103
  multiple personality disorder, 78–79
  narcissistic personality disorder, 97,
    103–104
  obsessive-compulsive personality
    disorder, 97, 105–106
  paranoid personality disorder, 96–97
  passive-aggressive personality disorder,
    97, 106–107
  schizoid personality disorder, 96–98
  schizotypal personality disorder, 96, 98
Phenelzine (Nardil), 151t
Phenobarbital (Luminal), 154–155, 154t,
  298
Phenothiazine(s), 143–148, 147t, 156
Phobia, 40, 71–72
Phobic behavior, 207–208
Phobic disorder(s), 71–72
  agoraphobia without history of panic
    disorder, 72
  panic disorders with agoraphobia, 72
  panic disorders without agoraphobia, 72
  simple phobia, 72
  social phobia, 72
Photosensitivity, as side effect of major
  tranquilizers, 146

Physical appearance. *See* Personal
  appearance/hygiene
Physical coercion, 190
Physical effects, of alcohol abuse, 289
Physical restraint, 190–191
Physical symptoms
  charting of, 134–135
  in conversion disorder, 34–35, 75–77
  of depressed patient, 221
  of elderly patient, 308–310, 314
Physically abusive behavior, 193–194
Physically destructive behavior, 189–191
Piperacetazine (Quide), 147t
Placidyl. *See* Ethchlorvynol
Post-traumatic stress disorder, 74
Postural hypotension, as side effect of
  major tranquilizers, 145
Posture, as nonverbal communication,
  122–123
Prazepam (Centrax), 149t
Prealcoholic symptomatic phase of
  alcoholism, 290
Preschool period
  discipline during, 17–18
  ego development during, 17–18
  masturbation during, 19
  personality development during, 17–19
  superego development during, 17–18
Primary degenerative dementia, 310
Primary gain, 75
Privacy, 56
Privilege(s), of patient, 195
Privileged communication, 53
Problem drinker, 284
Procedures manual, 50
Prochlorperazine (Compazine), 147t
Prodromal phase of alcoholism, 290
Prognosis
  in anorexia nervosa, 270–271
  in bulimia nervosa, 274
  in compulsive overeating, 278
Projection, 35–36, 92, 213
Prolixin. *See* Fluphenazine
Prolixin D. *See* Fluphenazine
Promazine (Sparine), 147t
Propanediol(s), 149t
Protriptyline (Vivactil), 151t
Prozac. *See* Fluoxetine
Pseudoparkinsonism, as side effect of
  major tranquilizers, 145
Psychogenic amnesia, 79–80
Psychogenic fugue, 78, 80
Psychopathology, 27–28
Psychosis, 39–42, 41t, 67
  behavior and problems frequently seen
    in, 136–137
  functional, 85
  organic, 85
  schizoaffective disorder, 89–90
  schizophrenic disorders, 86–90
  toxic, 85

Psychotherapy, 175–176
Psychotic maladjustment, 31
Psychotropic drug(s), 143–159
Puberty, 20–21
Public drunkenness, 292
Purging. *See* Bulimia nervosa

Question(s), techniques for effective use
    of, 126–130
Quide. *See* Piperacetazine

Rationalization, 33
Reaction formation, 37–38
Reality
    contact with, 40
    denial of, 33–34
    loss of contact with, behavior of patient,
        247–250
Recording patient information, 130–135
Recreational therapy, 178
Refusal of treatment, 55
Regression, 38
Relaxation technique(s), 205
Religious delusion, 215
Reorganization phase of crisis, 323–324
Repoise. *See* Butaperazine
Reporting patient information, 130–135
Repression, 32–33
Restitution, 39
Restless behavior, 205–206
Restraint, physical, 190–191
Retirement, 307–308
Rigidity, catatonic, 88
Ritualistic behavior, 73–74, 206–207
    in schizotypal personality disorder, 98
Role model, staff as model for patient,
    128, 188
Role playing, 194

Sadism, sexual, 108–109
Safe environment
    for elderly patients, 313
    for patient with neurologic deficit,
        255–259
    for suicidal patient, 232–239
Scanning, in anxiety disorders, 71
Schizoaffective disorder, 89–90
Schizoid personality disorder, 96–98
Schizophrenic disorder(s)
    behaviors associated with, 247–250
    catatonic schizophrenia, 86, 88, 144
    disorganized schizophrenia, 86, 89
    paranoid schizophrenia, 86, 88–89,
        91–92
    schizoaffective disorder, 89–90
    undifferentiated schizophrenia, 86, 89
Schizophrenic reaction

acute, 86
chronic, 87
Schizotypal personality disorder, 96, 98
School-age period
    personality development during, 19–20
    social interactions during, 19–20
Seclusion room
    for aggressive patient, 190
    for suicidal patient, 236–238
Secobarbital (Seconal), 154t, 298
Seconal. *See* Secobarbital
Secondary gain, 75
Sedation, as side effect of major
        tranquilizers, 146
Sedative, 153–154, 154t
    nursing considerations in, 158
Selective amnesia, 80
Self-deception, 33
Self-determination, 54, 56
Self-esteem, 124–125, 224, 231
    of elderly patient, 307–308
    of obese patient, 277–278
    promoting in anorexia nervosa, 270
Self-fulfilling prophecy, 187
Self-image, 31
    of patient with eating disorder, 265–278
Self-mutilation, 101
Self-reliance, development in toddler
        period, 16
Self-worth. *See* Self-esteem
Senile brain atrophy, 309–310
Serax. *See* Oxazepam
Serentil. *See* Mesoridazine
Sex education, 20
Sexual development, during adolescence,
        20–21
Sexual disorder(s), 107–108
    exhibitionism, 108–109
    fetishism, 108–110
    frotteurism, 108, 110
    pedophilia, 108, 110
    sexual masochism, 108–109
    sexual sadism, 108–109
    transvestic fetishism, 108
    voyeurism, 108–109
Sexual dysfunction, 108
    decreased interest, as side effect of
        major tranquilizers, 146
Sexual masochism, 108–109
Sexual sadism, 108–109
Sexually aggressive behavior, 196–197
Side effect(s)
    of anticonvulsants, 154–155
    of antidepressants, 150, 152
    of antiparkinsons, 155
    of barbiturates, 153
    of hypnotics, 155
    of lithium carbonate, 155
    of major tranquilizers, 145–146

of minor tranquilizers, 148–149
of sedatives, 153
Signs and symptoms
of alcohol abuse, 293–294
of anorexia nervosa, 267–268
of bulimia nervosa, 272
of compulsive overeating, 275–276
of drug abuse, 299
Silence, in staff-patient conversations, 129
Simple phobia, 72
Sinequan. See Doxepin
SIRS. See Suicidal Intention Rating Scale
Situational event, 322
Sleep disturbance, 222, 232, 314
Social crisis, 322–323
Social interaction, promoting in obese
patient, 277
Social phobia, 72
Socialization
in infancy and childhood, 17
in school-age period, 19–20
Sociopathic personality, 17
Sociopathic personality disorder. See
Antisocial personality disorder
Somatic delusion, 91
Somatization disorder, 75, 77–78
Somatoform disorder(s), 74–75
body dysmorphic disorder, 75, 77
conversion disorder, 75–77
hypochondriasis, 75, 77
somatization disorder, 75, 77–78
somatoform pain disorder, 75, 78
Somatoform pain disorder, 75, 78
Somnos. See Chloral hydrate
Sparine. See Promazine
Spending spree, 81
Splitting, 101–102
Spouse abuse, 99
Staff-patient relationship(s). See also
Communication
communication in, 123–126
dating, 125
discussion of personal lives of staff, 125
trust in, 123–126
Stalking, 90
Stare, paranoid, 88, 215
Stealing behavior, 30, 99, 192–193,
297–298
Stelazine. See Trifluoperazine
Streaking fad, 30
Stress
during crisis, 321–326
effect on mental health, 6
Sublimation, 38–39
Succinylcholine chloride (Anectine), 155
Suicidal Intention Rating Scale (SIRS),
234–238
Suicidal patient(s), 82, 221–222
adolescent, 231
with antisocial personality disorder, 100

behaviors of, 229–238
with borderline personality disorder, 101
communication of intention to commit
suicide, 231
completed suicide, 229
drug therapy for, 153
elderly, 309
motivational factors in suicide, 230–231
schizophrenic, 88
Suicidal Intention Rating Scale, 234–238
treatment of, 230–231
creating a safe environment, 232–239
drug therapy, 233
recognizing behavioral clues, 231–232
techniques for effective interaction
with, 233–238
unsuccessful attempts at suicide, 229
Superego, 17–18
Supervision of patient(s), 54–55
Surmontil. See Trimipramine
Suspicious patient(s), behaviors of,
213–216
Symptom complex, 68
Symptoms. See Signs and symptoms

Takedown of patient, 191
Talk therapy, 175–176
Terminally ill patient(s), 230–231
Tetracyclic antidepressant(s), 151t
Therapy
adventure, 178
ancillary, 224
art, 178
auxiliary, 178–179
behavior, 176–178
communication skills needed in, 121–137
drug, 143–159
electroconvulsive, 165–170
family, 176
group, 194
music, 178
occupational, 178
patient's right to refuse, 55
recreational, 178
talk, 175–176
treatment protocols, 66
Thioridazine (Mellaril), 147t
Third-party reimbursement, 65–66
Thorazine. See Chlorpromazine
Thought content, of schizophrenic, 87
Thought process(es), of patient, 133
Tindal. See Acetophenazine
Toddler period
personality development during, 16–17
toilet training during, 16–17
Tofranil. See Imipramine
Toilet training
regression in, 38
during toddler period, 16–17

Toxic psychosis, 85
Tranquilizer(s)
major
dosage of, 147t
indications for, 144
nursing considerations in, 156–157
patient teaching for use of, 146–148
route of administration of, 147t
side effects of, 145–146
minor
abuse of, 298
dosage of, 149t
indications for, 148
nursing considerations in, 157
patient teaching for use of, 149–150
route of administration of, 149t
side effects of, 148–149
in treatment of alcoholics, 294
Transsexualism, 108
Transvestic fetishism, 108
Tranxene. See Chlorazepate dipotassium
Tranylcypromine (Parnate), 151t
Trazodone (Desyrel), 151t
Treatment protocol, 66
Tricyclic antidepressant(s), 151t
Trifluoperazine (Stelazine), 147t
Triflupromazine (Vesprin), 147t
Trilafon. See Perphenazine
Trimipramine (Surmontil), 151t
Trust
development in infancy, 15
in staff-patient relationship, 123–126

Uncertainty, 69
Uncooperative behavior, 194–196

Undifferentiated schizophrenia, 86, 89
Undoing, 39
Urecholine, 145

Valium. See Diazepam
Verbal communication, 121–122, 132
Verbally abusive behavior, 187–189
Vesprin. See Triflupromazine
Vigilance, in anxiety disorders, 71
Violent behavior, 189–191
Vistaril. See Hydroxyzine
Vivactil. See Protriptyline
Voluntary admission, 51
Vomiting, self-induced, 271–272
Voyeurism, 38, 108–109

Warning, duty to give, 52–53
Waxy flexibility, 88
Weapon(s), potential, for suicidal patient,
232–238
Weight gain, as side effect of major
tranquilizers, 145–146
Well-being, promoting in obese patient,
277–278
Wernicke-Korsakoff syndrome, 294
Whiskey nose, 287
Wino, 284
Withdrawal, in schizoid personality
disorder, 97–98
Withdrawal symptoms, from alcohol,
293–294
Written communication, 121–122

Xanax. See Alprazolam